ALFRED CORT HADDON

Anthropology's Ancestors

Edited by Aleksandar Bošković, University of Belgrade; Institute of Archaeology, Belgrade; Max Planck Institute for Social Anthropology, Halle/Saale

As anthropology developed across geographical, historical, and social boundaries, it was always influenced by works of exceptional scholars who pushed research topics in new and original directions and who can be regarded as important ancestors of the discipline. The aim of this series is to offer introductions to these major figures, whose works constitute landmarks and are essential reading for students of anthropology, but who are also of interest for scholars in the humanities and social sciences more generally. In doing so, it offers important insights into some of the basic questions facing humanity.

Volume 5
Alfred Cort Haddon: A Very English Savage
Ciarán Walsh

Volume 4
Mary Douglas
Paul Richards and Perri 6

Volume 3
Françoise Héritier
Gérald Gaillard

Volume 2
William Robertson Smith
Aleksandar Bošković

Volume 1
Margaret Mead
Paul Shankman

ALFRED CORT HADDON
A Very English Savage

● ● ●

Ciarán Walsh

berghahn
NEW YORK · OXFORD
www.berghahnbooks.com

First published in 2023 by
Berghahn Books
www.berghahnbooks.com

© 2023 Ciarán Walsh

All rights reserved. Except for the quotation of short passages
for the purposes of criticism and review, no part of this book
may be reproduced in any form or by any means, electronic or
mechanical, including photocopying, recording, or any information
storage and retrieval system now known or to be invented,
without written permission of the publisher.

Library of Congress Cataloging-in-Publication Data
Names: Walsh, Ciarán (Curator), author.
Title: Alfred Cort Haddon : a very English savage / Ciarán Walsh.
Description: New York : Berghahn Books, 2023. | Series: Anthropology's ancestors ; Volume 5 | Includes bibliographical references and index.
Identifiers: LCCN 2023000968 (print) | LCCN 2023000969 (ebook) | ISBN 9781800739826 (hardback) | ISBN 9781800739840 (paperback) | ISBN 9781800739833 (ebook)
Subjects: LCSH: Haddon, Alfred C. (Alfred Cort), 1855–1940. | Photography in ethnology—History. | Ireland—Civilization—19th century. | Anthropologists—Great Britain—Biography.
Classification: LCC GN21.H22 W35 2023 (print) | LCC GN21.H22 (ebook) | DDC 301.092 [B]—dc23/eng/20230413
LC record available at https://lccn.loc.gov/2023000968
LC ebook record available at https://lccn.loc.gov/2023000969

British Library Cataloguing in Publication Data

A catalogue record for this book is available from the British Library

ISBN 978-1-80073-982-6 hardback
ISBN 978-1-80073-984-0 paperback
ISBN 978-1-80539-371-9 epub
ISBN 978-1-80073-983-3 web pdf

https://doi.org/10.3167/9781800739826

For Nuala Finn

CONTENTS

• • •

List of Figures	iv
Preface	xi
Acknowledgements	xiii
List of Abbreviations	xvi
Introduction	1
Part I. Becoming an Ethnologist	
Chapter 1. Becoming an Anthropologist	27
Chapter 2. Lessons from Utopia	46
Chapter 3. Becoming an Ethnologist	65
Part II. The Skull-Measuring Business	
Chapter 4. Ethnical Islands	89
Chapter 5. The Laboratory	109
Chapter 6. Fieldwork	127
Part III. The Fifth Field	
Chapter 7. Tedious Texts	155
Chapter 8. The Magic Lantern	176
Chapter 9. The Last Dance	205
Conclusion	230

References 251

Index 279

FIGURES

Figure 1.1. Anon., *Dredging party, 1885, with friends [plate 16] sitting, left to right: A. C. Haddon (in front of light suit), S. Haughton, W. S. Green, C. B. Ball; standing: Sir D'Arcy W. Thompson (light suit), Sir R. S. Ball (yachting cap), Valentine Ball (at end of trawl)*, 1885. Digital scan of silver gelatine print. Permission of the Royal Irish Academy © RIA. 26

Figure 4.1. A. F. Dixon, *Untitled*, 1890. Digital scan of silver gelatine, glass-plate negative (Ciarán Walsh, Ciarán Rooney, 2019). The original negative is held in the School of Medicine, Trinity College, University of Dublin. © curator.ie. 88

Figure 6.1. A. C. Haddon and C. R. Browne, *Anthropometry in Aran*, 1892. Digital scan and print of silver gelatine print (Timothy Keefe, Sharon Sutton, Ciarán Walsh, Ciarán Rooney, 2011). Courtesy of the Board of Trinity College, University of Dublin. 126

Figure 6.2. Schedule of measurements taken from Tom Connelly in 1892. Permission of the School of Medicine, Trinity College, University of Dublin. 126

Figure 6.3. C. R. Browne, *The People*, c.1897. Digital scan and print of silver gelatine photographic prints pasted into an album (Timothy Keefe, Sharon Sutton, Ciarán Walsh, Ciarán Rooney, 2011). Courtesy of the Board of Trinity College, University of Dublin. 129

Figure 7.1. A. C. Haddon, *Michael Faherty, and two women, Inishmaan, Faherty refused to be measured, and the women would not even tell us their names*, 1892. Digital scan of silver gelatine print (Timothy Keefe, Sharon Sutton, Ciarán Walsh, Ciarán Rooney, 2011). Courtesy of the Board of Trinity College, University of Dublin. 154

Figure 7.2. A. C. Haddon, *Colman Faherty, Thomas, aged about sixty years, Oghil. Michael O'Donnell, John, No. 25, Oghil*, 1892. Digital scan of silver gelatine print (Timothy Keefe, Sharon Sutton, Ciarán Walsh, Ciarán Rooney, 2011). Courtesy of the Board of Trinity College, University of Dublin. 156

Figures 8.1–8.10. A. F. Dixon, *Untitled*, 1890. Digital scans and prints of silver gelatine, glass-plate negatives (Ciarán Walsh and Ciarán Rooney, 2019). The original negatives are held in the School of Medicine, Trinity College, University of Dublin. © curator.ie. 180

Figure 8.11. 1895: a timeline. © curator.ie. 186

Figure 9.1. A. C. Haddon, *The Dance of the Zogo Le*, 1898. Digital scan of a frame from the short film that Haddon made of the dance of the Malu Zogo-Le on the island of Mer (Murray), Torres Strait. Permission of National Film and Sound Archive of Australia. 204

Figure 9.2. John Millington Synge, *An Islander of Inishmaan*, 1898. Digital scan and print from glass-plate negative (Timothy Keefe, Sharon Sutton, Ciarán Walsh, 2009). Courtesy of the Board of Trinity College, University of Dublin. 226

PREFACE

● ● ●

'The life history of Alfred Cort Haddon', Alison Hingston Quiggin (1942, ix) wrote in the preface to the sketch of her comrade, 'is to a great extent, the life history of modern anthropology'. It was a forlorn claim at the time. In the 1970s, James Urry (1972) began rewriting the history of British anthropology from within the library of the Anthropological Institute of Great Britain and Ireland and, in 1982, noted with some irony how Haddon, one of the first historians of anthropology, had been written out of the story of modern anthropology. Urry, along with Henrika Kuklick and George W. Stocking Jr, was responsible for reinstating Haddon as a pivotal figure in subsequent histories for all the wrong reasons.

In 2008, Henrika Kuklick reviewed the history of the British tradition in anthropology and sealed Haddon's fate by affirming the common sense that Haddon opened the way to the creation of 'an anthropology very different from his' (Kuklick 1991: 139). Haddon was different because he studied zoology in Cambridge, and this became a baseline for most assessments of his contribution to anthropology in scholarship that has accumulated since the 1990s. In this context, the time he spent in Ireland is generally regarded as too closely tied to zoology to be relevant, and the history of modern anthropology begins in the wake of the 1898 Cambridge Anthropological Expedition to Torres Strait.

I propose instead that Haddon was a modernizer whose achievements in anthropology become visible only when conventional histories of anthropology and photography – those preoccupied by race, bracketed by evolution and colonialism – are turned upside down, that is, when Haddon's experiments in photo-ethnography in Ireland between 1890 and 1895 are situated in a post-evolutionist critique of orthodox anthropology by an artist who became fascinated with the people he encountered at the very edge of the so-called civilized world.

This particular version of Haddon emerged from a discussion with David Shankland about the meaning of 'radical' and 'post-evolutionist' that took place during my defence of my doctoral thesis in January 2020. I set out to disrupt conventional accounts of Haddon's involvement in the skull-measuring business in Ireland in the early 1890s, using facts gleaned from an 'Irish' reading of the Haddon Papers and related records and, by the way, filling in some significant gaps in the Irish section of Quiggin's biography. The current text started from a different premise as Haddon's legacy came into focus in conversations with David Shankland, Herbert Lewis and Frederico Delgado Rosa, in the context of a more general review by the History of Anthropology Network of the relevance of the generation that preceded Radcliffe-Brown and Malinowski in relation to the modernization of anthropology.

Shortly afterwards, Aleksandar Bošković asked me to look at Haddon from this perspective, and what follows is a recovered history that credits Haddon with the development of visual and cultural anthropology and pivots on his role in an anticolonial movement that divided organized anthropology in the 1890s. Given the space available, there are a lot of loose ends that are left to stand as provocations, the main one being that Haddon remains relevant because his critique of a restricted orthodox anthropology is being replayed in the current stand-off between 'traditional' and 'practical' anthropology. The wheel turns full circle and Quiggin's claim gets a new life while the evolutionist narratives that negated it are consigned to history.

ACKNOWLEDGMENTS

• • •

This book is the outcome of independent post-doc research and would not have been possible without the support of Nuala Finn, who, apart from emotional and intellectual support, carried the financial burden for the year spent researching and writing the manuscript.

I thank Tom Bonnington and the team at Berghahn Books, especially series editor Aleksandar Bošković, Keara Hagerty and Harry Eagles. Doreen Anderson at Arc Indexing. David Shankland (Royal Anthropological Institute of Great Britain and Ireland) provided valuable advice, and conversations with Herb Lewis kept the exercise in perspective. My collaboration with Frederico Delgado Rosa, Christine Laurière and Anabel Vazquez of the Bérose Encyclopaedia of International Histories of Anthropology provided an invaluable opportunity to test my findings and fine-tune the tone of my arguments. Matthew Cheeseman and Carina Hart helped with the technical side of writing up the first draft of those arguments while Mark Maguire (Maynooth University) and Rob Kevlihan supported the research that underpins them.

Alfred Cort Haddon: A Very English Savage is a continuation of an exploration of colonial legacies commenced with the 'Irish Head-Hunter' project I developed with Dáithí De Mórdha between 2010 and 2015 in partnership with Felicity O'Mahony, Jane Maxwell, Timothy Keefe (Trinity College, University of Dublin) and Amanda Ryan (Heritage Council). The transition to *Alfred Cort Haddon* was made possible by people connected with Haddon in Cambridge. I thank Aidan Baker (Haddon Librarian), who first invited me to Cambridge in 2013. John D. Pickles (Cambridge Antiquarian Society) guided me through the uncatalogued Irish component of the Haddon Papers and Frank Bowles and Katrina Deane facilitated my research in the Department of Manuscripts in Cambridge University Library over a period of five years. Rebecca Hayes, Archivist and Curator at the Grand Lodge of Freemasons of Ireland, clarified aspects of Haddon's initiation into and progress through the freemasons in Ireland and the UK.

The story of *Alfred Cort Haddon* is organized around a set of photographs Haddon and Andrew Francis Dixon took in the Aran Islands in 1890, and I thank Ciarán Rooney (Filmbank) for digitizing the original negatives and producing the first set of prints since the 1890s. Ciarán and I worked with Timothy Keefe and Sharon Sutton on the digitization and printing of Charles R. Browne's photograph albums in 2011, and we developed a methodology that remains at the core of my work as a curator, archivist and public historian. This seemed like a fairly esoteric skill set until 2020, when Niamh Brennan, Archivist with Donegal County Council, and Caroline Carr, Curator with Donegal County Museum, named it and added public engagement to the set, thereby recognizing a key working principle of the writing of *Alfred Cort Haddon*. Likewise, Marie Coyne's tireless efforts to have the remains of Inishbofin islanders stolen in 1890 repatriated by Trinity College Dublin (TCD) has brought Haddon's legacy into the public domain and provided a focus for further engagement with the descendants of the people he studied in the 1890s.

Making sense of the Haddon-Dixon photographs in relation to a selfie Haddon and Charles R. Browne took while measuring the skull of Tom Connelly would not have been possible without access to and permission to use Haddon's papers, and I acknowledge the enormous contribution of the Syndics of Cambridge University Library in this respect. Likewise, I acknowledge the assistance of the archivists and librarians who searched for material used in this book. They include Haddon Librarian Meg Westbury, Frank Bowles at Cambridge University, Sarah Walpole at the Anthropological Institute, Melinda Robertson at the National Film and Sound Archive of Australia, Ciara Daly at Trinity College, University of Dublin, Natasha Serne at the Royal Dublin Society, Meadhbh Murphy and Rebecca Cairns at the Royal Irish Academy and Melissa Flynn at the Linen Hall Library, Belfast.

Finally, Aidan Baker introduced me to Margaret Rishbeth, Haddon's granddaughter, in 2013, and since then Margaret and her sister-in-law Pril Rishbeth have provided valuable information on the Haddon family.

Míle buíochas.
Thank you.

ABBREVIATIONS

APS	Aborigines Protection Society
BAAS	British Association for the Advancement of Science
BNFC	Belfast Naturalists' Field Club
EASA	European Association of Social Anthropologists
CI	Cephalic Index
JAI	Journal of the Anthropological Institute of Great Britain and Ireland
LGBTQI+	Lesbian, Gay, Bisexual, Transgender, Queer, Intersex plus
LMS	London Missionary Society
N&QA	Notes and Queries on Anthropology
ODNB	Oxford Dictionary of National Biography
RIA	Royal Irish Academy
RDS	Royal Dublin Society
TCD	The University of Dublin, Trinity College

A Note on Place Names/*Logainmneacha*

Many of the place names featured in this study have changed since the 1890s. For instance, the Isles of Arran was popular before the 1890s and was one variation on a theme that was gradually replaced by the Aran Islands. The islands are now called Oileáin Árainn, which translates as 'the Islands of Aran'. Árainn, the northern island, was renamed Inishmore and is now known as Inis Mór, the big island. Inishmaan, the middle island, is now called Inis Meáin and so on. I have used the version of the place name or *logainm* that is used in texts quoted.

INTRODUCTION
ANCESTRAL KNOWLEDGE

● ● ●

Alfred Cort Haddon was written out of the story of anthropology for the same reasons that make him interesting today. He was passionately committed to the protection of simpler societies and their civilizations from colonists and their supporters in Parliament and the armed forces. He grew up in a nonconformist family that was active in humanitarian campaigns, literature, art, progressive education and politics. His grandparents campaigned for the abolition of slavery, his mother was a writer, his father a publisher and illustrator, his brother an artist and two of his aunts socialists and founding members of the Fabian Society. Haddon was partly home-schooled, worked briefly in the family publishing business and studied art part-time before attending Cambridge and graduating in Zoology and Comparative Anatomy in 1879. He secured a teaching job at the Royal College of Science in Dublin after one of his professors lobbied Thomas Henry Huxley on his behalf, and he spent the next twenty-one years working as a part-time Professor of Zoology in the city before taking up a part-time University Lectureship in Ethnology at Cambridge University.

This monograph concentrates on what happened during those twenty-one years and begins more or less with Haddon's decision to switch from zoology to ethnology in 1887. There is an Irish proverb that says *briseann an dúchas trí shuile an chait*, which translates as 'heritage breaks through the eyes of a cat', and this could be used to explain what happened after Haddon decided to undertake an eight-month-long ethnological exploration of the Torres Strait and adjacent parts of New Guinea for the British Museum, even though he was supposed to be studying coral reefs for Huxley. From the outset, the collection of information that James G. Frazer sought on magico-religious rituals filled his journal, sketchbooks and photographs at the expense of data on the structure of coral reefs that Huxley requested in a research brief. Haddon also befriended James 'Tamate' Chalmers, a missionary and ethnologist who advocated a native mission and a New Guinea for the New Guineans (Porter 2004), and together they explored parts of New Guinea that had not been fully colonized. On his return to London, he joined a movement of social reformers, utopians and anarchists who looked to anthropology for inspiration in their search for an alternative to dog-eat-dog capitalism. He decided to abandon his faltering career in marine biology in 1889 and go into anthropology instead. He spent the next ten years fighting on two fronts. In Ireland he was opposed by a scientific establishment that deployed anthropology as a practical science in defence of the oldest colony. In England he had to negotiate with anatomists who restricted academic anthropology to the study of bodies and were determined to keep Haddon and his radical ideas out of Cambridge University.

The war on terror has ensured that the word radical has become closely associated with extremism (see Elshimi 2017), but the word has an older meaning that derives from Latin and, in Haddon's case, describes a desire to bring about a root-and-branch reform of the institution of anthropology in response to his experience of colonialism in Oceania. Haddon approached the problem in two ways. First, he joined Patrick Geddes, Henry 'Havelock' Ellis and their anarchist associates in a movement – the very definition of being a radical, according to the Oxford English Dictionary – to deconstruct anatomical anthropology and reconstruct anthropology as an instrument of scientific social reform, although the influence of Freemasonry ensured that this was a philosophical rather than ideological project. Two, Haddon sought to thoroughly modernize ethnography and adopted the slideshow as a form of engaged ethnography. Photography has been mentioned in passing, but archival material relating to his discovery of the Aran Islands in 1890 would have established Haddon as a pioneer of visual anthropology had his experiments in ethnographic form not been overwritten by anthropologists who assumed a 'hard' science attitude and, according to Margaret Mead (1995), adopted a word-based methodology in the first two decades of the twentieth century. What gets lost as a consequence is Haddon's decision in 1890 to switch from text to photography as the methodological and epistemological basis of his version of ethnology, which he defined as cultural anthropology in his *History of Anthropology*, obliquely in the first edition (Haddon and Quiggin 1910: 128) and unequivocally in the second edition (Haddon 1934: 100). That experiment culminated in the first use of a kinematographic camera by an ethnographer in the field, and I propose that the circumstance of that experiment entitles Haddon to be regarded as a modernist. Furthermore, I propose that his adoption of the slideshow as a form of anticolonial activism positively influenced key players in cultural nationalism and literary modernism in Ireland, and this overturns thirty years of scholarship based on a constructed antagonism between the political effect of Haddon's ethnological experiments and the aims of those movements.

The problem here is that Haddon's advocacy on behalf of colonized civilizations took the form of articles in popular journals and slideshows that have left few traces in the archives mined by disciplinary historians in the 1990s. They zeroed in on Haddon's brief involvement in zoology and used this to set him up as an evolutionist foil for the university-educated social anthropologists who followed him into the field in the first two decades of the twentieth century and produced two ethnographic texts that defined modern anthropology in Britain, A. R. Radcliffe-Brown's *Andaman Islanders: A Study in Social Anthropology* (1922) and Bronisław Malinowski's *Argonauts of the Western Pacific* (1922). Thus, the twenty-one years Haddon spent in Ireland became a sort of historiographical limbo that ended when Haddon left Dublin as a much-fêted anthropologist in the wake of his second expedition to the Torres Strait and founded the discipline of anthropology in Cambridge. Ten years of anticolonial activism, formal experimentation and increased marginalization within a hostile academy were forgotten in the process. The reason, I will argue, has less to do with the availability or accessibility of archival evidence than a determination to shoehorn Haddon into a story structured around Thomas Kuhn's (1970) work on scientific revolutions, the lens through which influential historians like Ian Langham (1981), Henrika Kuklick (1991) and George W. Stocking Jr (1995) examined the modernization of British anthropology.

The scale of the error, historiographically speaking, is best described by explaining the subtitle of this monograph. Alexander Macalister, Professor of Anatomy at Cambridge and President of the Anthropological Institute, addressed the split between ethnologists and anthropologists in a sectoral review in 1894. He acknowledged that Haddon was an experienced scientist who had 'become acquainted with savage men and their ways' (*JAI* 23 [1894]: 412), implying in the racist language of colonialism that Haddon had 'gone native' in the field and returned as a very English savage whose interest in the ethics of colonialism belonged in the realm of philosophy, and as such was incompatible with scientific anthropology. Macalister subsequently blocked Haddon's appointment to the first University Lectureship in Anthropology at Cambridge, a disruptive little fact that makes these histories read more like disciplinary folklore, and are treated as such.

Reinstating Haddon in the story of the modernization of anthropology in Ireland and England requires clear thinking about the political significance of anthropology and ethnology in the 1890s. This requires, by way of introduction, the definition of key terms in line with debates that manifested a culture war in organized anthropology. That in turn requires the recovery of narratives that have been written out of the history of anthropology because of a preoccupation with evolution bracketed by race and empire. This leads into a discussion of what Thomas Hylland Eriksen, speaking in a webinar in November 2021, labelled 'structural amnesia'. That phrase summarizes a core theme of my doctoral research, in which I investigated the forgotten spaces of Anglo-Irish anthropology. The key question was what anthropology meant in a historical context, and the current question of ancestry is bound up in what we think anthropology means in a contemporary context. If Haddon's story tells us anything it is that the assumption that we know what anthropology is and where it came from is false, that the meaning of anthropology was contested ever since the word first entered modern English in the sixteenth century. That search for definition was the first task Haddon set himself after he decided to go into anthropology in 1889, and I have taken this as the starting point of this monograph.

KEY WORDS

In November 1895, Haddon published a short article on 'The Study of Anthropology' in an obscure journal dealing with extramural studies in and around Cambridge. He filed a copy with other newspaper cuttings and Edith Fegan and John D. Pickles listed it under 'Articles and Notes' in their 1978 *Bibliography of A.C. Haddon*. It would be easy to miss the article except that Haddon incorporated it into his introduction to *The Study of Man* (1898), a mishmash of reprinted articles and reports published between 1891 and 1897 that dealt with practical aspects of physical anthropology and folklore collection.

Haddon's file copy of 'The Study of Anthropology' provides the textual foundation for many of the arguments advanced in this monograph, and this reflects the importance I attach to his journalism. I also share the disruptive intent Haddon revealed in the opening paragraph, in which he acknowledged a lack of recognition of the full 'scope and significance of Anthropology' (Haddon 1895a: 25) and the difficulty of approaching such a complex subject 'from a dispassionate point of view'. 'Dispassionate' is the key word here because it suggests conflict, and the timing of Haddon's article is important in this regard. Two months earlier, Haddon delivered an unequivocal critique of the genocidal consequences of British imperialism at a public meeting of the anthropological section of the British Association for the Advancement of Science in Ipswich (BAAS 1895: 832), and his credibility as a scientist first and anthropologist second was questioned in the press. I regard this as a pivotal event in Haddon's story and, for now, it serves to illustrate that Haddon's definition of key words is in essence a definition of the contrary political positions adopted by anthropologists and ethnologists in the 1890s. This, I propose, is the key to understanding his practice as it developed in Ireland in the 1890s and its significance in terms of contemporary debates about the scope and meaning of anthropology.

Haddon wrote:

> At the risk of being tedious I think it is desirable to define our terms at the outset. On the Continent the term anthropology is restricted to what we in England term Physical Anthropology or Anthropography, that is, the study of man as an animal. This comprises not only the comparative study of the structural differences between members of different races of mankind, but also the comparison of man with the higher apes. We prefer to retain the word Anthropology for the study of man in its wider aspect. (Haddon 1895a: 25)

He then set out what this meant. Ethnography was 'the description . . . of a small tribe, the natives of a restricted area or a large nation'. Ethnology was the 'comparative study of human groups and ha[d] for its aim the elucidation of inter-relationships of tribes, races and other bodies of men'. Sociology was 'the study of human communities, both simple and complex'. Archaeology attempted 'to reconstruct the ancient history of man from the remains of the past that are brought to light in various ways'. He added that it would be better 'to recover what they thought and believed', as the non-material aspects of a people's existence 'are the most important departments of human life'.

He set out two methods for generating knowledge in this department. The first was the study of culture, but he warned that organizing this around 'a rigorously defined order of evolution' in the stages of culture had its dangers and the comparative method of studying 'customs, modes of thought and religion' had to be used with circumspection. The second was 'folk-lore'; he preferred the hyphenated form because it was closer in meaning to 'the lore of the folk', the folk being traditional communities that survived in more or less developed societies. He dismissed the tendency of some to deride 'folk-lore' 'as being concerned with ghosts, fairy tales and old wives' superstitions' and represented it as a reserve of ancestral thought and belief that survived on a local (folk) and global (savage) level. In this context, art – pattern and designs – was 'replete with human interest, as being associated with some of the deepest and most subtle ideas'. He pulled it all together by stating that anthropology happened wherever people are, not just in the 'uttermost part of the earth' but 'in our own nurseries, the playground, on the village-green – even in our cities.'

As a body of text, 'The Study of Anthropology' amounts to a little less than an A4 page of typescript and cannot be compared with Radcliffe-Brown's *Andaman Islanders* or Malinowski's *Argonauts of the Western Pacific* in terms of foundational texts. That is not my intention, however. Haddon published the article to put his vision of what modern anthropology could be into the public domain and, on that basis, I treat it as a manifesto. Haddon probably wrote it in 1890 after Ellis commissioned a study of anthropology as the epistemological anchor for the Contemporary Science Series, a collection of utopian, anarchist and reformist treatments of subjects relevant to scientific social reform. That places Haddon in the vanguard of advanced thinking on anthropology and the text, despite its brevity, lives up to this in terms of its modernity. Haddon humanized and socialized anthropology, deterritorialized the ethnographic 'field' and incorporated an anthropology of affect in the study of the imaginative lives – art, craft and dance – of *other* civilizations, the very terms used adding an agency to the ethnographic subject that was groundbreaking at a time of imperialist expansion and genocide in the colonies. Furthermore, Haddon included sociology as a major area of study and tagged his explanation with a reference to Pëtr Kropotkin's theory that the study of social organization proceeds from the simple to the complex. Kropotkin was an influential Russian anarchist living in exile in London and Geddes introduced Haddon to Kropotkin's work in 1889. Haddon also substituted the modern concept of development as an explanation for the difference between simple and complex societies, explicitly rejecting a hierarchy of civilization, the orthodox taxonomy of evolutionary stages in culture and the comparative method used to study them.

Beyond the document itself, Haddon and his network thought of anthropology and sociology as interchangeable terms closely linked to a revamped version of political economy. In 1903, Geddes wrote a letter to Haddon in which he acknowledged that Haddon had 'approached sociology through anthropology' while Geddes had approached 'anthropolo. through socio.'. That letter started a process that culminated in Haddon and Geddes joining a working group that organized the inaugural meeting of the Sociological Society, the occasion, according to Chris Renwick (2012: 128–40), of a showdown with Galton and his Eugenics movement. This also explains the 'we' of 'we prefer', 'we' being a heterodox network of utopians, feminists, socialists, anarchists, revolutionaries and third-way reformists that Geddes created in the 1880s and Haddon joined in 1890. 'We prefer' was also a wonderfully understated acknowledgement of the culture war that split the small community of three hundred or so individuals that populated organizations active in the field of anthropology in Ireland and the UK. Haddon usually referred to this as 'Anthropology', and I use 'organized anthropology' for the sake of clarity. Haddon's membership of the Anthropological Institute, Folk-Lore Society and Royal Society of Antiquaries of Ireland was indicative of Anthropology in 'in its widest aspect', and he demonstrated what this meant in practice in an ethnographic survey of the Aran Islands in 1892 (RIA 3,2 (1891–93): 768–830), when he combined geography, anthropology, sociology, political economy, archaeology, folklore and ethnology under the organizing formula of 'Place-Work-Folk', which Geddes adapted from a synthetic, social survey model developed by Frédéric Le Play in France.

Haddon's manifesto had no effect on the trajectory of anthropology in the short term. In 1898, Cambridge University created the first University Lectureship in Anthropology in the Department of Anatomy and conceded a freestanding, part-time University Lectureship in Ethnology in 1900 after Frazer organized a lobby in support of Haddon and redefined anthropology-in-its-widest-aspect as ethnology. Ten years later, Haddon and Quiggin published the first history of anthropology in book form and defined ethnology as an alternative designation for those branches of cultural anthropology that 'deal with comparative sociology and magico-religious data' (Haddon and Quiggin 1910: 128), while anthropology retained the same meaning it had when it entered modern language in the sixteenth century as *Anthropologium*, a Latin word meaning the study of 'man's bodily structure' (ibid.: 6), which, of course, incorporated an evolutionary version of comparative anatomy. Haddon and Quiggin merely restated what Haddon proposed in 'The Study of Anthropology', but the implication of their argument goes against the grain of subsequent histories. The intention of this monograph is to trace the history of that argument and use it to construct a new version of Haddon's contribution to the modernization of anthropology and, by way of conclusion, to situate his preference for anthropology in its widest aspect within contemporary debates about the restriction of the scope of anthropology in a neoliberal academy.

CHANGING THE NARRATIVE

Representing Haddon as a progressive and formally innovative modernizer required forgetting large parts of his story as it has evolved to date, hence the absence of a conventional literature review. I disregard Haddon's background in zoology and drop Huxley from the role of a mentor who shaped Haddon's understanding of anthropology. I replace him with a heterodox network of mentors and collaborators, the key actors being William Henry Flower, James 'Tamate' Chalmers, James G. Frazer, Patrick Geddes, Henry 'Havelock' Ellis and Laurence Gomme – all men, but this was the nature of the power structures in organized anthropology in the 1890s. Haddon challenged discrimination on grounds of gender through his collaborations with Alice Shackleton, Clara Patterson and Alison Hingston Quiggin, as well as his articles on gendered science in his column in the *Irish Daily Independent*. Moreover, the influence of Elizabeth Cort, Caroline Haddon and Caroline Waterman is highlighted as I shift the epistemological focus from science to art, philosophy and political activism and introduce Haddon's family as the primary influencers in this context. I highlight his reading of Kropotkin as a major influence on his understanding of the task of the ethnographer and the purpose of ethnology. I also acknowledge Haddon's initiation into Freemasonry as a triggering event in terms of his switch from zoology to ethnology in 1888, that is, from science to art and philosophy, a route prepared by Frazer. Finally, I move the site of intellectual and practical development away from Cambridge in the wake of the 1898 anthropological expedition to the Torres Strait and back to the Aran Islands in the wake of his first expedition ten years earlier.

The key events in this new narrative include:

1887 Working with Flower and Samuel McFarlane on the ethnological component of his oceanographic expedition to the Torres Strait.

1888 Abandoning marine biology more or less as soon as he arrived there.
Meeting Chalmers.

1889 Co-curating an exhibition with Flower at the British Museum in October.
Deciding to go into anthropology in December.
Linking up with Geddes and reading Kropotkin and Elie Reclus.

1890 Adopting the magic lantern as an instrument of anti-racism activism.
Collaborating with Ellis on *The Study of Anthropology*.

INTRODUCTION

Visiting the Aran Islands for the first time during a government-funded survey of fishing grounds, discovering instantaneous photography and losing his job as a government scientist.

1891 Setting up an anthropometric laboratory in Dublin in partnership with Daniel J. Cunningham and Francis Galton.

1892 Writing a critique of imperial policy for popular journals. Experimenting with a social survey model in the Aran Islands and, paradoxically, becoming a craniologist.
Losing his job as a lead ethnographer for the Anthropological Laboratory.

1893 Mobilizing a popular ethnographic movement in Belfast. Conducting an ethnography of singing games with Clara Patterson.

1895 Leading an insurrection by anticolonial ethnologists in Ipswich.

1898 Breaking a BAAS embargo on funding for a second expedition to Oceania.

1898 Filming the last dance of the Malu Zogo-Le.

1899 Publishing a photographic manifesto in *Notes & Queries on Anthropology*.

1900 Becoming a part-time teacher of ethnology at Cambridge.

The key drivers of change include (1) his first experience of the Malu cult in 1888, (2) his collaboration with Geddes and Ellis, (3) conflict with the British Administration in Ireland during fisheries research in the Aran Islands in 1890, (4) his adoption of the slideshow as his primary ethnographic method between 1890 and 1895, (5) a confrontation with Huxley that forced him into the skull-measuring business in 1892, and, finally, (6) his anticolonial speech in Ipswich and the sanctions that followed in the wake of a very public controversy.

This, then, is a story with many plots and subplots, too many in fact to cover in the space allowed. There are, however, four consistent threads that tie all these events together, and these are

(1) Haddon's profound commitment to anticolonial activism, (2) his relentless experimentation with ethnographic form, (3) his fascination with the meaning of art and dance across space and time and (4) his involvement in the skull-measuring business in Ireland. The last is, from a historiographical perspective, extraordinarily problematic in terms of making the case that Haddon was a modernizer, and the structure of this monograph pivots around this question. Some background will explain why.

I first encountered Haddon in 2009 when I discovered a photograph of Haddon and Charles R. Browne, who was measuring Tom Connelly's skull in the Aran Islands in 1892 (Figure 6.1). Browne pasted the photograph into an album in 1897, one of three albums in the Manuscript Library in TCD that hold the photographic archive of the Irish Ethnographic Survey (see de Mórdha and Walsh 2012). I had just curated an exhibition of John Millington Synge's photographic documentation of life in the Aran Islands in 1898 (see Bruna 2017: 61–62) and Browne's albums provided an opportunity to compare the record of an anthropologist with that of a literary modernist. The photograph of Connelly submitting to measurement initially confirmed a narrative of an English 'head-hunter' and his Irish proxy searching for Irish aborigines. However, Browne's sustained and systematic documentation of social conditions in remote communities in the west of Ireland was unique, and Dáithí de Mórdha, an ethnologist descended from people Browne surveyed in Dún Chaoin in 1897, and I selected fifty photographs and showed 'The Irish Head-Hunter' exhibition in the same communities, terminating the tour in the Haddon Library in 2013.

In preparation for the opening, Aidan Baker, the Haddon Librarian, searched for Haddon's copy of 'The Ethnography of the Aran Islands' and discovered a file of material from an earlier survey of the islands. The file was separated from the rest of his papers in 1913 and contained a ten-page extract from a journal he kept while working on a survey of fishing grounds in 1890, filling a gap in the papers held in Cambridge University Library. His fascination with the people and their way of life contrasted sharply with the tables of anthropometric data that dominated the ethnography he wrote with Browne two years later. This gap widened in 2014 when a search of the Anatomy Museum in TCD uncovered a box of photographs that Andrew Francis Dixon took in the company of Haddon in 1890. There was nothing in any of the material recovered to suggest that Haddon had any interest in skull-measuring, and the focus of research switched to the Irish component of the Haddon Papers in an effort to find out why he measured Tom Connelly and twenty-six other islanders in 1892.

Haddon's 'Irish' papers were uncatalogued at this time and it appeared that they were rarely consulted. For instance, a search in 2017 for the manuscript of Haddon's 1891 critique of the Imperial Institute revealed that it had been misfiled, possibly after Stocking transcribed it in the 1970s (see Stocking 1995: xix; Stocking and Haddon 1993). This illustrates how much of what was written about Haddon was based on primary research undertaken by Stocking. Indeed, Stocking's mining of anthropological archives and personal papers in Britain prompted James Urry (1989: 364) to describe him as the 'doyen of studies of the anthropological past', who, according to Clifford Geertz (1999: 305), had 'an enormous impact on the way anthropologists see themselves and their profession'. It is hardly surprising then that Stocking's 1995 study of the emergence of modern anthropology in *After Tylor*, supplemented with Quiggin's 1942 biography, provided a road map for my research in Cambridge.

Discrepancies quickly emerged between significant aspects of Stocking's treatment of Haddon and the source material in Cambridge. For example, Stocking (1995: 105–6) quoted a draft of a letter Haddon wrote in May 1891 in response to a letter Ellis sent offering to support any movement to reconstruct anthropology and asking Haddon to write a study of anthropology for the Contemporary Science Series. Haddon's draft consisted of little more than a series of quick notes that summarize information from a range of viewpoints and relied heavily on analogy and quotation to address Ellis's request for a biological treatment of anthropology. Geddes put Ellis in contact with Haddon, and 'biological' can be interpreted as a metonym for biosociality and, as such, refers to the latter's interest comparative sociology. Stocking, however, missed this, bypassed the study of anthropology, and considered instead *Evolution in Art*, which Ellis reluctantly agreed to as a substitute in 1891. Haddon summarized the idea of this book in 'The Study of Anthropology'. He stated:

> The origin, evolution and migration of designs and patterns is a fascinating subject, and is repleted with human interest, as being associated some of the deepest and most subtle ideas. (Haddon 1895a: 25)

Stocking (1995: 106), however, concluded that 'Haddon insisted on casting his arguments in "biological" terms', and so consolidated the trope of a former zoologist with a biological understanding of the study of culture. Taken in context, Stocking would have seen that Haddon, Geddes and Ellis used evolution as a metonym for the human capacity to adapt and innovate and, in a post-evolutionist environment, tried to harness this natural force as a driver of scientific, social reform. Ellis presented their arguments in the Contemporary Science Series, which he launched in 1889 with *The Evolution of Sex* by Geddes and Thomson.

There are other examples of similar discrepancies. Haddon pitched an article to a few popular journals in 1891 in which he critiqued the link between racism, genocide, colonial administration and imperial policy. He proposed a bureau of ethnology that would act as a humanitarian agency and end a policy that actively facilitated colonists who exterminated 'slowly or rapidly, unintentionally or by force the inhabitants of the countries we annex' (Haddon MS 1891, Critique of Imperial Institute: 10). Haddon pulled no punches. He declared that 'the general public, the legislators & the executive' were complicit in these acts of 'legalized murder'. Stocking published a transcript in the *History of Anthropology Newsletter* in 1993 and commented that 'Such language was used by the founders of the Aborigines Protection Society' (Stocking and Haddon 1993: 3), which, incidentally, is not surprising given that Cruft (1915: 55) admired John Haddon and Elizabeth Cort's involvement in the anti-slavery movement that led to the formation of the Society in 1837. Stocking (1995: 101–3) edited this comment out of his analysis in *After Tylor* and concluded that the proposal was a scheme for 'enlightening imperial self-interest'. Stocking wasn't alone. Henrika Kuklick (1991: 50) first interpreted Haddon's proposal as 'a systematic basis for enlightened colonial administration' and this line of argument became an academic trend when repeated by James Urry (1993: 103) and Stocking. Greta Jones (1998) added a variation to the theme. She also consulted the same sources as Stocking and argued that Haddon and John Millington Synge operated in contested cultural and political territories that coincided geographically with the Aran Islands. Her description of Haddon as a 'Darwinist evolutionist par excellence' (ibid.: 195) was authoritative and, therefore, influential in generating a common sense that Haddon's biological project was the antithesis of Synge's literary modernism and, in subsequent scholarship, Douglas Hyde's cultural nationalism (see for example Beiner 2012; Ó Giolláin 2017). Emilie de Brigard (1995) applied a similar logic in her analysis of Haddon's cinematographic experiment and Alison Griffith (1996) added additional layers of instrumentality, gaze and orientalism when she looked at the problem of Haddon's films 'through the lens' of theories developed by Michel Foucault and Edward Said. Jones (2008) and Griffiths (2002) subsequently wrote more sympathetic treatments of Haddon, but the trope of a former zoologist with a biological understanding of the study of culture remained as an epistemological bottom line.

To summarize, there is a discernible pattern in these knowledge-making strategies, and Joan Leopold (1991: 315–17) provided an interesting perspective on its origin when she reviewed Stocking's 1987 study *Victorian Anthropology*. She detected a determination to establish evolutionism as *the* dominant organizing logic in Victorian anthropology, and I contend that the examples above establish this as a wider academic trend, which I have characterized as a preoccupation with evolution bracketed by race and empire in the context of a scientific revolution. Consequently, 'The Study of Anthropology' was forgotten in the sense that Guy Beiner (2006) used the term to describe the obsolescence of events in preferred histories that are necessarily selective. Thomas Hylland Eriksen, speaking at a webinar organized by the History of Anthropology Network on 19 November 2021, diagnosed the cumulative effect of strategic forgetting as a form of 'structural amnesia', and the results can be seen in Ó Giolláin's introduction to *Irish Ethnologies* (2017). This presents a synthesis of authoritative and trusted scholarship and, as such, locates the cause of this 'amnesia' in key texts from a historicist tradition that has dominated the history of anthropology since the 1990s and, ironically, derives its authority from its unprecedented study of primary sources. Discovering these discrepancies altered the trajectory of my research and I went back to the same sources to see what else had been forgotten.

REMEMBERING

Recovering the 'forgotten' events of Haddon's practice involved a multilayered 'Irish' reading of the Haddon Papers and related records, including photographic collections in Dublin, Cambridge and London. The first task was to photograph every document and document every photograph and then connect this archive to institutional records and newspaper reports using online archives like the Biodiversity Heritage Library (BAAS, RIA, RDS and BNFC proceedings and reports), the proceedings of the Royal Anthropological Institute and Royal Irish Academy, the Folklore Society, *Nature* – Haddon was a regular contributor – and the British Newspaper Archive (British Library and Find My Past). Newspapers were especially valuable in filling gaps in institutional records and constructing political contexts for various incidents in the daily lives of ethnologists and anthropologists. Archive.org and Hathi Trust digital libraries provided access to the first editions of many important texts and the *Oxford Dictionary of National Biography* (ODNB) was a useful source of biographical detail that added nuance to the lives of actors in networks connected to Haddon.

Regarding Haddon's papers, the TROVE portal managed by the National Library of Australia provides online access to the papers, and it was a pleasure to be able to 'leaf' through his sketchbooks on one screen while reading his record of making the same sketches on a second screen, a process enhanced significantly in 2020 by Anita Herle and Jude Philp's publication of *Recording Kastom*, an annotated and thoroughly illustrated transcription of Haddon's Torres Strait and New Guinea journals. Haddon and Mead argued that words cannot give the full sense of a dance performed, and Haddon's films can be viewed online at the National Film and Sound Archive of Australia. The associated sound recordings can be streamed on the British Library website. Michael Eaton combined both in his 2010 film *Masks of Mer*, and the National Museum of Ireland gave me access to dance 'toggery' Haddon collected in 1888, adding a material dimension to this multimedia research and recapitulating Haddon's use of this material in slideshows in Dublin in 1890.

The second task involved organizing this material around key events, and this required timelines and organizational charts that tracked the flow of ideas, money and influence, a methodology that drew on my experience as an organization and methods analyst in the Department of Justice *fadó fadó* (a long time ago). The information produced required several revisions over a four-year period as new facts disrupted emerging narratives. For instance, the last document I accessed in Cambridge University Library was Haddon's 'little black book'. He listed Douglas Hyde among regular contacts in the period under review, thereby triggering a late detour into the field of Anglo-Irish folklore and the discovery of a link between Haddon's first experience of a Malu ceremony in 1888, his collaboration with Clara Patterson in Belfast in 1893 and his filming of a Malu dance performance in 1898 (see Walsh 2021c).

This illustrates how my research process became a form of spatial historiography, the scope and complexity of the sources generating a multidimensional and mobile epistemology in which new material comes online constantly. For instance, the British Newspaper Archive recently uploaded the *Optical Lantern and Kinematograph Journal*, which published a review of Haddon's films in 1906. Likewise, discovering a recently uploaded copy of

Cruft's 1915 history of the Haddon family filled significant gaps in my research in relation to (a) linking Haddon's humanitarian activism to the Aborigines Protection Society and (b) tracing the origin of Haddon's interest in art. Finally, I found a letter Haddon wrote to Geddes on 25 December 1887 on TROVE – the original is held in Strathclyde University Archive Department – while checking quotes during the copyedit phase of this publication and it confirmed Haddon's interest in art and the importance of Geddes as a mentor, which points to opportunities for further research in this and other related archives. Finding this material involved some creativity with keywords in an effort to disrupt the algorithms that build internet searches around account histories, and this added a post-human dimension to the process. Further disruption is inevitable as new material comes online, and this monograph constitutes a time-specific epistemological screenshot of sorts, a conditional epistemology that contrasts sharply with the certainty, fixed perspectives and determined 'forgetfulness' of the historicist tradition that has dominated the history of anthropology for three decades.

Regarding these histories, the main problem was reconciling Haddon's involvement in the skull business with the discovery of Kropotkin's influence. This exposed a yawning gap in mainstream histories, and Kenneth Maddock's article 'Through Kropotkin to the Foundation of Radcliffe-Brown's Anthropology' (1994) makes one wonder why more researchers haven't investigated 'Anarchy' Brown more thoroughly. If they had, they might have discovered that 'Anarchy' Brown was secretly wearing Haddon's theoretical undergarments. Moreover, there is plenty of material in the wider literature on utopianism and anarchism that explains why Haddon was so influenced by Kropotkin. To begin with, Norman MacKenzie's 1975 study of the origins of the Fabian Society includes a brief but valuable account of Haddon's father's sisters, Caroline and Margaret. Neil Weir's 2006 ODNB biography of Margaret (Haddon) Hinton's husband James adds further detail in terms of Caroline Haddon's sponsorship of Ellis's medical training in preparation for his groundbreaking study of sexuality. Likewise, Anna Clark adds detail to that relationship in her 2017 study *Alternative Histories of the Self: A Cultural History of Sexuality and Secrets*. Caroline Haddon also features in outline in Susan Hinely's study 'Charlotte Wilson, the "Woman Question" and the Meaning of Anarchist Socialism in Late Victorian Radicalism' (2012), as well as Nan Sloane's *The Women in the Room: Labour's Forgotten History* (2018). Lawrence Davis and Ruth Kinna's collection of essays *Anarchism and Utopianism* (2009) updated Mackenzie, and Judy Greenway contributed an essay that deals specifically with sexual politics in 'Speaking Desire: Anarchism and Free Love as Utopian Performance in *Fin de Siècle* Britain'. The 'Miss Haddons', as MacKenzie (1975: 51) called them, do not feature, but Greenway provides additional context for their nephew's advanced thinking on gender, sex and sexuality. Similarly, Tom Steele's (2007) work on Élisée Reclus, Patrick Geddes and links between radical French Freemasonry and popular education movements helps explain Haddon's commitment to the university extension movement and his participation, with Geddes and Reclus, in the Science and Art Meeting in Edinburgh in 1895. Federico Ferretti's work 'Anarchist Geographers and Feminism in Late 19th Century France: The Contributions of Élisée and Élie Reclus' (2016) provides a good description of the radical milieu that Haddon associated with when he decided to go into anthropology. Gerry Kearns's work on Kropotkin in 'The Political Pivot of Geography' (2004) provides a framework for constructing a similar pivot in organized anthropology and, with Ferretti, provides a basis for reconnecting ethnology to its roots in geography. Han Vermeulen's (2015b) study of the origin of ethnology in the German Enlightenment extended the timeframe of anti-imperial thought in ethnology. Jack Morrell and Arnold Thackray's brief study of ethnology in the 1830s in *Gentlemen of Science* (1981) is a valuable prequel to Chris Renwick's study *British Sociology's Lost Biological Roots* (2012), essential reading in relation to differences Geddes had with Huxley and Galton. Similarly, Erin McLaughlin-Jenkins's 2001 investigation of an exchange of articles in the press between Huxley and Kropotkin makes it possible to connect a class war in science in the 1880s to the culture war in organized anthropology in the 1890s. Similarly, Clifford O'Connor's *A People's History of Science: Miners, Midwives and Low Mechanics* (2005) revealed to me Huxley's mobilization of science in support of capitalism, which is especially interesting in the context of Haddon's attempt to move anthropology out of a restricted form of natural history and into sociology.

Haddon was not an anarchist. He was a philosophical reformist, and the need for clarity around terms like 'radical' arose in conversation with David Shankland[1] and fed into a longer conversation with Mark Maguire[2] about the power of anthropology and the anthropology of power. This led to an engagement with a new historiography of anthropology that has gathered momentum around questions of modernity before and beyond Malinowski. Shankland (2014) and Vermeulen (2015a) were instrumental in reviving the History of Anthropology Newsletter and reformulating it as the History of Anthropology Network (HOAN), which organized a wider review of pre-Malinowskian ethnography at the 2020 conference of the European Association of Social Anthropologists (EASA). The HOAN continued the process of remembering in 2021 with Thomas Hylland Eriksen's webinar on forgotten anthropologies, which set up the publication of Vermeulen and Delgado Rosa's 2022 collection of essays on ethnography before Malinowski. However, a decision to exclude recent scholarship on Haddon and his associates – the foundations of the book were laid down in 2018 – has rendered this akin to a discussion of Hamlet without the Prince. Delgado Rosa and Christine Laurière offset this to some extent when they commissioned a contemporaneous review of Haddon's life and work for the Bérose International Encyclopaedia of Histories of Anthropology (Walsh 2022), which drew on research for this volume.

To conclude, historiography is a dynamic and often contrary process and this volume, written by an outsider in terms of academic traditions and networks, continues in that spirit. Accordingly, the question of Haddon's ancestry is framed by a fundamental shift from history as the construction of disciplinary traditions to history as part of a process of engagement with colonial legacies in the wake of the murder in police custody of George Floyd. Haddon makes most sense in the latter context. He envisaged a new anthropology as a response to the genocidal logic of colonialism, the destruction of Oceanic civilizations and, with it, the loss of ancestral knowledges that bridged the extremes of humankind and contested European ethnocentricity. He drew inspiration from the anti-slavery activism of his grandparents John Haddon and Elizabeth Cort, who fostered a tradition of nonconformism that continued through the radical feminism of his aunts Caroline Haddon and Margaret Hinton and the humanitarian activism of their nephew and his associates in a loose network of anarcho-utopian activists who imagined another anthropology. The memory of that anthropology may have skipped a generation or two, but the unsettled state of the historiography of anthropology today provides a useful vantage point to recall the ancestral knowledges that influenced it.

This story of that other anthropology is told (with the aid of photographs) in three parts of three chapters and subchapters each, three being a magical number in Celtic mythology. The first part deals with Haddon's decision to go into anthropology in 1889 and argues against the common sense that he experienced an anthropological epiphany in the Torres Strait during the 1888 expedition and bided his time in Dublin before returning to Cambridge and leading an anthropological expedition back to the Torres Strait in 1898. This is the essence of the 'taking anthropology out of the armchair' trope that is so central to the folklore of disciplinary anthropology, for which Haddon is partly responsible, it must be said. Dismantling that trope was relatively easy, but it is way beyond the wordcount of this project, and I have chosen instead to deal with it in terms of the following conundrum: Haddon's papers clearly show that he abandoned marine biology upon reaching the Torres Strait in 1888, decided to go into anthropology in 1889 and became the anthropological lead in an anarchism-inspired social reform movement in 1890. So, how did he become a part-time ethnologist in 1900 after a craniologist became the first full-time anthropologist at Cambridge University?

The second part goes back to the Aran Islands in 1892 and the problematic 'selfie' of Haddon and Browne measuring Tom Connelly's skull in a mobile version of Galton's anthropometric laboratory. This photograph places Haddon's practice firmly in the realm of scientific racism, but this 'selfie' has a long history and its function as a demonstration of advanced practical science in action is inextricably tied up with the wider political response of a Tory government to a campaign by Irish nationalists to exit the Union with Great Britain. Practical science in the fisheries sector brought Haddon to the west of Ireland two years earlier and he discovered a seemingly undisturbed ethnological zone that was the perfect testing ground for a reconstructed anthropology. The question here is why he set up and mobilized an anthropometric laboratory in a partnership with Galton and Daniel J. Cunningham, Professor of Anatomy at TCD and a staunch defender of British rule in Ireland.

The third part takes its cue from a subversive act that points to the most innovative aspect of Haddon's work as an ethnologist. Haddon included in the report of the 1892 ethnographic expedition to the Aran Islands a photograph that documented the refusal by Michael Faherty and two women – they withheld their names – to submit to measurement. It was a study in native agency and affect that materialized an earlier decision to adopt 'instantaneous' photography over 'tedious' text as his ethnographic method of choice. It also recorded a 'little war' in the daily life of the colony and so materialized Haddon's anticolonial attitude. He had already adopted the magic lantern – literally and metaphorically – as an instrument of anticolonial activism and incorporated this into a performed ethnography that culminated in the filming of the last dance of the Malu Zogo-Le. One year later, Haddon published a manifesto on photography as the fifth field of anthropology and created a foundation for visual anthropology that was thoroughly buried under the discipline of words Mead described in 1975. The question here is whether this is sufficient reason to claim that Haddon was a modernist – not just a modernizer – who ought to be remembered as a pioneer of modern anthropology and the man who pointed Synge towards the Aran Islands.

This question goes to the heart of any discussion of ancestry. It is inextricably tied to the question of what anthropology meant in 1890 and how that relates to what anthropology means in 2023. The main finding of this study is that the conflict between radical and reactionary forces in the 1890s is being re-enacted in a stand-off between exponents of 'traditional' and 'academic' anthropologies in which debates about restricted knowledge production are enlivened by a renewed engagement with structural racism and colonial legacies in the wake of the murder of George Floyd. It seems that the history of anthropology has at last caught up with Haddon.

NOTES

1. David Shankland, Director, Royal Anthropological Institute for Great Britain and Ireland, acted as external examiner for my PhD thesis.
2. Mark Maguire, Dean of Social Studies, Maynooth University, supervised my doctoral research.

PART I

• • •

BECOMING AN ETHNOLOGIST

Figure 1.1. Anon., *Dredging party, 1885, with friends [plate 16] sitting, left to right: A. C. Haddon (in front of light suit), S. Haughton, W. S. Green, C. B. Ball; standing: Sir D'Arcy W. Thompson (light suit), Sir R. S. Ball (yachting cap), Valentine Ball (at end of trawl)*, 1885. Digital scan of silver gelatine print. Permission of the Royal Irish Academy © RIA.

CHAPTER 1

BECOMING AN ANTHROPOLOGIST

● ● ●

Anthropology and photography take up a good deal of time but it is mainly in the evening. Summing up my work to the end of October I fancy a fair verdict would be (1) Coral reef investigation – much less done than I should have liked, but I am making a start. (2) General marine zoology about as much as I could reasonably expect to do. (3) Anthropology much more than I anticipated.

—A. C. Haddon, Torres Strait and
New Guinea Journal (October 1888).

Haddon arrived in Oceania on 8 August 1888, and began the long journey back to Europe on 15 April 1889, having spent eight months exploring the Torres Strait and adjacent parts of New Guinea. By his own record, anthropology took up much more time than the investigation of coral reefs, which had been the focus of research proposed for the expedition. On his return to London, he spent the summer in the British Museum sorting through the material he collected and writing up his fieldnotes. From September onwards, his accounts of native life in the Torres Strait and New Guinea appeared in reports of the proceedings of Section H – Anthropology of the British Association for the Advancement of Science, the Anthropological Institute of Great Britain and Ireland, and the Folk-Lore Society. In December, he told his friend Patrick Geddes, the biologist turned sociologist, that he had decided to 'go into Anthropology', as Geddes phrased it in a follow-up letter. There were no jobs in anthropology at the time, and Haddon returned to Dublin, where he taught zoology at the Royal College of Science until 1901, when his election as a Fellow of Christ's College at Cambridge University made it possible for him to accept an offer of a part-time University Lectureship in Ethnology.

These events provide the bare bones of a well-established narrative of a decade-long transition from zoology in Dublin to disciplinary anthropology in Cambridge. However, a closer look at Haddon's own record of the 1888 expedition suggests rupture rather than transition. This created two main tasks in respect of the research presented here. The first was deciding when Haddon actually became an ethnologist and the second involved unravelling what he meant when he told Geddes that he had decided to 'go into Anthropology' – deciding, in effect, where zoology finished and anthropology began. My analysis of Haddon's journal and the papers he published after the expedition indicates that he abandoned zoology as soon as he reached the Torres Strait at the beginning of August 1888 and acknowledged as much when he reviewed fieldwork undertaken up to the end of October 1888. The problem here is that Haddon disguised this abrupt change in direction as an unintended consequence of his encounters with the islanders and stated, by way of justification, that he was so struck by evidence of population decline and cultural disruption that he felt obliged to collect information on 'old habits and beliefs' (*JAI* 19 [1890]: 297–98) before they vanished, along with the people themselves. It was inevitable then that epiphany and salvage would become associated with Haddon's entry into anthropology and become a part of the original narrative of disciplinary anthropology at Cambridge.

I have constructed an alternative narrative that begins with Haddon's faltering career as an academic zoologist and his attempt to revive it by going on expedition to Oceania. This activated a long tradition of linking oceanographic and ethnological research and created the conditions under which Haddon decided to leave zoology aside and focus instead on ethnology. That switch makes sense when one considers the evidence of a well-planned ethnological component to the research proposed and, in this context, I focus on Samuel McFarlane (sometimes spelled MacFarlane), a missionary and ethnologist who advised Haddon prior to departure. McFarlane's association with the British Museum brings William Henry Flower, director of the museum's Natural History Department, into play and opens a route to argue that Haddon was acting as an agent for the British Museum, with the inevitable consequence that he decided to go into anthropology in December 1889.

LEAVING ZOOLOGY

Haddon announced his imminent departure for the Torres Strait while reading a paper at a meeting of the Royal Dublin Society (RDS) in June 1888, the first of a series of planned communications 'on the Sea Anemones of the British Seas' (RDS 4,2 [1888–92]: 297). He stated that he had to interrupt this work because of the difficulty of procuring specimens and added that he was 'leaving Ireland for some time, and it may be a considerable period before I shall be able to conclude this series of Papers' (ibid.: 301). The following month Haddon boarded a ship in the Port of London and sailed to the Torres Strait, arriving on 8 August. He returned to his teaching job in Dublin in January 1890 and resumed his revision of the taxonomy of sea anemones in February 1891, at the same time that Cunningham and Haddon acceded to a request by Galton and presented the Royal Irish Academy and the Anthropological Institute with a plan to establish an Anthropometric Laboratory of Ireland at TCD and undertake an associated programme of ethnographic surveys in the west of Ireland (*JAI* 21 [1892]: 35–39).

This outline of a timeline registers the impact of the 1888 expedition. Within two years of his return from Oceania, Haddon was working with two of the most powerful players in organized anthropology in Ireland and England. However, his collaboration with the founder of eugenics and an anatomist who set a baseline for the anthropometric investigation of anthropological problems relating to comparative anatomy seems to support the narrative of a transition from zoology to a hybrid of biology and anthropology that owed much to Darwin in spirit and Huxley in practice and was tainted with scientific racism by association with Galton. For instance, Emilie de Brigard (1995: 16–17) described Haddon as 'a former zoologist' who made the first ethnographic film, while Greta Jones (1998: 201) interpreted his experiments in ethnological fieldwork in Ireland as 'a form of cultural zoology' that constituted the antithesis of literary modernism and cultural nationalism. This way of thinking about Haddon has, as discussed in the introduction, become orthodox since the 1990s, and the problem with this accumulated historiography (see Kuklick 1991; Urry 1993; Stocking 1995; Kuper 2001; Beiner 2012; Brannigan 2014; Ó Giolláin 2017) is that it assigns too much significance to Haddon's training as a zoologist.

Haddon entered Christ's College, Cambridge in 1875 to read Natural Sciences. He specialized in Zoology and Comparative Anatomy and graduated in 1879. He applied for a job at the British Museum but failed the qualifying examination. He spent six months in the Zoological Station in Naples and then worked at Christ's College as Curator of the Zoological Museum and a Demonstrator in the Zoology Department. Alfred Newton, his Professor of Zoology, lobbied Huxley on Haddon's behalf and Huxley arranged for an appointment in 1880 to the Chair of Zoology at the Royal College of Science in Dublin. Huxley also put him in charge of reorganizing the natural history collections in the Museum of Science and Art in Dublin. As a government scientist and a member of Huxley's network, Haddon got involved in fisheries research. He took part in dredging expeditions off the south-west coast of Ireland in 1885 and 1886 (see Praeger 1949: 186–87) and was chief scientific officer on a government-funded survey of fishing grounds in the west of Ireland in 1890 (see Green in RDS 127 [1890–91]: 29–66; RDS 128 [1891–92]: *23–72*). The dredging expedition provides a fascinating piece of evidence of Haddon's relations with other academics at the time. He posed as an outsider in a photograph taken at the launch of a survey of fishing grounds (Figure 1.1), representing himself as a mariner among academics – including Haughton, President of the Royal Irish Academy, on his left – and, by looking off-camera, very deliberately set himself apart from the rest of the company. At some stage over the winter, he founded the Dublin Naturalists' Field Club and his involvement in the field club movement in Ireland became a counterpoint to his progress as an academic scientist in zoology and a substitute for non-existent jobs in ethnology.

As an academic zoologist, Haddon was in trouble. He specialized in sea anemones and was not doing well in comparison with his contemporaries. Geddes, who became a close friend and collaborator after they briefly shared a laboratory in Cambridge, discovered a reciprocal arrangement between algae and marine invertebrates that guaranteed the survival of both. Karl Brandt was engaged in a parallel investigation in Berlin and published a paper in 1881 in which he labelled this type of interspecies cooperation 'symbiosis', a term coined by botanist Anton de Barry in 1877 (Renwick 2012: 77). This gave Brandt priority in the discovery of symbiosis and his paper (Brandt 1881) has become one of the most cited in the literature 'on modern coral reef taxonomy' (Bowen 2015: 84–85). This did not affect Geddes so much. He took a different track after he discovered social theories that resonated with his pioneering work on biosociality (Renwick 2012: 19–42). Haddon's 1888 revision of sea anemones was, however, unremarkable except for his collaboration with Alice Shackleton, whom, according to a report in the *Freeman's Journal* in November 1890, he introduced as the first woman to present a scientific paper to the Royal Dublin Society (RDS 4,2 [1888–92]: 673–701). This may place him in the vanguard of gender politics in science but, in March 1887, he failed to secure a teaching post in the School of Biology at the University of Melbourne (see *Report of the Proceedings of the University of Melbourne for the Year 1887–88*), and that was the most likely motivation for his first expedition to the Torres Strait, on the basis that it would demonstrably enhance his reputation in the new field of systematic biology and thereby improve his future prospects of employment. It is worth noting in this context that biology was undergoing a methodological transformation that Edmund B. Wilson (1901: 19) has memorably described as a battle between 'bug hunters' and 'section cutters', and Haddon, who studied in Michael Foster's physiology laboratory in Cambridge, was definitely a section cutter. Haddon met Huxley over dinner and worked on a proposal for an investigation of coral reefs and, according to Quiggin (1942: 80), Haddon's first draft stated:

> I propose to investigate the fauna, structure and mode of formation of the coral reefs in Torres Straits, ... With the information thus obtained to study the raised coral formation on various islands and on New Guinea so as to be able to approximate the exact conditions under which the various formations were found.

Huxley had his own motives. John Murray, a member of the HMS *Challenger* expedition, had controversially challenged the correctness of Darwin's theory of coral reef formation and Huxley, who earned the nickname 'Darwin's Bulldog' for his forceful defence of Darwin's theory of evolution, seems to have taken Haddon's difficulty as an opportunity to settle the row. He arranged for Foster, in his capacity as Secretary of the Royal Society, to organize part of the funding for the expedition and, on 7 September 1889, the *Illustrated London News* reported on the controversy between Huxley and Murray and the reporter noted that 'Scientists are at work in Torres Straits and elsewhere on the coral reefs'.

Before he left Ireland, Haddon told the members of the Royal Dublin Society that the expedition was essential to his study of specific variation in sea anemones because:

> The most satisfactory way to accomplish this is to go to the original locality and collect specimens there. Then, having recovered it, the type must be subjected to anatomical investigation. (RDS 4,2 [1888–92]: 297–98).

In 1891, Cunningham and Haddon presented the following rationale for an ethnographic survey of 'original' localities in Ireland:

we have in Ireland certain very old colonies. These ethnical islands, if we may so term them, require to be very carefully studied, and will no doubt afford valuable information concerning the persistence or otherwise of racial characters. It has therefore occurred to us that we might employ anthropometric methods for the purpose of giving some assistance to the anthropologist in his endeavours to unravel the tangled skein of the so-called "Irish Race". (*JAI* 21 [1892]: 36)

It is not difficult to see how Haddon's decision to go into anthropology could be interpreted as a logical transition from zoology: swapping sea anemones for humans and developing a mobile anthropometric laboratory to generate anatomical data from Irish aboriginals. However, the anthropologist's endeavour 'to unravel the tangled skein of the so-called "Irish Race"' was specific to debates about Home Rule, and Haddon's decision to engage in ethnological research during his first expedition was rooted in an older tradition of oceanographic research and, as such, grounded in geography rather than biology.

The study of non-Europeans by natural scientists developed as a component of oceanographic research. Bronwen Douglas (2008), for instance, credits George Cuvier, the French zoologist and explorer, with setting a benchmark in the development of field anthropology in 1829 when he celebrated recent conquests of geography that included the study of the languages and customs of the inhabitants of Oceania. Cuvier, according to Douglas (ibid.: 99), ensured that Oceania became a focus of empirical research in the 'classic era of scientific voyaging between 1766 and 1840 ... not least in the natural history of man and the nascent discipline of anthropology'. Huxley was a product of this system. He met Australian aboriginals and made sketches of Papuans while working as an Assistant Surgeon on the HMS *Rattlesnake* expedition, which charted a route through the Great Barrier Reef between 1846 and 1850 and spent time in the Torres Strait. Ethnographic material from the HMS *Challenger* expedition of 1872–76 was also sent to the Natural History Department of the British Museum, and it may be that Huxley envisaged a similar arrangement for Haddon's expedition. The circumstances of Haddon's correspondence with McFarlane in 1887 provide convincing evidence of such an arrangement.

PLANNING AN EXPEDITION

Samuel McFarlane was the first London Missionary Society (LMS) evangelist to reach the Torres Strait in 1870 and he established a regional base on the island of Mer (Murray) in 1871. He retired to England in 1886 and Haddon consulted him in 1887 in relation to the best site for his study of coral reefs. McFarlane wrote to Haddon on 2 December 1889 and advised him to 'make the Mission Station at Murray Island your headquarters and spend August September, October and November there & New Guinea'. Quiggin (1942: 77–80) thought McFarlane's advice decisive and speculated that contact between McFarlane and Haddon originated in missionary networks connected to the Haddon family and its publishing business. Cruft (1915: 53) described how John Haddon printed literature for Baptists for use in their missions, and this developed into an agency of sorts when other goods were routinely sent with this material. Quiggin, however, missed the fact that McFarlane donated over two hundred ethnological specimens from the Torres Strait and New Guinea to the British Museum between 1876 and 1886. Given that Huxley (a) served as a trustee of the British Museum between 1883 and 1886, and (b) was instrumental in having Flower appointed as Director of the Natural History Department in 1884 (see Huxley 1900: 71, 204), it is safe to assume that Flower and McFarlane, like Haddon, were part of Huxley's network and, in that capacity, were involved in planning the ethnological and anthropological component of Haddon's oceanographical expedition. In effect, Haddon was acting as an agent of the British Museum, and this might explain why he made no reference to coral reef investigation in the first paper he presented to Section H – Anthropology in September 1889 (BAAS 1890: 786).

He corrected this oversight in his inaugural paper at the Anthropological Institute in November:

> In the summer of 1888 I went to Torres Strait to investigate the structure and fauna of the coral reefs of that district. Very soon after my arrival in the Straits I found that the natives of the islands had of later years been greatly reduced in number, and that, with the exception of but one or two individuals, none of the white residents knew anything about the customs of the natives and not a single person cared about them personally. When I began to question the natives I discovered that the young men had a very imperfect acquaintance with the old habits and beliefs, and that only from the older men was reliable information to be obtained. So it was made clear to me that if I neglected to avail myself of the present opportunity of collecting information on the ethnography of the islanders, it was extremely probable that that knowledge would never be gleaned – for if no one interested himself in the matter meanwhile, it was almost certain that no trustworthy information could be collected in, say, ten years' time. This being my opinion, I felt it my duty to fill up all the time not actually employed in my zoological researches in anthropological studies ... (*JAI* 19 [1890] 297–98)

Haddon reversed the order of work he recorded in his journal in October 1888, and the reason for this spin is most evident in a letter he wrote three years later. Haddon wrote to Foster on 7 May 1891 and asked him to fund the publication of a monograph on the islanders. He explained that he had 'employed the time not otherwise devoted to my zoological and geological investigations in studying the natives & in making an ethnographical collection and in taking photographs'. Haddon used the spin to cover the fact that money Foster provided for oceanographical research at Huxley's request had, by Haddon's own account, been diverted into the collection of ethnological material.

Haddon recorded in his journal that his first act on reaching the Torres Strait was to undertake an exploration of the islands in the company of Hugh Milman, an acting police magistrate based on Thursday Island. He described his first encounter with 'natives' on Nagir Island on 13 August 1888, and, from that point on, his journal becomes a record of seeking out and collecting ethnological information and artefacts. Quiggin (1942: 82) explained the collection of artefacts as a means to defray the cost of the expedition through the sale of curios and, indeed, Haddon referred to curios in his journal, although usually in inverted commas. He recorded on page four that he always carried a supply of tobacco, tomahawks and knives because he was 'anxious to get a supply of implements and "curios" generally'. He clarified on page eight that 'curios' were 'ethnological specimens' like masks used in dance performance and other objects that materialized important ethnological information. He reviewed his collection on page twenty-four and argued that there was 'no merit in mere collecting'.

> After our return from the first cruise we had several days at Thursday Island before starting again. I was very glad of this time in order to go over my 'curios' and get them properly labelled and named. I find I have nine different kinds of arrows. My Thursday Island friends are wonderfully struck by my good luck and they assure me that they have never seen such a collection as I have already collected and I haven't done yet. But I value the information I have gathered concerning the things as being of more value. There is no merit in mere collecting and I have been fortunate enough to have the benefit of Mr Milman's knowledge and authority and to arrive at a time when the old order is changing giving place rather to a negation than to a 'new'. (Haddon 1888–89 Torres Strait and New Guinea Journal: 24)

Haddon valuing 'the information I have gathered concerning the things as being of more value' becomes a theme of sorts in subsequent writing, especially his statement in 'The Study of Anthropology' that however important archaeological evidence was, it was better 'to recover what they thought and believed' (Haddon 1895a: 25). The commercial value of specimens was not lost on Haddon, however. He sold a collection of skulls to TCD after Cunningham outbid Charles Stewart of the Hunterian Museum. He also earned £10 – worth approximately €1,186 in 2023 – from the sale of thirty or so objects to the Museum of Science and Art in Dublin. However, any doubt about the priority he attached to ethnological research and the commercial trade in 'curios' is cleared up in his correspondence with McFarlane.

Haddon filed two letters from McFarlane and, although Haddon's side of the correspondence has not yet been found, it is clear that he informed McFarlane of his plan to bring an artist with him, whom he identified in an earlier letter he wrote to Geddes on 25 December 1887 as 'Wm Thomas, a great friend of ours'. McFarlane advised against it on the grounds that it altered 'the conditions entirely.' Travelling alone, Haddon would be treated as a guest, but:

> If you take an Artist or anybody else, you will probably be regarded as collectors & have to stay at the Hotel at Thursday Island wh will cost abt £3 per week & then you will have to pay a high price for boat & crew for your work. (McFarlane to Haddon, 28 December 1887)

This letter confirms that McFarlane understood that Haddon was acting as an ethnologist rather than a collector, and in this context, two other details stand out. The first is that, from the outset, Haddon thought of ethnography as a visual process. The second is that McFarlane's advice was aimed at saving money by exploiting the missionary infrastructure. The first point will be developed in Part III. The second point speaks to the way the expedition was set up and challenges the common sense that Haddon was dependent on colonial officials and missionaries and limited his research to heavily colonized and missionized populations. Malinowski, for instance, criticized early anthropologists – Haddon and Rivers, according to Langham (1981: 174) – who operated from a 'comfortable position in the long chair on the veranda of the missionary compound, Government station, or planter's bungalow' (Malinowski 1954: 122–23).

Haddon's record of his 'first cruise' shows that this jibe was unjustified. Granted, Haddon acknowledged in *Head-Hunters: Black, White, and Brown* the importance of logistical support provided by the LMS and colonial administrators. 'All travellers to British New Guinea', he wrote, 'receive many benefits directly and indirectly from the New Guinea Mission of the London Missionary Society' (Haddon 1901: xi), adding that 'the great assistance afforded us by the late Rev. James Chalmers deserves special recognition'. Haddon recorded in his journal that he first met Chalmers on Thursday Island in September 1888 and 'got a good deal of valuable information from him' (Haddon 1888–89 Torres Strait and New Guinea Journal: 30). He subsequently arranged to explore New Guinea with Chalmers (ibid.: 68–69). Chalmers was a nativist who, Andrew Porter (2004) noted, distinguished between evangelism and Anglicization, and advocated for a native church and a 'New Guinea for the New Guineans'. Porter also noted that New Guinea was considered dangerous for Europeans because of the threat from 'reputedly wild and cannibalistic tribes' (ibid.), and this adds some nuance to the plan proposed by McFarlane and the ethnological partnership Haddon established with Chalmers.

In 1888, the Torres Strait represented the edge of civilization and beyond it lay uncolonized and dangerous territory. In October 1889, around the time Flower and Haddon exhibited ethnological material from the expedition in the British Museum, a report from the Torres Strait began circulating in the press about a massacre of a missionary party. The *Glasgow Herald* ran the story on 31 October 1889 under the headline 'Terrible Massacre in New Guinea' and relayed reports of an attack on 'the Rev. Mr Savage, of London Missionary Society, the native teachers under him and the crew of the society's cutter'. Haddon met Edwin Savage four days after arriving in the Torres Strait. The reports turned out to be false on this occasion but, twelve years later, Chalmers, the Rev. Tomkins and twelve native mission students were 'captured, clubbed, killed, and eaten' (Prendergast 1969) while, according to an obituary Haddon (1901b: 33) wrote for *Nature*, 'endeavouring to stop a tribal fight on the Aird River, a region which, had not yet come under missionary influence and over which the Government had no control.' The point is that McFarlane advised Haddon to use the missionary station on Mer as a base because it gave him access to New Guinea, and Chalmers acted as his guide in territories that had not been fully missionized or colonized.

As I write, I am struck by how far coral reefs have faded into the background and a well-planned ethnological experiment begins to dominate Haddon's own account of his first expedition to the Torres Strait and New Guinea. It may have been facilitated by missionaries and colonial administrators, but it was an innovative ethnological enterprise, and the thrill of his encounters with head-hunters and cannibals propelled him to the forefront of organized anthropology.

BECOMING AN ANTHROPOLOGIST

It could be argued that Haddon became an anthropologist in October 1888 when, by his own account, his interest in the customs and beliefs of the people he met in the Torres Strait and New Guinea overwhelmed his interest in coral reefs and sea anemones. However, the distinction between becoming an ethnologist and an anthropologist is important, and this section considers the latter in terms of Haddon's induction into organized anthropology in 1889. He returned to the British Museum in London with thirty-four crates of mostly ethnological material, an unprecedented haul by a relentless and persuasive collector, which is how Haddon described himself in his journal. For instance, he recorded what happened when he entered a dwelling for the first time on Nagir Island:

> Mr Milman at once spotted a mask, then another was discovered and two drums. These I also bought when their re-

spective owners turned up, but a drum and a mask belong [*sic*] to one of the old boy's son[s] who was away working on the mainland, but the father took upon himself to trade for his absent son. I also bought 3 tobacco pipes of bamboo – 3 amulets and mass of grass bangles worn on the leg, 2 shell breast ornaments, a basket and a lot of bows and arrows. (Haddon 1888–89 Torres Strait and New Guinea Journal: 6)

He subsequently convinced Maino, the Chief of Tud, to part with a headdress that belonged to his father, even though it went 'greatly against the grain' (ibid.: 66). Haddon prevailed with a promise that it would 'be exhibited in a big museum in England where plenty people could see his father's things'.

Haddon spent the summer of 1889 in the 'big museum' sorting through this material. He also wrote up his notes. On 16 September, he read 'On Some Former Customs and Beliefs of the Torres Straits Islanders' (BAAS 1890: 786) into the record of Section H – Anthropology of the BAAS at its annual meeting in Newcastle upon Tyne. It was one of forty-one papers and reports presented over four sessions and was exceptional because it described the cultural consequences of colonization by 'white men' (ibid.) in terms that were at variance with the anthropological attitude of most contributions. The meeting opened on 12 September with the first of two reports by Galton, who argued that a test of bodily efficiency was a principle and a method 'of no small interest to anthropologists' (BAAS 1890: 474). William Turner, Professor of Anatomy at the University of Edinburgh, presided over the meeting and picked up on Galton's work on heredity (ibid.: 757). He treated it as a biological problem that overlapped with the anthropological problem of variation, a proposition predicated on his definition of anthropology as a 'branch ... of biological science'. Cunningham, who worked as a demonstrator under Turner in the 1870s and replaced him in Edinburgh in 1903, presented a preview of a comparative study of the vertebral column in 'the Ape and different races of Men' that he wrote for the *Journal of Anatomy and Physiology* (ibid.: 777). This session set the tone for the remainder of the meeting and Haddon's paper was one of only six ostensibly ethnological reports from naturalists in the field, including an appended report on the Indians of British Columbia that Franz Boas prepared for a committee chaired by Edward Burnett Tylor and tasked with the collection of information on the 'North-Western Tribes of the Dominion of Canada' (ibid.: 797–900).

Haddon moved centre stage in October, when Flower fulfilled Haddon's promise to Maino and curated an exhibition of material from the expedition in the British Museum. *Nature* published a short piece in 'Notes' on 24 October 1889 and reported that 'special interest' attached to the anthropological specimens that Haddon brought back from the Torres Strait, a reference possibly to forty skulls, some of which he procured in New Guinea. Several newspapers published extracts of a review written by an anonymous correspondent but the *Colonies and India* newspaper in London published the full copy on 23 October. The author noted that seven or eight of these skulls had 'lenticular holes made by the club that killed them', and later in the article described another 'hardwood weapon on which 11 successive knotches indicate the heads which the owner has cut off'. The correspondent described other skulls used in ceremonies and divination, before outlining the craniological significance of the collection. The author then switched to the ethnological material, writing that 'Among the most striking of the objects exhibited are the huge eccentric masks employed in semireligious and secular dances' and thereby registered a shift in the focus of public interest from head-hunting and cannibalism to the customs and beliefs of the islanders that is a feature of the summaries published by other newspapers. The full copy of the *Colonies and India* review establishes that Haddon guided the journalist around the exhibition, and it stands as a remarkable account of the expedition from Haddon's perspective. The journalist noted Haddon's use of photographs and quoted his intention to publish his 'full journal and observations, especially as he made a large number of coloured drawings on the spot'.

Haddon became an anthropologist on 12 November, when he was elected a member of the Anthropological Institute, and two weeks later, he read 'The Ethnography of the Western Tribe of Torres Straits' into the record. Haddon stated in his introduction that 'In the first or general part I have followed the order of the sections in Part II, Culture, of that invaluable little book, "Notes and Queries on Anthropology"' (*JAI* 19 [1890]: 300), adding that he 'was also indebted for many hints to the excellent list of "Questions on the Manners, Customs, Religion, &c.," drawn up by my friend J. G. Frazer' and subsequently published in the *Journal of the Anthropological Institute* (*JAI* 18 (1889): 431–40). Haddon's ethnography was more anthropological in format than his earlier report 'On Some Former Customs and Beliefs' and, as such, comparable in scope and scale to that of the report Boas presented to Section H in September. There are, however, some striking differences in tone and emphasis. Haddon's tone was much more familiar and reflected a significant difference in the time both authors spent in the field. Haddon passed over language and grammar entirely and showed far more interest in art – promising a separate publication on the subject (*JAI* 19 (1890): 298) – and dance. Boas provided considerable detail on physical characteristics while Haddon glanced over the topic, telling members of the Institute 'that before I left home I had no intention of seriously studying the natives, or I would have endeavoured to prepare myself for the work' (ibid.). This statement is interesting because it confirms that, from the outset, Haddon thought of ethnology and anthropology as distinct. It also confirms that Haddon was well prepared to undertake ethnological work before he left for the Torres Strait, and there is no such evidence in relation to anthropology. Rather, Haddon recalled in 1935 that Flower dissuaded him 'from taking measurements of natives' (Haddon 1935: xi), and he never delivered a report on 'the physical characteristics of the islanders' that he promised members in 1889. The difference between Haddon and Boas in this regard is most visible in the illustrations they published in their respective papers. Boas provided illustrations of twelve skulls while Haddon provided thirty-five of his own drawings of people and artefacts, some drawn from life and others based on photographs he took. This is remarkable given that Boas reported to Tylor, an ethnologist, and Haddon to Flower, an anatomist. Finally, Boas's report was less 'historical' in nature and more orthodox in terms of the scope of Section H – Anthropology and the operation of a four-field syllabus encompassing physical anthropology, ethnology, philology and paleo-archaeology. A notable element in Haddon's paper in this context was his reference to the legends and myths he presented to the Folk-Lore Society, which published the material in March 1890 in the first volume of its revamped journal and added a second collection in June. One year later, Laurence Gomme, President of the Folk-Lore Society, congratulated the Society on its 'veritable capture' of Professor Haddon, who 'went out to the Torres Straits on an expedition on behalf of natural science; he returned an ardent folklorist, and immediately joined us' (FLS 2,1 [1891]: 13).

In December 1889, Haddon informed Patrick Geddes that he had decided to 'go into Anthropology', and Geddes asked him how in practice he would become an anthropologist: would he join Flower and Turner in 'the skull-measuring business' or join Geddes and his anarcho-solidarist associates in a great scientific movement developing around comparative sociology in France? Their correspondence points to the latter, as Geddes set about persuading Haddon to move to Paris.

And what of sea anemones? Haddon did not abandon natural science altogether. He published 'Zoological Notes from Torres Straits' in *Nature* in January 1889, and, in May, he attended the Royal Irish Academy and read a report on sea anemones collected during a dredging expedition in Ireland in 1888. He apologized for the incomplete nature of the study, as he received the material shortly before his departure for the Torres Strait and did not have 'time to submit the actiniae to anatomical investigation' (RIA 3,1 [1889–91]: 374). He co-authored a paper on the anatomy of fishes (Bridge and Haddon 1889) for the Royal Society in June and his focus then shifted to the *former* customs and beliefs of the Torres Strait and New Guinea.

CONCLUSION

To summarize, Haddon reached the limit of his interest in zoology in the autumn of 1888 and his apology, one year later, for abandoning his systematic study of sea anemones effectively marks his departure from marine biology. Haddon, however, spun this as an anthropological epiphany, but the reality was a little more prosaic. In the tradition of oceanographic research, Huxley seized upon Haddon's plan for an expedition as an opportunity to collect anthropological information and mobilized Flower, his man in the British Museum, to induct Haddon into the field of ethnology. Haddon became a determined collector of materialized ethnological knowledge and his unprecedented haul of objects and pictures from the land of head-hunters and cannibals caught the attention of the scientific community and propelled him into organized anthropology, his election as a member of the Anthropological Institute merely formalizing his decision taken two years earlier to become an ethnologist.

Haddon's abrupt departure from marine biology and his almost total engagement with ethnology during the 1888–89 expedition cancels out his training as a zoologist as a central feature of his historiographical identity. Enacting his decision to go into anthropology was not, as Geddes warned, straightforward. Huxley, Galton and Cunningham may have advocated a biological mindset and quantitative methodology but Haddon, despite collaborating on various projects with each of them, showed no interest in their version of anthropology. His fascination with former customs and beliefs placed him at the sociocultural end of a wide spectrum of scientific interest in humans and thus closer to Tylor and Boas. However, his total lack of interest in physical characteristics and linguistics makes his emerging sense of anthropology far less orthodox in terms of the four-field model that Boas presented at the meeting of Section H in 1889. Similarly, Haddon's interest in sketches and photographs emerges as a definite and distinctive feature of his practice.

'On Some Former Customs and Beliefs' was a deceptively modest affair that masks the truly innovative nature of Haddon's exploration of 'uncivilized' lands in the company of Chalmers. The word 'former' codified the critical cultural loss that followed 'intercourse with the white man' (BAAS 1890: 786) and Haddon used this to problematize the scope and function of anthropology in 1889. This caught the attention of a heterodox network of utopians and social reformers who found inspiration in lessons learned from the scientific study of simpler societies.

CHAPTER 2

LESSONS FROM UTOPIA

• • •

> I am very glad indeed that you are going into Anthropology, but I am sure it is your human sympathy & power of interpretation which is leading you, & not the mere desire of measuring skulls. It is my fancy to ask how?
> —Geddes to Haddon, 11 December 1889.

Haddon entered organized anthropology in September 1889 with a modest ethnological study of the people inhabiting the edge-lands of the British Empire where, as the rumoured massacre of Savage and his missionaries indicated, head-hunters remained hostile to the agents of European 'civilization'. Geddes identified the most innovative aspect of this study as the 'human sympathy & power of interpretation' that manifested in Haddon's identification with these head-hunters and his determination to prevent the destruction of what remained of their *former* civilization. Geddes understood the disruptive force of these ideas in a European context and asked Haddon to join a sociological movement that had the capacity to revolutionize anthropology.

In practical terms, Geddes asked Haddon to choose between craniology and sociology, and that choice is, in many ways, the foundation of many of the arguments put forward in this monograph, especially those that relate to Haddon's role in the modernization of the idea, practice and purpose of anthropology. Geddes encouraged Haddon as follows:

So you will get beyond Turner's & Flower's notion of the study of anthropology just as you have in fact & practice. In a word the skull measuring business if and when done, is now done by the 'Germans', so to speak – I mean the hewers of wood and drawers of water. while of the ~~xxx~~ professors, every one I have yet heard more of less has risen from the anatomical √$^{\&\text{ static}}$ standpoint to the physiological ~~xxx~~ & dynamic one, & from the ~~xxx~~ individual study of the man as the unit ~~xxx~~ to the standpoint of Comp. ~~psychology~~ sociology. Altogether ~~xxx~~ a great scientific movement is beginning in France, & more every year as the men whose characters were disciplined by the disasters of 70–71 come to the front, & get in their hand. (Geddes to Haddon, 11 December 1889)

'Hewers of wood and drawers of water' was a biblical reference to menial drudges and labourers. 'The disasters of 70–71' referred to the Paris Commune. Geddes informed Haddon in another letter that he was in contact with former Communard and renowned geographer Élisée Reclus and the exiled Russian geographer Kropotkin, both of whom the French state identified as leaders of anarchism in Europe (see Kearns 2004). Geddes and Kropotkin were allies. Kropotkin wrote a series of press articles between 1888 and 1891 in which he challenged Huxley over evolution and its implications for social and political reform, a rerun of an argument Geddes had with Huxley in the 1870s. Ten years on, Geddes set out his position in a revised entry on 'Evolution' in *Chambers's Encyclopaedia* (Geddes and Thomson 1889b) and the social reformer and his anarchist associates formed one axis of this 'great scientific movement'. This correspondence picks up on a discussion of art, evolution and sociology contained in a letter Haddon wrote to Geddes on 25 December 1887, while planning his expedition to the Torres Strait and New Guinea. Haddon wrote that he was delighted Geddes was not 'following the orthodox lines in "Evolution"', adding that he had 'long felt that there are higher aids to evolution than mere struggle' (original emphasis). The word 'struggle' situates that discussion in the exchange between Huxley and Kropotkin, and Haddon's decision 'to go into Anthropology' four-years later provided Geddes with the opportunity to develop his biosocial arguments on a new axis that ran from anthropology to sociology.

This is important for two reasons. One, it highlights a class war within organized science that was fought between Huxley as an advocate of survival-of-the-fittest capitalism and Kropotkin as an advocate for mutual assistance (communalism in simple societies) as a natural alternative to unnatural competition. Two, it signals the beginning of a post-evolutionist phase in anthropology in the sense that the human capacity to adapt and change becomes a factor in debates about social evolution and the lessons that could be learned from the an-archic – as defined by Proudhon's 1863 reworking of an-archy as self-government (Proudhon 1863: Part 1, Chapter 2) – societies that both Kropotkin and Haddon had studied. That marks the point where both axes meet and the logic of describing Haddon's position at this time as radical is established in terms of his association with the leaders of anarchism in Europe and his commitment to a root-and-branch reform of anthropology grounded in comparative sociology. Therefore, 1889 is presented here as a watershed between an evolutionist anthropology that aligned practical science with liberal economic policies and colonial expansion on one side, and on the other, an aspiration for a sociologically oriented anthropology that aligned social science with a heterodox social reform movement inspired in part by former Communards and revolutionaries.

The idea of revolution runs counter to the methodological gradualism and political acquiescence that Kuklick presented in *The Savage Within* (1991), the most cited study of the origins of social anthropology in Britain. She argued that natural scientists like Haddon preferred the logic of evolution over sudden or catastrophic changes in the social ecology of Britain in the second half of the nineteenth century. She set out the terms of an evolutionist creed (ibid: 116–18) that Haddon came to personify and, in the process, defined the terms of an epistemological orthodoxy that became consolidated in key works that followed from Stocking (1995) and, in an Irish context, Jones (1998). The impact is apparent in the scholarship that has accumulated since, which, in effect, constitutes a historiographical tradition with its own conventions in the form of tropes that bracket evolution with race and empire.

Accordingly, this chapter steps outside 'traditional' histories of anthropology and attempts to remember what was behind the 'how' in the question Geddes put to Haddon in 1889, using what remains of their correspondence to reconstruct a conversation about the nature of anthropology. This leads into an examination of their place in a system of interlocking assets that Huxley used to revolutionize the natural sciences in Britain and the class war that followed, thereby providing a context for (a) examining the political nature of the conversation and (b) testing the extent of Haddon's association with the leaders of anarchism in Europe. That opens a way into an exploration of a long-forgotten collaboration between Haddon and Ellis in May 1890, when Ellis asked Haddon to write a study of anthropology that would draw on the lessons he learned in Oceania and serve as an anarcho-utopian manifesto for a movement for scientific social reform.

A CONVERSATION WITH GEDDES

Haddon's entry into anthropology was the subject of an extended conversation with Geddes that took place between December 1889 and May 1890. The letters Geddes wrote are held in Cambridge University Library and Haddon's part of the conversation is extrapolated from these. Geddes wrote an undated note to Haddon trying to set up a meeting in London to 'talk things over' and, in case they missed one another, emphatically advised Haddon to 'take Flowers' advice' and become an anthropologist. He acknowledged the financial risk involved and advised Haddon that his 'prospects will come all right in the end even if you don't proceed in a worldly way'. Haddon took his advice and Geddes asked him in a letter dated 11 December how he intended to become an anthropologist. Did he intend to indulge his desire for measuring skulls and follow Turner and Flower into anatomical anthropology? Or did he intend to follow his instincts and join Geddes in a movement for scientific and social reform? The exchange identified two potential consequences of Haddon's decision, one economic and the other political.

Regarding economics, proceeding in a worldly way meant securing an alternative to his part-time teaching job in Dublin. Frazer informed Galton in 1897 that Haddon was 'a poor man with a small professional income (£200 a year from Dublin) and, I believe, very small private means' (Ackerman 2005: 101). The biggest problem Haddon faced was that anthropology had a singular presence in universities at that time. Oxford appointed Tylor as Reader in Anthropology in 1883 and, as Haddon (MS 1891. Critique of Imperial Institute: 13) noted, it remained the only teaching appointment in anthropology in the British Empire. Worse still, as it was an optional subject in the School of Natural Science, no student had enrolled in the course or presented for examination. Nevertheless, the possibility of a similar appointment in Cambridge must have appeared to be a real possibility in the wake of Haddon's spectacular entry into anthropology in 1889, Flower's encouragement that he become an anthropologist and Haddon's subsequent anthropometric collaboration with Galton in 1891.

It was, as Geddes predicted, a gamble and it did not 'come all right' for a long time. Haddon struggled to create opportunities for employment in Dublin and eventually secured a foothold at Cambridge University in 1893, where he taught Physical Anthropology on a part-time and freelance basis in Macalister's Department of Anatomy. As meagre as it was, he lost his foothold in 1898 while leading the Cambridge Anthropological Expedition to Torres Strait. Macalister used his absence to organize the appointment of a craniologist to the first University Lectureship in Anthropology. Frazer and his allies lobbied for an equivalent post in Ethnology for Haddon and, in 1900, university managers offered a standalone and part-time position with a small annual income. In January 1901, Haddon drafted an angry letter to his friend Charles S. Myers, a member of the psychology team he assembled for the 1898 Cambridge Anthropological Expedition, in which he wrote that 'unless I get something more in Camb. I must give up the struggle and return to Dublin, a very few weeks must decide me'. Haddon's exasperation is clear in a note he wrote in the margin: 'But all this is visionary – who cares for Anthropology? there's no money in it.' Shortly afterwards, he got that 'something more' when he was elected a Fellow of Christ's College, his alma mater, and he resigned his Professorship in Dublin in 1901. These facts, even arranged as a bare chronology, contradict the common sense that Haddon's Lectureship in Ethnology constituted an acknowledgement of his leadership of the 1898 expedition and represented the beginning of disciplinary anthropology in Cambridge. I will return to that story in the next chapter and, for now, turn to the problem of Haddon's politics and how they limited his ability to secure employment in anthropology between 1889 and 1901.

I have interpreted the 'great scientific movement' Geddes referred to as a reference to solidarism, a social concept that developed into a political movement in the 1890s in France. Leon Bourgeois, a reformer and politician, formalized the idea of social solidarity as solidarism in 1896 as a third way between the individualism of liberalism and the collectivism of socialism (Béland 2009). Hayward (1959), however, described solidarism as a protean term that encompassed a range of economic, social and philosophical thought and practice, and I propose that Geddes was on the left of this spectrum on the basis of his enthusiasm for the involvement of people 'whose characters were disciplined by the disasters of 70–71', namely Reclus and Kropotkin. Geddes informed Haddon in an undated letter in the same series that he had travelled to Switzerland to meet Reclus and was greatly influenced by him. He also drew Haddon's attention to Kropotkin, reminding him that he had lent him 'a letter to Kropotkine [*sic*] on the teaching of biology', which incidentally, coincides with the row between Kropotkin and Huxley. This correspondence connects Haddon directly to a strand of anarcho-solidarist activism, and the reference to activists being 'disciplined' is worth developing as a pretext for claiming that Haddon's entry into anthropology was a radical affair.

Reclus fought in defence of the Paris Commune and survived the purges that followed its bloody suppression. He escaped transportation for life because European scientists appealed to the French government to commute his sentence (Kearns 2004: 340) and he went into exile in Switzerland. He was included in an amnesty in 1879, but, three years later, the government identified Reclus and Kropotkin as leading promoters of anarchism and jailed Kropotkin for three years. On his release, Kropotkin made his way to London and joined a lively socialist scene that included the Social Democratic Federation, the breakaway Socialist League and Fabian Society, whose founding members included Caroline Haddon and Margaret Hinton (see MacKenzie 1975; Ferretti 2017; Morris 2018). Kropotkin regularly travelled to Edinburgh to consult with Geddes and Anna Morton, his wife and cofounder of the Edinburgh Social Union (Renwick 2012: 91). Reclus travelled to London in 1895 to receive a gold medal from the Royal Geographical Society and address the Sixth International Geographical Congress. He then embarked on a lecture tour to promote anarchy in the UK and the *Glasgow Herald* reported that he joined Geddes and Haddon at the ninth Summer Meeting of Art and Science in Edinburgh in 1895, an event that coincided with the end of the lecture tour.

There is a further connection between Haddon and Reclus. Both were involved in Freemasonry, although they were moving in opposite directions. Reclus joined the Freemasons in 1858, and Tom Steele (2007b: 1–12) describes him as being a former Freemason when he launched his New University in Brussels in 1894, albeit in a lecture theatre provided by local Freemasons. Haddon joined the Freemasons in Dublin in 1888 and progressed to the office of Worshipful Master in 1918, the highest honour awarded to members of a lodge. Reclus established the New University to advance the provision of popular education, and Steele describes his alliance with Kropotkin in this context as 'A curious example of the conjunction of an even more extreme freemasonry and social sciences' (ibid.: 6). Haddon was also involved in the provision of popular education through university extension schemes in Dublin and Belfast, extramural lectures that he exploited to get around class and gender barriers to access in science education – and, as I will argue later, he used the scheme as a platform to mobilize a popular ethnographic movement in Belfast in 1893. Steele (2007a: 130) describes how the exclusion of dogma and religion in the university extension movement in Britain was noted by the promoters of the Free University in Brussels, which offered Reclus a professorship before revoking it after an attack on the French parliament provoked a backlash against anarchists, which Federico Ferretti (2018) documented as the 'Reclus incident' that led to the establishment of the breakaway New University in 1894. Clearly, Haddon and Reclus were operating on a common platform, but I have not found any evidence that Haddon supported the extreme version of French Freemasonry that Steele described. It is far more likely that Haddon, like most British and American Freemasons (Steele 2007b: 4), was more moderate. Nevertheless, Haddon's conversation with Geddes is evidence that a combination of social science, anarchism and Freemasonry influenced Haddon as he set about becoming an anthropologist, and this, I propose, set the scene for a confrontation with Huxley.

CULTURE WARS

Political dissent ceased to be a feature of organized anthropology in the 1840s when ethnologists associated with the Aborigines Protection Society – in some ways an early version of the Black Lives Matter campaign – were quickly brought into line by the managers of the BAAS. Ethnology was 'stripped of its dangerous features' (Morrell and Thackray 1981: 283–84), repackaged as anthropology and incorporated as a branch of biological science. Huxley emerged as a leader of anthropology in 1871 when he negotiated a deal between the Ethnological Society of London (founded by ethnologists associated with the Aborigines Protection Society) and the breakaway Anthropological Society of London, under which the societies amalgamated as the Anthropological Institute of Great Britain and Ireland (see Stocking 1971). The deal establishes Huxley's credentials as a reformist, but I will argue that it would be an error to mistake him for a liberal, on the basis that Huxley was determined to limit the scope of anthropological enquiry in response to social reforms sought by the working-class Chartist movement in the 1840s; this politicization of anthropology led to his confrontation with Kropotkin in 1891.

Huxley revolutionized public science in the nineteenth century. He neutralized the influence of the Church, broadened the social base of participation in scientific research, professionalized training and ushered in an era of practical science. This made him a hero to reformists, a point acknowledged by both Ellis (1890: 5–6) and Haddon (Haddon and Quiggin 1910: 50). Ellis identified Huxley as 'one of the most militant and indefatigable exponents of the scientific spirit in the last half century', and, as such, the instigator of a revolution that created the necessary conditions for scientific social reform in the last decade of the century. I have no argument with that. I concentrate instead on one small and, I think, neglected aspect of Huxley's work in anthropology: his decision to deploy evolutionist theories in defence of capitalism.

Huxley emerged as a political activist in the 1850s, when the political landscape of England was changing in the aftermath of the Chartist protests of 1848 (White 2003: 114; O'Connor 2005; Renwick 2012: 24–25). Chartism was a working-class movement that mobilized in 1836 to demand better political representation. Parliament rejected its final petition for electoral reform in 1848 and violence associated with the protests that followed made some opponents regard it as a revolutionary movement. Huxley approached the leader of the anti-Chartist Christian Socialists and offered to align his teaching of natural history with its aim of counselling English workers against revolution. For the next two decades, he used 'Working Men's Lectures' to counter calls for radical social reform with an evolutionist doctrine of survival of the fittest in a stable capitalist system (White 2003: 114). Erin McLaughlin-Jenkins (2001: 451–53) has described how socialists fought back in the working-class press. In 1884, for instance, the Socialist Democratic Federation published in its newspaper *Justice* a translation of Kropotkin's 1880 appeal 'Aux jeunes gens', an appeal to young people to study 'socialist' science and thereby counter Huxley's 'advocacy of nature as a blueprint for progress and democracy' (ibid.). In 1888, Huxley published 'The Struggle for Existence: And Its Bearing upon Man' in *The Nineteenth Century* and Kropotkin countered with 'Mutual Aid among Savages' in 1891. The row pitted one of the leaders of anarchism in Europe against the acknowledged leader of science in Britain, whose appointment as Fisheries Inspector in 1881 confirmed his influence in government circles, which sets the scene for his connection to Geddes and Haddon. They personify many of Huxley's reforms and the political tensions that emerged during his stewardship of British science.

Geddes and Haddon were among a new generation of academically trained natural scientists that Huxley, operating from his base at the Royal School of Mines in London, inducted into a complex system of interlocking marine biology assets that operated as follows: specimens were collected and classified by zoologists on expedition or working in universities and associated laboratories. The collections were sorted and displayed in natural history museums, which functioned as centres of specialist research and public instruction from an evolutionist perspective. Huxley decided who got jobs and he illustrated his power with an anecdote in a letter to Joseph Dalton Hooker in 1888. Robert Lowe, Chancellor of the Exchequer, asked Huxley what he should do with the natural history collections in the British Museum and Huxley suggested that he 'put Flower at the head of it and make me a trustee to back him' (Huxley 1900: 71, 204). Lowe duly appointed Huxley as an *ex officio* trustee in 1883 and Flower as Director in 1884. Similarly, Newton wrote to Haddon to assure him that he would get a job in Dublin or the officials in the Department of Science and Art would 'have Huxley to tackle'. Haddon duly became Professor of Zoology at the Royal College of Science and curator of the natural history collections in the Museum of Science and Art. He took part in fisheries research organized by the Royal Dublin Society and funded by the Royal Irish Academy (Praeger 1949: 186–87). He lodged his specimens with the Natural History Department of the Museum and presented his findings at the Royal Dublin Society, the Royal Irish Academy and meetings of Section D – Biology at the BAAS.

Geddes entered Huxley's system in 1874 when he enrolled in a course in natural science at the School of Mines in London. Huxley gave him a job as a demonstrator and Geddes went to Cambridge in 1876 to study embryology in Foster's laboratory, where he met Haddon. Quiggin (1942: 31) underlined the innovation involved with a footnote crediting Huxley and Foster with 'revolutionising the teaching of science by their insistence on practical work'. It was a pivotal experience for Geddes. Chris Renwick (2012: 193, fn. 24) speculates that Foster introduced Geddes to the work of Herbert Spencer, and he became interested in relating 'the natural sciences to social and ethical processes'. Geddes was especially interested in Spencer's critique of imperialism (ibid.: 41). When Geddes returned to the School of Mines, Huxley was, according to Renwick (2009: 43; 2012: 76), determined to keep his 'enthusiasm for evolution within the bounds of anatomical analysis and the biological sciences as a whole' and, in 1878, he encouraged Geddes to undertake further research in France, where two factors combined to exacerbate his differences with Huxley. First, he discovered evidence of interspecies cooperation – symbiosis – and developed a theory of biosociality in opposition to Huxley's evolutionist doctrine of competition. Second, he met Edmond Demolins of the Société d'Economie Sociale, who introduced him to 'attempts being made to develop a Le Playist social science dedicated to securing peaceful social evolution in the future' (Meller 2008). The fact of evolution was not an issue. Huxley and Geddes differed over the political implications of evolution as a biosocial process. In 1889, Geddes and J. Arthur Thomson, a Scottish naturalist, revised the entry on 'Evolution' in *Chambers's Encyclopaedia* and Renwick described the result as

> A profoundly un-Darwinian yet Spencerian account of evolution [in which] individual competition was subordinated

to social and reproductive ends, and interspecific competition to cooperative adaptation. (Renwick 2012: 86)

It was at this point that Geddes engaged Haddon in a conversation about what it meant to become an anthropologist.

That conversation eliminates Huxley as an influence on Haddon's engagement with the idea of anthropology and replaces him with Reclus, Kropotkin and Le Play. Kropotkin's influence can be detected in 'Incidents in the Life of a Torres Strait Islander', which Haddon wrote in 1889 for *Lippincott's Monthly Magazine: A Popular Journal of General Literature, Science, and Politics*. Haddon defined the social function of ethnology as follows:

> The solidarity of the human race is still for the majority a theory, not a belief which determines actions. An intimate and friendly acquaintance with savages breaks down many prejudices, and while it often reveals modes of thought and traits of character which are all but incomprehensible to us with our specialized Aryan civilization, yet human nature is displayed at every turn, and common impulses and sympathies link the extremes of human kind. (Haddon 1890a: 567)

Four years earlier, Kropotkin defined the third task of geography in general education as:

> that of dissipating the prejudices in which we are reared about the so-called 'lower races' – and this precisely at an epoch when everything makes us foresee that we soon shall be brought into a much closer contact with them than ever. (Kropotkin 1885: 942–43)

Haddon developed the idea of an 'intimate and friendly acquaintance with savages' in a critique of the Imperial Institute, which he pitched to a number of journals in 1891, including the journal that published the exchange between Huxley and Kropotkin.

This article has entered the history of anthropology as a proposal to establish an Imperial Bureau of Ethnology, which Haddon designed to promote solidarity with fellow subjects in the colonies and, as stated earlier, end a policy that permitted the Anglo-Saxon to 'slowly or rapidly, unintentionally or by force, exterminate the inhabitants of the countries we annex' (Haddon MS 1891, Critique of Imperial Institute: 10). To be clear about Haddon's intentions, consider the statement that followed this sentence:

> The ~~history~~ story of our Colonial administration is sad & humiliating. If an impartial foreigner were to write the true history of our dependencies, he would be branded as inaccurate & prejudiced. The blame lies alike with the general public, the legislators & the executive. Ignorance engenders callousness, which is the fertile mother of injustice, cruelty, & legalized murder. (ibid.)

Rather naively, he sought Huxley's help after the journals rejected the article. Huxley replied in January 1892, stating that the proposal

> would not have the slightest chance of being taken in hand by the Government and I cannot advise you to publish your paper, with that view. (Huxley to Haddon, 1 January 1892)

Huxley presented Haddon with a stark choice: work within a biological system that guaranteed him employment as a government scientist and a place in anthropology, or publish and risk government censure.

Haddon, like Geddes before him, had run afoul of Huxley's regulation of the political scope of anthropology, and Geddes took Haddon's decision to become an anthropologist as an opportunity to wrest anthropology from the bony grasp of anatomists and transform it into an instrument of scientific social reform. To advance his agenda, Geddes put Haddon in contact with Ellis and, by the time Huxley suppressed Haddon's article, they had already set to work on reconstruction of the institution of anthropology.

A NEW SPIRIT

Ellis was a utopian, writer, critic and author of the first scientific study of homosexuality. He features in the history of anthropology because A. R. Radcliffe-Brown was recorded by historians as citing Geddes, Ellis and Kropotkin as important influences (Langham 1981: 371; Stocking 1995: 304–5; Maddock 1994: 14–15; Maddock 2002: 702). Indeed, Radcliffe-Brown reviewed the state of anthropology at the hundredth meeting of the BAAS in 1931 (see this volume: 235–37) and counted Ellis, Kropotkin and Spencer among those who influenced him. He did not refer to Haddon in this context, although he acknowledged that Haddon's method of interpreting culture favoured psychology and so constituted an approach that belonged to sociology. He concluded that this 'came too soon in the history of anthropology' (BAAS 1932: 155–57), and I have already argued that Stocking (1995: 104–6) and Jones (1998: 195) took the correspondence between Ellis and Haddon out of context and, effectively, wrote Haddon out of more recent histories as anything other than an evolutionist foil for those who came after him. I now revisit the correspondence and elaborate on its original context to argue that Haddon, working with Ellis, took the lead in a root-and-branch reconstruction of the institution of anthropology, and thus support my earlier claim that, in 1890, Haddon was in the vanguard of advanced thinking on anthropology.

Ellis wrote to Haddon on 8 May 1890, stating that Geddes had informed him of Haddon's plan to study anthropology in Paris and that he had been 'in Paris for some months chiefly with the same object in view'. Ellis continued:

> The condition of anthropology and anthropological teaching in England is deplorable in the extreme, & I should be very glad indeed to cooperate in any movement for putting anthropology in England in its proper position. It seems to me indeed, that the 'psychological moment' has now arrived. In my series I am giving the first place to the anthro-

pological sciences, & I do not find that it is more unpopular on that account, it has, indeed, been extremely successful. (Ellis to Haddon, 8 May 1890)

The letter makes it clear that Ellis thought that Haddon was already involved in a 'movement for putting anthropology in England in its proper position' and he wanted to get involved too. 'My series' was a reference to the Contemporary Science Series, which he edited for the Walter Scott Company. Ellis wrote *The New Spirit* in 1890 and, although it was not part of the series, the introduction serves as a manifesto of sorts. He identified imperial expansion, the revolutionary rationalism forged by Huxley and the concept of evolution as forces that had revolutionized every department of organic science, especially where it touched upon humans. The emphasis on interlocking social, political and scientific revolutions is derived in part from his intention to mark the centenary of the French Revolution and use this as a pretext to describe the beginning of a new era that demanded a new approach to anthropology. He wrote:

> The great and growing sciences of today are the sciences of man – anthropology, sociology, whatever we like to call them including also that special and older development, now become a new thing, though still retaining its antiquated name of Political Economy. It is difficult for us to-day to enter into the state of mind of those who once termed this the dismal science; if the question of a man's right to a foothold on the earth is not interesting, what things are interesting? Our hopes for the evolution of man, and our most indispensable guide, are all bound up with all that we can learn of man's past and all that we can measure of his present. (Ellis 1890: 5–6)

Ellis wrote this during the period in which Haddon read 'On Some Former Customs and Beliefs of the Torres Straits Islanders' into the record of Section H and incorporated an oblique plea for the right of those islanders to 'a foothold on the earth'. I will argue later that this vision of anthropology, augmented by the methods of Kropotkin and Le Play, provided Haddon with a template for his ethnographic study of the Aran Islands in 1892. For now, the passage illustrates what I mean by a post-evolutionist understanding of the function of anthropology, which Haddon expanded considerably in his article on 'The Study of Anthropology' three years later. In this context, Ellis's hopes for the evolution of humankind tags him as a utopian rather than a revolutionary.

Ellis remained loyal to idealists in the Progressive Association when its members separated by agreement in 1883 and formed the utopian Fellowship of the New Life and the socialist Fabian Society (see MacKenzie 1975). The Contemporary Science Series reconstituted a Manuscript Club that distributed literature among its members and was, according to Mackenzie (ibid.: 32–33), a precursor of the Progressive Association through which many of the future members of Fellowship and Society met. Will Dircks was a founding member of the Manuscript Club and held a senior position in the Walter Scott Company. It seems likely that he put Ellis in charge of a publishing venture designed to extend the reach of Club to include the general public, with the aim, according to a press release in the *Journal of Mental Science*, of investigating

> all the questions of modern life – the various social and political-economical problems of to-day, the most recent researches in the knowledge of man, the past and present experiences of the race, and the nature of its environment. (*Journal of Mental Science* 36,153 [April 1890]: 265)

The 'social and political-economical problems' of the day were at the heart of the venture and, as a post-evolutionist, Ellis maintained a core Spencerian (see 1873: 366–67) tenet of the New Lifers, that is, that social reconstruction 'should proceed by only such revolutionary means as are consistent with the natural development of the community, and that social development can only advance side by side with individual development' (Henry Hyde Champion quoted in MacKenzie 1975: 36).

However, a thread of anarchist thought ran through his arguments, which is consistent with the overlap between utopianism and anarchism in the 1880s (see Davis and Kinna 2009). For instance, Ellis (1890: 14) argued that representative government was ineffective and social reconstruction required that every person 'be a member of government', a superficial reworking of Proudhon's 1863 definition of anarchy as 'the government of each by each – an-archy or self-government' (Proudhon 1863: Part 1, Chapter 2). Ellis also adopted Kropotkin's idea that the study of social organization proceeds from the study of simple to complex societies, stating, in relation to feminism, that simpler societies were 'as lamps to us in our social progress' (Ellis 1890: 9). Haddon picked up on this when he checked out the series in response to the first letter from Ellis. He filed a rough draft of his reply, in which he stated that he noted a definite 'zeitgeist' in Geddes and Thomson on sex (1889), Taylor on Aryan origins (1889) and Gomme on village communities (1890). By 'zeitgeist' Haddon meant works of practical value in the reconstruction of institutions and, in this context, the influence of Kropotkin on Gomme's treatment of *The Village Community* is especially interesting. Gomme reworked Seebohm's 1883 study of the same subject and, according to a notice in *Folklore* (FLS 1,1 [1890]: 127) used 'folk-lore to prove that the English village community is not simply an economical institution, but one which contained much of the old tribal religion'. Gomme adopted Kropotkin's model of the progressive study of social organization, treating village communalism as a primitive (pre-Aryan) form that evolved into a democratic model of open, self-governing and self-supporting communalism 'not very far removed from the Socialism of today' (Gomme 1890: 18). Ellis developed this theme in 1891 with *Primitive Folk: Studies in Comparative Ethnology* (1891), a translation of Élie Reclus's *Les Primitifs: Études d'Ethnologie Comparée* (1885), which Geddes and Haddon referred to in their correspondence. Brian Morris (2018) described it as one of the earliest manifestations in print of the affinity between anthropology and anarchism. Finally, Haddon finished the draft letter with the following declaration:

I am increasingly seeing the importance of anthropological work and heartily echo your wish 'to cooperate in any movement for putting anthropology in England in its proper position'. (Haddon to Ellis, 14 May 1890)

Ellis responded by asking Haddon to write a study of anthropology along the lines of Spencer's 1873 volume *The Study of Sociology*.

Stocking and Jones missed the zeitgeist and focussed instead on Haddon's proposal to write from 'a biological point of view and not as is usually done from the "anthropological" standpoint'. They interpreted his heavily hedged definition of folklore as 'psychological palaeontology' as firm evidence of an evolutionist mindset and a biological approach to the study of culture. They missed the fact that the letter was a rough list of contemporaneous themes, that Haddon used inverted commas a lot and, most importantly, the significance of the distinction between 'biological' and 'anthropological'. The last point is, perhaps, the most important given that Geddes, Haddon, Kropotkin and Ellis were engaged in a discussion of biosociality as a theoretical alternative to Huxley's anthropological doctrine.

Haddon and Ellis abandoned their project in May 1891. Ellis acknowledged the difficult nature of the book and, noting Haddon's fascination with 'the earliest origins of art among savages', commissioned *Evolution in Art* instead.

CONCLUSION

To summarize, Haddon's conversation with Geddes places him in a network of utopians, anarchists, socialists and solidarists who drew inspiration from the Paris Commune, and he set about reconstructing the institution of anthropology as an instrument of scientific social reform. At this point, Haddon's entry into anthropology turns into a narrative of intentional disruption. Political dissent was suppressed in the 1840s after ethnologists associated with the Aborigines Protection Society were disciplined. Huxley deployed evolutionist arguments as a weapon against socialism in the 1850s and, despite his connections with the Ethnological Society, situated anthropology firmly within biology in 1871. His dispute with Kropotkin in the 1880s manifested a class war in science and Geddes, Huxley's protegee, aligned himself with Kropotkin, recruited Haddon and introduced him to Ellis, a utopian who perceived the beginning of a new era that demanded a new approach to anthropology. He asked Haddon to write a manifesto for the movement and all that remains of that project is an introductory essay that transformed anthropology into a sociological study of culture, wherever and however culture happens.

Huxley rather than Geddes is usually associated with Haddon's entry into anthropology, mainly because Huxley recruited Haddon in 1880 and sponsored his expedition in 1888. Huxley's investment in Geddes was of a different scale altogether and that places Haddon on the margins of Huxley's system of patronage and power. Thus, Geddes, as friend and mentor, displaces Huxley as the key player in Haddon's initiation as a member of organized anthropology. The effect is immediately apparent in Haddon's journalism. Kropotkin's anti-racism strategy frames Haddon's treatment of the consequences of colonialism in 'Incidents in the Life of a Torres Strait Islander' and the anti-racism theme was amplified in his 1891 critique of the Imperial Institute. Huxley suppressed this in 1892 and, in so doing, revealed a continuing intolerance for political dissent. Haddon, however, was talking to Ellis, and their shared optimism for 'the great and growing sciences' of anthropology and sociology stands in stark contrast to Huxley's reaction.

To finish, Haddon entered anthropology fighting on two fronts. Haddon, Geddes and Ellis agreed to work together to reconstruct the institution of anthropology and Haddon's confrontation with Huxley underlines the essentially political nature of their project. The movement for reform gathered momentum after Tylor re-emerged as a leader in 1891 and launched a decade-long struggle between 'cultural' and 'physical' factions that reached a disciplinary denouement of sorts when Haddon became an ethnologist.

CHAPTER 3
BECOMING AN ETHNOLOGIST

• • •

We venture to think that the present moment would be singularly opportune for founding a lectureship in these branches of study, which on the continent are generally classed together under the name of Ethnology in contradistinction to Anthropology, which foreign experts commonly limit to the study of the physical side of man's nature.
—Memorial to the General Board of
Cambridge University, November 1899

Frazer drafted this memo in 1899 to have Haddon appointed to a University Lectureship in Ethnology, and it posed the following conundrum: if Haddon decided to become an anthropologist in 1889, how did he become an ethnologist in 1899? Haddon had not changed, and the situation is partly explained by the circumstances of the memo. Frazer drafted the text and twenty-one leading academics at Cambridge University signed the memo before it was submitted to university managers in response to their decision to (a) establish disciplinary anthropology in Macalister's Department of Anatomy and (b) appoint W. L. H. Duckworth, an anatomist and craniologist, to the first University Lectureship in Anthropology. In effect, the managers had decided to restrict disciplinary anthropology to 'the study of the physical side of man's nature'. Frazer appealed that decision and asked the managers to make equal provision for the wider, sociocultural approach developed by Haddon over the previous decade.

In some ways the memo represents the end of the optimism manifested in 'The Study of Anthropology' project Haddon and Ellis launched in 1890. Haddon was, as we know from his letter to Myers in 1901, prepared to abandon anthropology altogether, but Frazer never gave up. He used little-Englander rhetoric to attack an orthodox albeit foreign system of limiting anthropology to the study of bodies, thereby making the case for ethnology as the home of English anthropology in 'its widest aspect'. Frazer glided over the fact that Geddes, Haddon and Ellis derived their inspiration from former Communards, French solidarists, a Russian anarchist-in-exile and a French school of comparative sociology. That did not matter. He was engaged in academic politics and his aim was to correct a reversal in an institutional row between ethnologists and anthropologists that engulfed anthropology after Tylor emerged from a form of epistemic exile in 1891 and called for parity of esteem for ethnologists. That triggered an escalation in a long-running fight between 'physicals' and 'culturals' – labels Tylor devised – for control of organized anthropology.

I use the word 'escalation' because the tension between biology and geography, science and humanities had divided ethnologists and anthropologist since the 1830s. It took institutional form in England in the 1840s when the Ethnological Society of London broke away from the Aborigines Protection Society and sought recognition from the BAAS, which shuffled ethnology between biology and geography over four decades. The Ethnological Society split in 1863 and anthropological members set up their own society before reconciling with the ethnologicals and forming the Anthropological Institute in 1871, although the choice of Anthropological for the name was a source of disagreement (see Stocking 1971). The differences persisted into the 1880s and can be detected in debates over the relative efficacy of craniology and philology as defining methods of the new science, which Tylor placed on the record at the inauguration of Section H – Anthropology in 1884 when he dismissed craniology as an imperfect method of studying problems better suited to philology. Ironically, that speech marked the beginning of an era of complete domination by anthropologicals, and the underlying tension exploded into public controversy when Haddon revived his 1891 critique of imperialism as a rallying call for an insurrection by ethnologicals at a meeting of Section H – Anthropology in Ipswich in 1895. The consequences of that speech constitute the back story to Frazer's memo and set the scene for a pivotal event in the development of disciplinary anthropology in Britain.

A recurring theme of this monograph is the failure of conventional histories of anthropology to see beyond evolutionism and the disappearance of the insurrection in Ipswich in evolutionist historiography is a case in point. Ipswich, however, verifies the existence of a demand for the discussion of a range of social, political, philosophical and moral topics under the banner of anthropology. That movement can be traced back to the humanitarian agenda of the first ethnologicals, and it received additional impetus from an emerging consensus that the argument over evolution had been settled. Attention turned to the implications of evolution for every aspect of life, from race, class and gender to sex, art, economics, social organization and governance; the anarcho-utopian agenda Ellis set out in *The New Spirit* and disseminated through the Contemporary Science Series. He hoped that Haddon's study of anthropology would serve as a manifesto, but that experiment failed and the reasons for this can be detected by reading between the lines of Frazer's memo: a culture war between ethnologicals on the left and anthropologicals on the right that has been overwritten in histories constructed around a theory of a shift from evolutionist scholarship to social science.

So, once again, we step outside of history in search of evidence that supports the idea of a post-evolutionist culture war in anthropology in the 1890s. Fortunately for me, Tylor inaugurated a system of annual reviews of the business of the Anthropological Institute that left a documentary trail of institutional infighting. A second historiographical windfall came by way of a debate sparked by the tenth anniversary of the establishment of Section H – Anthropology. A third windfall came courtesy of press coverage of Haddon's speech in Ipswich and the institutional record of the sanctions that followed. The search for evidence terminated in the Memorial to the General Board of Cambridge University, and this became the basis for a reconstruction of the circumstances under which Haddon became an ethnologist in 1899.

This story begins with a brief overview of the positions adopted by 'physical' and 'cultural' factions in the 1890s. That serves as a pretext for an analysis of the public controversy that followed when Flinders Petrie and Haddon organized a public debate about colonialism under the provocative billing of 'On Interference with the Civilisation of Other Races'. They provoked a hostile reaction from a scientific establishment that regarded Haddon as having become too familiar with savage people and their ways and, as a result, wandered out of science and into sociology. I finish with the consequences for Haddon as the managers of the BAAS attempted to contain the fallout and, in the process, defined the terms by which Haddon became an ethnologist and disciplinary anthropology became a function of anatomy.

'PHYSICALS' VS 'CULTURALS'

Frederick W. Rudler, a geologist, was elected President of the Anthropological Institute in 1898 and asked its members why the Institute attracted three hundred members in an empire of three or four hundred million inhabitants. Rudler blamed a lack of clarity over the purpose and practice of anthropology, arguing that:

> one set regards Anthropology as a formidable branch of biology – it's very name a stumbling block – representing a science to be comprehended only by those who have had the advantage of special training; whilst the other group regards Anthropology as an incoherent assemblage of odds and ends of knowledge, not yet sufficiently systematized to rank as a distinct science. (*JAI* 28 3,2 [1899]: 314)

This problem of definition was as old as organized anthropology itself. In 1894, on the tenth anniversary of the establishment of

Section H – Anthropology, Flower (BAAS 1894: 762–74) traced the origin of the organization to the establishment of the Ethnological Society in 1843 and summarized attempts to place its work within the sectional structure of the BAAS. Each science operated as a section of the Association and in 1843 there were seven sections:

- A Mathematical and Physical Science
- B Chemistry and Mineralogy
- C Geology and Physical Geography
- D Zoology and Botany
- E Medical Science
- F Statistics
- G Mechanical Science

Ethnology started out as a subsection of Section D – Zoology and Botany in 1846, moving to Section E – Geography and Ethnology in 1851, before returning to Section D – Biology as a Department of Anthropology in 1866, reverting to Ethnology in 1869, changing back to Anthropology in 1870 and, finally, being incorporated as Section H – Anthropology in 1884. Flower noted that ethnologists and anthropologists had operated side by side as members of the Ethnological Society before personal considerations and scientific ambitions led to the establishment in 1863 of a rival Anthropological Society, a split that was resolved, as stated, in 1871 with the establishment of the Anthropological Institute of Great Britain and Ireland. Flower rationalized the difference between the old and the new by arguing that the 'old term Ethnology' encompassed the comparative study of peoples or races, whereas 'Anthropology, now understood' investigated human origin and variation with the aid of zoology, comparative anatomy and physiology (BAAS 1894: 763).

Personal considerations and scientific ambitions are as close as Flower got to the bitter differences over evolution that set ethnology and anthropology alternating between geography and biology. Stocking summarized the situation as follows:

In this context of differences in scientific orientation, political attitudes, and organisational and personal style, it is not surprising that relations between the two groups were characterised by recurring conflict, bitterness, recriminations, and the failure of several attempts at reconciliation. (Stocking 1971: 381)

Stocking identified the BAAS as the main arena of conflict and, although the amalgamation of the ethnologicals and anthropologicals ended outright conflict, the shift towards biology as the natural home for the scientific study of 'man's place in nature' (ibid.: 387) generated, I propose, an underlying tension that framed contrasting statements by presidents of Section H – Anthropology in 1884 and 1894.

Tylor presided over the inaugural meeting in 1884 and set out the ethnological position as follows:

> To clear the obscurity of race-problems, as viewed from the anatomical standing point . . . we naturally seek the help of language. (BAAS 1885: 904)

Craniometry, he argued, had proven to be an 'imperfect science' and anthropologists turned to comparative philology in dealing with the 'anthropology of the old world'. Tylor and Boas employed this methodology in their survey of the north-western tribes of Canada and Boas provided a template with his 'First General Report on the Indians of British Columbia: Introductory Note' (BAAS 1890: 801–900).

Flower presided over the tenth meeting of the Section in 1894 and set out the anthropologist's position as follows:

> the complete history of any race of mankind, especially with regard to its relation to other races, must be based upon a knowledge both of its physical and psychical characteristics, and customs, habits, language, and tradition largely help, when anatomical characters fail to separate and define. (BAAS 1894: 763)

Flower acknowledged that ethnology came within the remit of anthropology but stated that the difficulty lay in setting legitimate boundaries between anthropology, archaeology, antiquarian studies and history. These boundaries had shifted over time, he argued, but were fixed in the organization of anthropological material by museums into separate anthropological and ethnological collections (ibid.: 764). Rudler subsequently argued that this separation could be measured in terms of 'a sharp interval of three or four miles' (*JAI* 28, 3,4 [1899]: 315) that separated the natural history and ethnological collections of the British Museum, and Rudler's logic could be applied to the collections Haddon sold in 1889 to Cunningham in the Anatomy Department at TCD and the Museum of Art and Science in Dublin, although the distance could be measured in hundreds of metres.

The position of ethnology in the Anthropological Institute was even more remarkable. Members elected 'anthropological' presidents on nine occasions between 1884 and 1894: Flower (1883–84), Galton (1885–88), Beddoe (1889–90) and Macalister (1893–94). The exception was Tylor. Members elected him president in 1891 and at the end of his first year in office he expressed satisfaction with the Institute's prosecution of 'physical, philological, archaeological, cultural and traditional lines of the study of Man'. He then added a caveat:

> We are not dissuaded by the views of respected fellow-students elsewhere in the world, who hold that anthropology should only concern itself with the physical structure of the human species. (*JAI* 22 [1893]: 384)

Incidentally, the principal 'fellow student' was one and the same as Frazer's 'foreign expert' whom, as we shall see, Edward Brabrook (*JAI* 25 [1896]: 399) named as Dr Paul Topinard, Director of the École d'Anthropologie and Secretary General of the Société d'Anthropologie de Paris. Meanwhile, Tylor pointed to the benefits of an interdisciplinary approach that could be achieved through 'a kind of anthropological rotation of crops', arguing that 'it is obviously advantageous in the present case that a physical should succeed a cultural President' (*JAI* 22 [1893]: 384), and, for the next ten years, the Institute operated this system of rotation. He amplified the effect of rotation with a second innovation. He changed the format of the presidential address, replacing learned lectures on specialist topics – Galton on statistics (1889) and Beddoe on the skull-measuring business (1890), for example – with a sectoral review of institutional anthropology, which was closer to the format used in Section H – Anthropology. From that point on, the legitimate scope, methodology and purpose of anthropology was contested by 'physical' and 'cultural' presidents in rotation and, thus, Tylor's innovation brought the institutional infighting into the open and, more importantly for this research, onto the record.

Macalister took over from Tylor in 1893 and reasserted 'physical' control of the Institute. He declared that anthropology 'was an integral part of anatomy' (*JAI* 23 [1894]: 411) and that anthropometry – comprising cranial and facial measurement – was the principal methodology of 'the great group of sciences which deal with the Natural History of Man' (ibid.: 402). Then, in a comment that might have been directed at Haddon, Macalister declared that the study of 'savage men and their ways' might add a 'living interest' to the teaching of anthropology but remained incidental to the scientific study of humans. He had little to say in relation to the 'ethical and metaphysical sides of the subject, which are probably the most important with which the Philosophical Anthropologist can be occupied' (ibid.: 414). Macalister's speech created two problems for members like Haddon. First, natural scientists were institutionally separated from the anatomists who operated in schools of physic – as schools of medicine were called – where dissection rooms doubled as anthropological laboratories. That allowed anatomists to claim that anthropology, unlike ethnology, was a laboratory-based practice and, therefore, a pure science (see Gooday 2012). Second, Macalister's dismissal of the ethical and metaphysical aspects of anthropology placed the study of 'savage men and their ways' outside of the legitimate scope of scientific anthropology.

The 'culturals' responded in 1895 when members elected Flinders Petrie as President of Section H – Anthropology, and he set about organizing a conference titled 'On Interference with the Civilisation of Other Races' scheduled for the next meeting in Ipswich in 1895. He invited Haddon to contribute and was very clear about the purpose of the conference. He wrote to Haddon on 24 April 1895 and acknowledged that anthropologists needed to foster 'a readier toleration of what does not fit our ideas in the races we now have to deal with'. He appealed to Haddon to use his experience of 'lower civilisations' to ensure a 'useful & also popular group of papers & discussion.' Haddon agreed and the Ipswich conference became a pivotal event in Haddon's attempt to become the first anthropologist in Cambridge.

IPSWICH

On 17 September 1895, Haddon stood before a packed session of Section H – Anthropology convened in the Working Men's College in Ipswich and delivered a speech on the consequences of Anglo-Saxon colonialism. The correspondence between Flinders Petrie and Haddon establishes that the intention was to raise a debate about the protection of human rights in the colonies; this was, as such, a political rather than a scientific event, a formulation I borrow from a speech Matthew Arnold gave in the same venue in 1879 (Arnold and Super 1973: 327). Haddon's presence, the provocative billing and the evocative location – one of the largest of the working-class clubs Huxley used to launch his campaign against socialism in 1855 – made it one of the most eagerly anticipated and widely reported sessions of the meeting.

Flower set it up in 1894. This may seem surprising, given the foregoing portrayal of Flower as a leading 'physical', but Flower and Haddon were close, and Flower used the closing section of his paper to present Haddon's argument for a humanitarian function for anthropology. Flower acknowledged that the rapid disappearance and modification of primitive societies was a well-recognized consequence of colonialism, and he reminded anthropologists of their duty in respect of the native populations that had been 'to use a current phrase "disestablished and disendowed" by our own countrymen' (BAAS 1894: 774). Flower explained exactly what he meant:

> the rapid spread of civilised man all over the world . . . has obliterated what still remains of the original customs, arts, and beliefs of primitive races; if, indeed, it has not succeeded – as it too often does – in obliterating the races themselves. (BAAS 1894: 774)

Flower effectively summarized the arguments Haddon drafted in his 1891 critique of the Imperial Institute and the above quote is merely a more diplomatic version of Haddon's charge that imperial policy actively facilitated genocide by accident or design, fast or slow. In effect, Flower acknowledged that the consequences of colonialism constituted an ethical problem for some members in the mid-1890s and, despite Topinard's objections, were a legitimate topic for discussion under the heading of anthropology.

Contrast this with the laissez-faire attitude of the 1880s. In 1886, the Anthropological Institute organized meetings at the Colonial and Indian Exhibition in London, and Galton reviewed the event in 1887. He noted the 'rapid diminution' in native populations in the colonies and added:

> They are to the new European lords of the soil of not much more consideration than the vegetation of the wilderness might be to the owner of a newly reclaimed and scientifically cultivated farm. (*JAI* 16 [1887]: 390–91)

The studied brutality of that statement still has the capacity to shock. Huxley was more subtle when he suppressed Haddon's critique of the Imperial Institute in 1892. He described depopulation as the rapid disappearance of 'wild races' and elsewhere (Huxley 1900: 284) relabelled the extinction of Tasmanians as extirpation, an evolutionist rationalization of extermination through competition, although, to be fair, he allowed scope for the charge of genocide by stating that British colonists were 'the main agents of their extirpation' (ibid.). Flower's choice of 'obliteration' was far less passive even if it fell short of Haddon's use of 'legalized murder'. Nevertheless, Flower's statement was extraordinary given that he was Huxley's man in the British Museum, and he used his presidency of Section H – Anthropology to set the stage for the 'culturals' to breach the ban on anti-imperial activism introduced in the 1840s in response to the humanitarian campaign waged by ethnologists associated with the Aborigines Protection Society (see Morrell and Thackray 1981: 283–84). The ban itself is considered in more detail in relation to the consequences Haddon suffered because of his speech, and the idea of a ban on dissent is introduced here to set up the event in Ipswich as a well-planned insurrection.

Haddon resurrected his 1891 critique of imperial policy for the occasion and incorporated the main points into a speech that constituted an unprecedented and very public attack on Anglo-Saxon values, British imperialism and the political culture of organized anthropology. The BAAS did not include Haddon's speech in its report of the meeting, but Haddon filed a pamphlet issued after the meeting – no publisher is listed on the cover – which included a transcription of each contribution and recorded the opening of Haddon's speech as follows:

> Professor Haddon said civilization did not consist of railways, telegraphs, representative government, nor even of those characteristic British exports – beer and Bible – (laughter) – but of right living and the cultivation of morality. The British people especially desired to crush other people into their own procrustean bed of belief and action. (*Discussion 'On the Contact of European and Native Civilisations'*: 16)

The reference to railways and telegraphs may seem odd, but the Tories fought a general election in 1895 and hoped that government investment in fisheries infrastructure in the west of Ireland would counter support for Home Rule in swing constituencies in England and so prevent the break-up of the United Kingdom of Great Britain and Ireland. Haddon's role in that campaign will be considered in more detail in Chapter 4 and the reference matters here because it registers the fact that Ipswich took place during a divisive debate about decolonization in the context of a general election. Two other factors make the timing even more interesting. Huxley died in June and, in August, Haddon participated in the Summer Meeting of Art and Science in Edinburgh alongside Geddes, Élisée Reclus and Demolins. The combination of these events may have prompted Haddon to disregard Huxley's earlier warning and revive the anti-imperial arguments couched in the provocative language of a campaigning journalist.

His portrayal of Anglo-Saxon civilization as a grubby mix of 'beer and Bible' was the perfect sound bite and the speech was widely reported in the press. Haddon kept clippings of some reports in a file on race relations, but I draw on other articles held in online newspaper archives. The *Dundee Courier* ran the story under the headline 'Debate on Savages – Missionary Tactics Condemned' and reported that the Working Men's Club was 'thronged this forenoon during a discussion in the Anthropological Section on "Interference with the Civilisation of Other Races"'. The correspondent noted that 'Ladies were present in large numbers', highlighted the 'beer and Bible' comment and quoted Haddon's statement that:

> Some people confounded clothing with morality, but if we wanted to extend our market for cotton goods let us do it honestly, and not under the pretence of religion. The extermination of the Tasmanians was a fearful blot upon our Colonial policy, and there was no doubt that irresponsible whites had inflicted heartrending atrocities upon savages. (*Dundee Courier*, 18 September 1895: 3)

The *Glasgow Herald* ran a story under the heading 'The British Association: Interference the Civilisation of other Races' and reported that 'Professor Haddon (Dublin)' described the Imperial Institute as a 'large carcass without a soul ... given over to exploiting native populations in the colonies'. The *Daily News* reported that 'Professor Haddon' made 'some rather contemptuous remarks on the efforts of the missionaries to induce the naked races to clothe themselves ... a sneer that probably drew from a gathering of anthropologists loud applause.' This correspondent concluded that the 'kind of talk which is indulged in at the Anthropological Section ... had no connection whatever with science' and rejected the version of anthropology presented by Flinders Petrie and Haddon. This statement is worth quoting at length:

> Anthropology may be defined as the Natural History of Mankind; and its scientific treatment is the study of mankind in the same sense and spirit as that in which Natural History describes the other creatures. The relations of the various races to each other, and the consequences and effects of the contact of the higher with the lower races, belong of course to the Natural History of Mankind and might throw much light on trade, on colonisation, on civilizing and missionary efforts if it was pursued in a scientific spirit, – that is, a spirit which looks only for the facts. But there has not been a trace of the scientific spirit in the discussions over which Mr. Flinders Petrie has been presiding. (*Daily News*, 18 September 1895: 4–5)

The identity of the special correspondent is unknown, although the statement is an effective reiteration of the uncompromising, biological view that Huxley imposed on Haddon in 1892 and Macalister presented at the Anthropological Institute in 1894. It is likely that the denunciation came from within organized anthropology and, even if it did not, it stands as a definitive statement of anthropological orthodoxy.

The Globe, a Conservative newspaper, also addressed the issue of scientific credibility in a report published on 18 September under the headline 'Conquest and Conscience' in which the writer advised readers interested in sociology, as distinct from the more exact sciences, that they 'could do no better than to devote attention to the Anthropological Section and the question of Interference with the Civilisation of Other Races'. The *Daily News* was more direct and warned that anthropologists who 'wandered' into sociology could no longer be regarded as credible scientists and, by implication, had no place in an association for the advancement of science. The threat may have been implicit, but the managers of the BAAS reacted accordingly, and retribution was swift.

CONSEQUENCES

Haddon's performance was controversial but, according to Huxley (BAAS 1879: 573), that was the nature of debates in anthropology. Indeed, Haddon cited Huxley in 1910 to highlight the role controversies played in shaping anthropology in the nineteenth century. Anthropology, he wrote:

> has always been regarded as a somewhat anarchical subject, advocating views which might prove dangerous to Church and State; and many are the battles which have raged within and without. Huxley attributed the large audiences which were wont to throng the Anthropological Section of the British Association to the innate bellicose instincts of man, and to the splendid opportunities afforded by Anthropology for indulging those propensities. (Haddon and Quiggin 1910: 50)

Haddon's performance in Ipswich was 'anarchical' and widely perceived as an attack on 'Church and State', but the Church did not matter as much in a secular scientific culture in the 1890s as the fact that Haddon had wandered into sociology and breached a ban on anti-imperial activism that had stood since the 1840s. This point needs some elaboration in order to put the consequences that followed Haddon's speech into perspective.

Haddon's speech revived the anti-imperial and anti-missionary agenda of ethnologists associated in the Aborigines Protection Society in the 1830s, and two points need to be noted here. The first is that John Haddon and Elizabeth Cort were involved in the anti-slavery movement that led to the formation of the Aborigines Protection Society. The second is Haddon's friendship with Chalmers, who advocated a native missionary as a way of limiting European interference with other civilizations (Porter 2004). This suggests that Haddon was aware of and sympathetic to a movement that drew on an ethnological tradition rooted in the humanities and the anti-imperialism of Enlightenment *philosophes* like Spencer, whose influence on Geddes via Foster also needs to be noted, especially in the context of Joan Leopold's argument that Stocking's focus on evolution in *Victorian Anthropology* discounted the influence of the 'culturalogical thinking' of *philosophes*, *ideologues* and 'other writers of the enlightenment' (Leopold 1991: 315–16). Accordingly, Haddon's speech carried a lot of tradition, and Morrell and Thackray's history of the BAAS provides valuable context in terms of the original humanitarian campaign by ethnologists in the 1830s and 1840s.

Morrell and Thackray (1981: 283) argued that the forced civilization of natives by colonists and missionaries in the 1830s ignited the 'political, social and religious tinderbox' that ethnology had shown British imperialism to be. In 1835, James Cowles Prichard, a physician and ethnologist, and Thomas Hodgkin, a physician and social reformer, lobbied the British government to establish a Select Committee

> to consider what measures ought to be adopted with regard to the native inhabitants of countries where British settlements are made . . . in order to secure to them the due observance of justice and the protection of their rights. (*Parliamentary Select Committee on Aboriginal Tribes* 1837: xii)

The Committee reported in 1837 and presented a lot of 'evidence as to the injustice and cruelty with which the Aborigines have hitherto been treated, and the pernicious effects which have resulted from their intercourse with European nations' (ibid.: v). Hodgkin founded the Aborigines Protection Society in 1837 to ensure that recommendations contained in the report were implemented and, with Cowles Prichard, pursued the same agenda at meetings of the BAAS, which refused to support ethnology until they abandoned overt criticism of British imperialism, missionary activities and even the Church itself (Morrell and Thackray 1981: 283–84). The Society split and Hodgkin set up the Ethnological Society on a platform of a science of facts, not inferences, of observation rather than ideas – what Morrell and Thackray memorably described as ethnology 'stripped of dangerous features' (ibid.). The BAAS responded positively and incorporated Ethnology as a subsection of Zoology and Botany, and its embargo on dangerous ideas held until the meeting in Ipswich. Haddon advanced similarly dangerous ideas in his first reports to Section H and the Anthropological Institute in 1889 and was more explicit in his journalism and slideshows. His proposal for a bureau of ethnology was a fit for the sort of measures the Select Committee recommended and his campaign to reconstruct anthropology represents a continuation of the campaign launched by Hodgkin and Cowles Prichard in the 1830s. Sixty years on, the managers of the BAAS attempted to use the same strategy to deal with Haddon and they got their opportunity when Haddon looked for support for a second expedition to the Torres Strait.

The General Council of the BAAS appointed a committee to consider 'The Necessity for the Immediate Investigation of the Biology of Oceanic Islands' with Flower in the Chair and Haddon acting as Secretary (BAAS 1895: xciii). Haddon presented a first report in 1896 to Section D – Biology (BAAS 1896: 487–89) and Section H – Anthropology (BAAS 1896: 929). He set out the necessity for prompt action, given the threat of extermination that colonization by invasive species posed to native flora and fauna. He then turned his attention to anthropology.

> The Tasmanians have entirely disappeared and we know extremely little about this interesting people. In many is-

lands the natives are fast dying out and in more they have become so modified by contact with the white man and by crossings due to deportation by Europeans, that immediate steps are needed to record the anthropological data that remain. Only those who have a personal acquaintance with Oceania, or those who have carefully studied the recent literature of the subject, can have an idea of the pressing need there is for prompt action. No one can deny that it is our bounden duty to record the physical characteristics, the handicrafts, the psychology, ceremonial observances and religious belief of vanishing peoples; this also is a work which in many cases can alone be accomplished by the present generation. (BAAS 1896: 488)

Haddon avoided the word 'extermination' in respect of humans. The Tasmanians had 'disappeared' and the natives of Oceania were 'being modified', 'dying out' or otherwise 'vanishing'. *Nature* published an edited version titled 'The Saving of Vanishing Knowledge' in January 1897 and a correspondent for *The Standard* pointed out that Haddon's plea for 'the preservation of vanishing knowledge ... speaks only of the scientific aspects of the effects which are being produced by rapidly extending civilisation'. That statement chimes with Morrell and Thackray's conclusion that Hodgkin stripped ethnology of its dangerous features in the hope of securing research funding from the BAAS. However, Haddon's use of the rhetoric of biological fact had little effect and he reported in 1897 that the Committee's appeal for funding had no practical effect (BAAS 1898: 352).

The BAAS strategy appeared to be working until Haddon dropped a bombshell. He reported that he was organizing an expedition with a committee in Cambridge 'for the purpose of continuing his researches on the Anthropology of the Torres Straits Islanders' (ibid.). Haddon had been looking for funding for an alternative expedition since 1895. Frazer wrote to Galton in October 1897 seeking advice on funding from the Royal Geographical Society and reminded him that they had spoken two years previously of 'an expedition to New Guinea, which my friend Prof.

Haddon and myself had some thoughts of making' (Ackerman 2005: 101); incidentally, Frazer decided to stay in his study and this is the origin of the 'taking anthropology out of the armchair' trope. Fundraising continued until, eventually, a deal was done with Cambridge. Haddon (1899, 413–16) set out the main object of the expedition in *Nature* in August 1899, stating that it was to 'verify and supplement the anthropological observations made in the Torres Straits in 1888–89 with a view to the publication of a monograph dealing with the anthropology of the islanders, *using that term in its widest sense*' (ibid., emphasis added). In Haddon's mind the 1898 anthropological expedition to the Torres Strait was in fact an ethnological expedition, although anthropology was included in deference to the 'physicals'. The ethnological orientation is significant, but more consequential by far was the fact that Haddon had broken the BAAS monopoly on funding and thereby disabled its main instrument of control over the scope and significance of anthropological enquiry.

The controversy had another positive consequence. It mobilized 'cultural' opposition to the restricted definition of anthropology that 'physicals' used to castigate Haddon in the press. Haddon published 'The Study of Anthropology' in the *University Extension Journal* in November and Edward Brabrook, a civil servant, folklorist and antiquarian who served as a 'cultural' president of the Anthropological Institute between 1896 and 1897, endorsed it in his presidential address in January 1896. Brabrook went further than Haddon and directly challenged the limits on anthropological enquiry that Frazer – probably quoting Brabrook – attributed to the influence of 'foreign experts'. Brabrook named the principal foreign expert as Dr Paul Topinard and told the members of the Institute that:

> I must separate myself from the doctrine of my valued friend Dr. Topinard. In his ardour to repress a tendency to the discussion under the name of anthropology of a variety of social, moral, and religious topics ... he would restrict general anthropology to the determination of the physical type of man as an animal and of his place in nature, and

special anthropology to the determination of the interrelations of the special physical types which distinguish particular races of men. (*JAI* 25 [1896]: 399)

'Special anthropology' was a specifically biological formulation of systematic, physical anthropology and Brabrook's emphatic rejection of Topinard's doctrine simultaneously summarized and politicized 'The Study of Anthropology'. More importantly, he used his authority as president to simultaneously forgive Haddon his political transgression in Ipswich and legitimize his vision of 'general anthropology' in its widest aspect.

The war was not over, however. The main prize was the control of anthropology as an academic discipline and the 'physicals' had one last card to play. With Haddon away in the field, Macalister persuaded the managers of Cambridge University to convert Haddon's part-time teaching post into the first University Lectureship in Anthropology, and he organized the election of Duckworth to the position. Frazer reacted angrily and informed Haddon that he was lobbying for 'a readership or professorship of ethnology'. He drafted a memo to the General Board and informed Haddon that he thought

> every one interested in anthropology could hardly decline to sign ... I have good hopes that the thing might be carried without opposition, perhaps with enthusiasm. (Frazer to Haddon, 14 November 1899)

'Enthusiasm' was hoped for and 'opposition' was expected, so Frazer's strategy was to represent Anthropology and Ethnology as complementary courses. He defined ethnology as the 'other and not less important branches of Anthropology which deal with the mental, moral and social aspects of primitive man, his customs, laws, institutions, religion, superstition, the growth of society and of all the arts of life'. William Ridgeway informed Haddon of some opposition from the Moral Science people, but the strategy worked and twenty-one academics signed. However, the General Board offered a part-time, standalone teaching position worth little more than what Haddon earned as a freelance lecturer alongside Duckworth in Macalister's department. To put this in perspective, the university offered Haddon £50, whereas a full-time job in Aberdeen attracted a salary of £700, and Haddon needed a minimum of £200 to survive in Cambridge. The university managers knew this. The memo referred to Haddon's financial position and emphasized the disinterested service he had given the university. Yet the managers conceded as little as possible to Frazer, his lobby and, most of all, Haddon.

Quiggin, whom Haddon recruited in 1904, described how for ten years or so 'lectures had to be given at odd times and in odd corners', such as a storeroom lined with shelves holding skulls in the Pathology Department (Quiggin 1942: 116). She described how, in 1909, the General Board of Studies recommended, against considerable opposition, that Haddon be appointed to a University Readership in Ethnology (see Macfarlane 2009). That indicates that an institutional determination to marginalize ethnology shaped the first version of academic anthropology, and despite the existence of an extensive paper trail, this story has disappeared from the history of disciplinary anthropology.

CONCLUSION

To summarize, the row between the Aborigines Protection Society and the BAAS exposed a political culture that defined ethnology as a threat to state, church and empire. Anthropology, redefined as a function of biology, emerged as an alternative and gained institutional supremacy in the 1880s. Ethnologists regrouped under Tylor, who described the split as a faction fight between 'physicals' and 'culturals' and instigated a form of positional rotation in pursuit of a multidisciplinary approach that chimed with a reformist vision of anthropology in its widest aspect. This gave reformists a forum to make the case for engaging with a range of social, cultural, political and ethical issues, and nothing was more ethical in a nakedly political way than the destruction of other societies and their cultures under the banner of Anglo-Saxon civilization. Haddon delivered an 'anarchical' speech in Ipswich in which he set out his vision of ethnology as a cultural project best suited to the protection of human rights in the colonies. The 'physicals' interpreted it as an insurrection by 'culturals' who had wandered out of science and into sociology. In response, the managers of the BAAS withheld funding from Haddon's second expedition to Oceania and Macalister, the leader of the 'physicals', removed him from the teaching of anthropology in Cambridge University. The 'culturals' rallied around Haddon, and he became an ethnologist, although the terms of that appointment exposed the limited effect of Frazer's lobby and confirmed the dominance of academic anthropology as function of biology in the form of anatomy.

At the core of this telling of that story is the substitution of ethnology with anthropology, which, when viewed alongside Huxley's deployment of evolutionary theory in defence of capitalism in the same period, can be interpreted as a victory for the political right over a spectrum of anti-slavery, humanitarian and anti-imperial activists that found common cause in human rights campaigns conducted under the banner of ethnology. In this context, anthropology became a reactionary will to limit dissent and, as such, remained the foundation of the political culture of organized anthropology into the early years of the twentieth century, as demonstrated by Huxley's suppression of Haddon's critique of the Imperial Institute in 1892, the codification of Topinard's doctrine within the institutions and the choice of biology as the foundation for academic anthropology in Cambridge. Flinders Petrie's decision to use Section H – a forum that had, for half a century, been the main arena of conflict between ethnologists and anthropologists – to stage a protest against the destruction of *other* civilizations by Anglo-Saxon colonists provided Haddon with an opportunity to align an anti-imperial tradition in ethnology with a 'cultural' demand for anthropology in its widest aspect and thereby to advance a humanitarian agenda that had been suppressed for over half a century. The backlash in the press and sanctions imposed by the BAAS and Cambridge exposed the limits of Huxley's revolution in terms of an underlying intolerance of any challenge to the status quo in the form of criticism of the Church, the state and empire. As such, the insurrection in Ipswich necessitates a shift in focus from evolutionist methodology to institutional politics as the governing dynamic of organized anthropology in the 1890s. That renders obsolete much of what has been written about Haddon.

To finish, institutional politics may have barred Haddon from an academic career in anthropology but, paradoxically, becoming an ethnologist was probably the best basis for claiming a stake in the modernization of anthropology. However, his involvement with Cunningham and Galton is a problem, and the photographs he took in the Aran Islands in 1892 of himself and Browne measuring Tom Connelly's head in a mobile version of Galton's laboratory (Figure 6.1) are clearly incompatible with such a claim and, in the context of a series on the ancestors of anthropology, cast him in the role of a rather disreputable predecessor whose lineage, despite some merit, was tainted by an association with scientific racism. Accordingly, this study now turns to Haddon's perplexing involvement in the skull-measuring business in Ireland.

PART II

• • •

THE SKULL-MEASURING BUSINESS

Figure 4.1. A. F. Dixon, *Untitled*, 1890. Digital scan of silver gelatine, glass-plate negative (Ciarán Walsh, Ciarán Rooney, 2019). The original negative is held in the School of Medicine, Trinity College, University of Dublin. © curator.ie.

CHAPTER 4

ETHNICAL ISLANDS

● ● ●

Anyone who has travelled through the country districts must be familiar with the very different types which are presented by the inhabitants. This is especially the case in outlying portions of the west coast and in the islands off the mainland.

—Cunningham and Haddon,
'The Anthropometric Laboratory of Ireland'

Having decided to go into anthropology, Haddon returned to Dublin in January 1890 and resumed his duties as a part-time Professor of Zoology. He put off his revision of sea anemones for a year and this suggests that marine biology was not uppermost in his mind. Gomme provides corroborating evidence. On 26 November, he thrilled the members of the Folk-Lore Society with the following account of its capture of Haddon:

> Professor Haddon went out to the Torres Straits on an expedition on behalf of natural science; he returned an ardent folk-lorist, and immediately joined us. As a scientific man, he knows the value of precision in recording facts, and I do not know a more perfect model of genuine story-collecting than his. He is now pursuing his folk-lore work in Ireland, and I, for one, expect great things from him. (FLS 2,1 [1891]: 13)

Haddon stated a preference for the hyphenated form of folklore in 'The Study of Anthropology':

> The second psychical probe into the past is folk-lore. One is too apt to dismiss this study with a smile of derision as being concerned with ghosts, fairy-tales, and old-wives' superstitions. What does the name imply? The 'lore of the folk.' But the folk bear the same relationship to educated people that savages do to civilised communities... and thus by this means we are largely enabled to study the practices and beliefs of our forefathers, for in an attenuated form many of these persist amongst us. (Haddon 1895a: 25)

'Derision' suggests that Haddon was already encountering opposition from anthropologists, and Gillian Bennett (Bennett and Stocking 1997: 122), drawing on the records of the Folklore Society – which discarded the hyphen from the name of its journal in 1958 and the society ten years later (see Cowdell 2015) – described Haddon and Gomme's efforts to organize an amalgamation of the Folk-Lore Society and the Anthropological Institute in 1893, noting how anthropologists treated the folklore movement with some disdain. Equally noteworthy is the correspondence, however clumsy to our ears, of savage and civilized peoples in terms of ancestral knowledges. This echoed Ellis's (1890: 9) declaration that simpler societies were 'as lamps to us in our social progress', which I have already argued was an idea borrowed from Kropotkin. Thus, Haddon's definition suggests that tension between a restricted, physical anthropology and an extended anthropology incorporating the study of folklore and informed by a blend of anarcho-utopian thought was already becoming ingrained in his thinking about practice. That tension complicates any analysis of the evidence that, within months of becoming an 'ardent folk-lorist', he got involved in the skull-measuring business.

Haddon's 'folk-lore work in Ireland' began in June 1890 when he joined the government-funded Survey of Fishing Grounds, West Coast and travelled to remote districts in the west of Ireland, many of which were only accessible by boat. He reached the Inishkea Islands on 8 July and recorded in his journal that quern stones were still used for grinding flour, commenting:

> It is most interesting to come across these relics of barbarism – Doubtless a more extended stay in some of these islands would yield many interesting facts – especially in archaic beliefs. Next week we shall be cruising off Connemara and round about Inishbofin and I am expecting to be able to record some fragments of Folk Lore. I have heard of a custom of courting by proxy about which I want to get fuller information. (SS *Fingal* Journal, 1890: 19)

He was also interested in craniology. He consulted Flower about measuring the people and, while in Inishbofin, he stole thirteen crania from a community burial ground. Haddon wrote an account of the theft, the first of a series of grave-robbing incidents that became a programme of 'collecting' Irish skulls from mediaeval ruins that served as community burial grounds (see Walsh 2021a, 2021b). It seems that Haddon had, as Geddes feared in his letter of 11 December 1889, yielded to 'the mere desire of measuring skulls', and that seems to be confirmed by his role in the mobilization of Galton's laboratory to assist anthropologists in their efforts to 'unravel the tangled skein of the so-called "Irish Race"', the standout statement in the proposal for an Anthropometric Laboratory of Ireland that Cunningham and Haddon presented to the Royal Irish Academy and the Anthropological Institute in February 1891. Further evidence is provided by a series of craniological studies he launched in 1892, and the inevitable question was whether the naturalist-turned-ardent-folklorist had flipped once again and become a craniologist.

That sounds rhetorical, given what has gone before, but it was the main problem I faced when I started investigating what Haddon was doing in the west of Ireland. A recurring theme of this monograph is that most histories of anthropology were written with the common sense that Haddon experienced an anthropological epiphany in Oceania in 1888 and bided his time in Dublin until the 1898 expedition opened a route into disciplinary anthropology in Cambridge in 1901. Historians usually left the telling of what happened in between to Quiggin, although my experience indicates that her biography has been largely forgotten because Ireland did not really matter in the grand narrative of the founding of British anthropology. Moreover, Quiggin's account of this period ends on a cliffhanger. She notes (1942: 70–71) that information about the skulls on Inishbofin 'aroused his head-hunting passion' and she quotes Haddon's account of stealing them. However, Haddon left Inishbofin and headed south to the Aran Islands and Quiggin did not have access to the section of Haddon's journal that records what happened there. Cambridge University Library holds forty-six pages of a fifty-six-page journal, which, in 2013, was scattered throughout a file of seemingly miscellaneous material relating to his work in Ireland. Ten pages were missing, and the gap corresponded to the time Haddon spent in the islands, according to a one-page chronology in the same file. The gap proved very problematic in explaining how the islands became the site of the first ethnographic survey conducted by Haddon in 1892 as a founding member of the Anthropometric Laboratory of Ireland. Aidan Baker, the Haddon Librarian, solved part of the problem in 2013 when he found Haddon's file on the islands. It contained the missing pages as well as sketchbooks, galley proofs of typical portraits and a commentary for a slideshow. In 2014, I discovered a collection of photographs at TCD that enabled me to reconstruct this slideshow and to see, for the first time ever, what Haddon was doing in the islands in 1890. The ten pages and forty-nine photographs record the discovery of a folk community (figure 4.1), a geographically bounded community that had escaped the worst effects of Anglo-Saxon colonization and, as such, constituted an undisturbed ethnological field less than a day away from Dublin. The shift from the study of folk and their lore to measuring skulls is registered six months later when he coined the phrase 'ethnical islands' (*JAI* 21 [1892]: 36) and identified them as sources of 'valuable information concerning the persistence or otherwise of racial characters'.

The problem here is that the appalling lack of social and economic development in the same 'ethnical islands' had generated a level of food insecurity that bordered on persistent famine, and this threat became the focus of political debates about the legitimacy of British rule in Ireland. The survey of fishing grounds was a critical part of the Tory strategy for defeating Home Rulers in a general election scheduled for 1892, although the Royal Dublin Society was nominally in charge. A search of its library produced two reports, a narrative account by William Spotswood Green as Director of the Survey (RDS 127 [1890–91]: 29–66), and an introductory note (RDS 7 [1891–92]: 221–24) to Holt's report (ibid.: 225–477) that Haddon wrote in his capacity as Naturalist to the Survey. The most striking aspect of the narrative account was evidence of Green's antagonism towards Haddon, and this became the basis of my telling of the end of Haddon's career as a marine biologist, which, in turn, provided a possible motive for his involvement in the skull-measuring business.

This chapter begins with Haddon's journey into the west, where the Survey of Fishing Grounds, West Coast led him into an undisturbed ethnological field on the western periphery of the UK. Haddon 'discovered' the Aran Islands and abandoned the survey for a week of ethnology. That was a mistake. The threat of famine in the islands had become a lightning rod for anti-government sentiment amongst the electorate and the survey was designed to counter that. Green took issue with Haddon's preference for ethnology over practical science and threw him overboard.

INTO THE WEST

Haddon boarded a train in Dublin on the morning of 26 June 1890, and arrived, ten hours later, at the end of the line in the town of Donegal. He transferred to a jaunting car (see Haddon 1898: 200–18 for a description of this) and travelled for two and a half hours to Killybegs, the main fishing port in the north-west. He boarded the SS *Fingal* and assumed responsibility for the biological programme of the Survey of Fishing Grounds, West Coast. Arthur J. Balfour, a Conservative MP and political head of the British Administration in Ireland, organized the survey after a combination of political circumstances threatened the Tory majority in the Imperial Parliament in London. The Tories came to power in 1886 in an election caused by the defeat of the Liberal Party's Government of Ireland (Home Rule) Bill, a legislative measure designed to end British rule in Ireland. Balfour was given the job of defeating Home Rule and earned the nickname 'Bloody' for his heavy-handed suppression of a popular land reform movement known as the Land League. At the same time, government inaction in response to the threat of famine in the west and south-west fuelled anti-government sentiment and the Tories lost seats in newly introduced local elections in England in 1889, a measure withheld in Ireland for a decade. Balfour switched tactics, scaling back on coercion and launching a programme of railway expansion and fisheries development in the west of Ireland that James Hack Tuke, a banker and anti-Home Rule activist, had been advocating for decades. Tuke led Quaker relief missions during the Great Famine of 1845–49 and the Second Famine of 1879–80. He earned the trust of the government with a rigorously empirical method for gauging the extent of famine and his efficient management of subsequent relief programmes. Balfour commissioned an assessment of the threat of famine in 1887 and Tuke, fearful of Home Rule, persuaded him of the political benefit of investing in railways and fisheries. Tuke brokered a deal with the Royal Dublin Society (RDS) whereby the government paid the Society half the estimated cost of a two-year survey – £600 – to oversee the project (Berry 1915: 134–36; Moriarty 1996: 162–65).

The RDS tasked Haddon with the organization of the Natural History Department (RDS 7 [1891–92]: 222) under the overall direction of Green, a fisheries expert who worked with Haddon in 1885 and 1886 (Praeger 1949: 186–87, Figure 1.1). In 1887, Green prepared a plan for fisheries development that was in line with Huxley's application of maritime research to the problem of developing economically sustainable fisheries in the wake of the International Fisheries Exhibition of 1883 (Berry 1915: 333–37; Moriarty 1996: 155–68). The deal Tuke brokered with the RDS was necessary to shield Balfour from accusations of market intervention and, worse still, state socialism. Balfour made Green a Commissioner of Irish Fisheries, the Irish equivalent of the post held by Huxley between 1881 and 1885. To put this into perspective, Green was Balfour's agent and Haddon, Huxley's man in Dublin, was Green's second-in-command (RDS 127 [1890–91]: 29–30), just two degrees of separation from Balfour, who went on to become prime minister. This arrangement illustrates the mix of political imperative and practical science that made Huxley's system so effective. Incidentally, Balfour's younger brother Frank studied under Foster at Cambridge and taught Haddon, who acknowledged the former's influence (see Quiggin 1942: 48–49).

Green commenced the survey on 1 May 1890, leaving Queenstown (Cobh) in the south and working his way north to Killybegs and a rendezvous with Haddon. The survey left Killybegs the following day and sailed south to Broadhaven Bay in Mayo, where bad weather prevented trawling and Haddon, accompanied by Ernest W. Holt, a marine biologist who deputized for him on the northward leg of the survey, headed overland to the town of Belmullet. Haddon described the country as wretchedly barren and covered in peat mosses, except for the odd crop of stunted oats. He then considered the inhabitants:

> The people I was informed are not so destitute as they seemed or many were not they lived in worse houses (huts or hovels would be a better term) than they might. The parish priest was my informant & he said that some to whom you might feel inclined to give 1/2d. had £200 in the bank. They are tall, dark usually black hair, occasionally red, say 1 or 2 % & light eyes. it struck me that the nose was often long. They are a hardy & strong race. (SS *Fingal* Journal, 1890: 2)

Once again, Haddon turned oceanographic research into an opportunity to collect anthropological information on land, but the circumstances of this research were slightly different. Haddon was now a member of the Anthropological Institute, and the influence of its president John Beddoe is apparent in the references to complexion and physiognomy. Beddoe operated a system of racial classification based primarily on hair and eye colour and, in 1891, he presented a paper on the state of craniology in Europe in which he noted that Ireland, 'that distressful country' (*JAI* 19 [1891]: 358), had contributed nothing, but given its history, promised much.

Haddon intended to fill that gap. He wrote to Flower in May and sought advice on the measurement of people. Flower replied that he 'had not much opportunity of making anthropological observations on the living' and added:

> I should think the people of the West coast of Ireland would offer good material for investigation, though very difficult probably to make them submit to the required observations & measurements. I expect that your trained eye as a zoologist will soon indicate the points in which they differ and resemble each other and that you will be able to get data perhaps on a better principle than hitherto required.
> (Flower to Haddon, 17 May 1890)

Haddon's interest in anthropology was short-lived. He reached the Inishkea Islands on 8 July and resumed a pattern of research established on Nagir in 1888. The Inishkea Islands were, Haddon recorded in his journal, very difficult to reach and 'the islanders take advantage of their insular position & defy the law' (SS *Fingal* Journal, 1890: 13). Green went there to warn the islanders to repay government loans for fishing gear 'or the Board of Works would be down upon them'. Haddon went looking for ethnological material and called at the house of the King of the North Island, drew a sketch and wrote that:

> half of the house ... was used as a cattle shed, thus one & the same room formed the dwelling place of man & beast. On the whole the houses in Torres Straits are better &

cleaner / & neater than those in the W. of Ireland. (SS *Fingal* Journal, 1890: 14)

The islanders were also 'noted for making the best poteen along the coast' and, after Green concluded his business, the King, knowing they 'were safe', unearthed a small barrel of poteen in their presence. These incidents of conflict with colonial agents and an-archy (self-government) are a recurring theme in Haddon's journal and he later coined the phrase 'little wars' to describe the constant friction between native conviction and imperial law that characterized daily life in the colonies (Haddon MS 1891 Critique of Imperial Institute: 19). An-archy and isolation also brought Gomme's work on village communities into play and the discovery of quern stones – relics of barbarism or pre-conquest civilization – alerted him to the survival of 'fragments of Folk Lore' (SS *Fingal* Journal, 1890: 19).

Inishbofin was disappointing in this regard, but Haddon recorded the theft, under cover of darkness, of thirteen crania from Teampall Colmáin (Colman's Monastery), a mediaeval abbey where human remains disturbed during burials were placed for safety. On departure, Haddon noted that the people were more truculent than elsewhere, and it is not clear if that was because of an earlier incident in which the islanders mistook the survey for a raid by tax collectors or because the islanders had discovered the theft of the skulls. I suspect the latter because the islanders refused to submit to measurement by Browne during an ethnographical survey in 1893 and thwarted his attempt to remove more skulls from Teampall Colmáin (RIA 3,3 [1893]: 334; De Mórdha and Walsh 2012: 51).

Either way, the survey eventually reached the Aran Islands and events there had profound consequences for Haddon's career as a marine biologist. Green used the islands as a base from 23 July to 12 August and Haddon was so struck by what he observed on his first tour of the islands that he took a week off from the fishing survey, and the next ten pages of his journal record a turning point like no other in his quest for anthropology in its widest aspect.

THE ARAN ISLANDS

Haddon, accompanied by Andrew Francis Dixon, left the survey on 30 July, and the SS *Fingal* sailed away, returning on 7 August to collect them. Dixon was one of Cunningham's students whose interest in embryology led him to Haddon and extra tuition at the Royal College of Science. He joined the survey on 11 July as a replacement for Holt, who returned to his laboratory in St Andrews, Scotland. Haddon and Dixon travelled through the islands making sketches, taking photographs and collecting information on customs and beliefs. Haddon summarized the experience as follows:

> The Arran Islands are in respects the most remarkable islands I have as yet come across anywhere. (SS *Fingal* Journal, 1890: 41)

It was an extraordinary statement, given his recent expedition to the Torres Strait and New Guinea. Nevertheless, the next ten pages of his journal document Haddon's growing fascination with the glaciokarst landscape, the distinctive appearance of the islanders, their way of life and the archaeology scattered throughout the islands, which was studied by an earlier generation of ethnologists who visited the islands during a BAAS meeting in Dublin in 1857 (Haverty 1859). They were more interested in archaeology as evidence of racial origins than they were in the people, while Haddon treated archaeology as evidence of the antiquity of island culture and he made the islanders and their way of life the focus of his attempts to reconstruct anthropology between 1890 and 1895.

The Aran Islands were also known as Arran, the Arran Isles and the Isles of Arran. The last, Green (RDS 127 [1890–91]: 44) noted, was closer in pronunciation to the Irish original, Oileáin Árann. The islands lie across the entrance to Galway Bay, about 29 miles and a four-hour journey by boat from Galway city. Haddon described them as follows:

The north island Inishmore ('Big Island') is the largest of the 3 main islands & has a population of over 2,000 souls. The middle island has about 800 inhabitants & the S. Island 450. (SS *Fingal* Journal, 1890: 41)

They were remote. Green (RDS 127 [1890–91]: 47) reported that the only means of communication with the mainland was a sailboat for mail that operated, weather permitting, three times a week. He recommended a telegraph connection in 1891 – the source of Haddon's reference in Ipswich – and Brian Harvey (1991: 240) documented a report from an inspector for the Royal Irish Constabulary who objected on the basis that, apart from fish, there was scarcely any trade with the islands and very few tourists. In 1878, John Murray published a handbook for travellers and warned those using the mailboat that they risked getting stranded (Murray 1878: 188). Mary Banim, a journalist and antiquarian whom Haddon tried to recruit as an ethnographer in 1893, visited the islands just before him. She travelled by paddle steamer that operated weekly excursions during the summer and still relished the risk of being stranded.

Banim wrote a series of articles for her travel column for the *Freeman's Journal* and the first instalment, illustrated with sketches by her sister M. E., appeared on 23 August, a week before the end of the survey. She recalled how the islanders struggled to get the owners of the islands to provide basic services like schools and described them as absentee landlords and rack-renters, labels used by Home Rulers to discredit the landlord system and thereby challenge the legitimacy of colonial rule in Ireland. The Digby family bought the islands in the 1870s (see Robinson 1997: 160) and, in 1890, according to an online database of landed estates maintained by the Moore Institute, the property was part of an extensive portfolio controlled by the Digby/Barfoot and St. Lawrence/Guinness families. Banim's description may have been politically motivated, but the facts were corroborated by William Frederick Johnson, a member of the Belfast Naturalists' Field Club who visited the islands with Haddon in 1895. He wrote a report that the *Belfast*

News-Letter published under the initials W.F. J. on 13 December, and he described the islanders as 'very poor, living solely by fishing in the bay ... They had no jail, no hospital and no workhouse'. Harvey reviewed the historical record in 1991 and added the lack of a midwife and local government works to the list, noting that the islands were well policed, with three barracks and eighteen policemen for a population of 3,163 (Harvey 1991: 239).

The most striking feature of the islands was a pastoral system adapted to the glaciokarst landscape, which, as Haddon explained in his journal, was made up of sheets of carboniferous limestone planed so smooth by glaciers that Atlantic storms prevented soil formation, except in some sheltered spots. Sheep grazed on grass and herbs that grew in fissures (grykes) between bare limestone slabs (clints) that were enclosed with rocks to make a 'field' and some fields were made into pastures. Green described how the islanders covered the bare rock with sand and seaweed 'till enough soil had been carried to it to grow a crop of potatoes, and afterward be turned into pasture' (RDS 127 [1890–91]: 51–52). Banim challenged the right of the Digbys to charge rent for this handmade land. Green also recorded that one in ten islanders depended on fishing 'though many look to fishing as their chief support for part of the year' (ibid.). Drownings ensured that the islands became synonymous with fisherfolk, and Banim's account of the islanders skilfully handling frail, canvas-skinned canoes or 'corrachs' (currachs) on stormy seas is an early example of the mythologizing of this aspect of island life. The same islanders ferried people, animals and goods between ship and shore and Haddon filed a photograph of three men in a currach pulling up alongside the SS *Fingal*, a picture that captures his first contact with these argonauts of the western isles.

Haddon and Dixon attended a regatta and watched currach teams race against each other. There was, Haddon noted, 'very little drinking during the day & scarcely any smoking', and he continued:

> I never was in a pleasanter crowd. The fine upright islanders with their fair hair & white & blue costumes were usu-

ally readily distinguishable fr. the men from other places. The Inishmaan (Central Island) men were as a rule larger & darker. The Connemara men had darker hair & wore grey frieze. The Galway men had black coats. (SS *Fingal* Journal, 1890: 48)

This encounter has, I propose, some significance in terms of interpreting what happened next in relation to Haddon's career as a marine biologist and his progress as an ethnologist operating within an anthropological community dominated by 'physicals'. Taking the second point first, Haddon acted on Beddoe's identification of a gap in anthropological knowledge and came up with the idea of an extended ethnographic study as part of Cunningham's plan to establish a branch of Galton's anthropometric laboratory in Dublin. He illustrated his contribution with a reference to the regatta:

To take one example: the fair slight men of the North Island of Arran offer a marked contrast to the dark burly men of the Middle and South Islands. (*JAI* 21 [1892]: 1892: 36)

Haddon appeared to have reverted to the anthropological approach adopted earlier in the expedition, as evidenced by his attention to complexion, physiognomy and stature. Appearances are deceptive, however.

Everything Haddon did in the islands, as recorded in his journal, sketches and photographs, conformed to the ethnological methods he developed during the 1888 expedition. When considered in the context of his conversations with Geddes and Ellis, this material records the discovery of the sort of an-archic (self-governing) folk community that fascinated his friends in various utopian and social reform movements. In other words, he had discovered an undisturbed ethnological zone that offered a chance to emulate Kropotkin's work in Siberia and thereby reconstruct anthropology along the lines agreed with Ellis. I think that is why Haddon described the islands as the most remarkable he had encountered up to that point. His sympathy for the islanders echoed that of Banim, and that was always going to be a problem, given that Balfour organized the survey to counter the Home Rule arguments she advanced in her column. Green acted for Balfour when he presented his first report to the Royal Dublin Society, and it provides a remarkable record of the end of Haddon's career as a marine biologist.

MAN OVERBOARD

Haddon's decision to leave the survey for a week was a mistake. However interesting the Aran Islands may have been to Haddon as an ethnologist, the survey was a political gamble, and the stakes were high. The 1892 election was shaping up as a referendum on Home Rule and Balfour needed to demonstrate that a Tory government was capable of tackling distress in Ireland or risk losing power to a Liberal–Nationalist alliance. Haddon's decision displayed a remarkable lack of political savvy and he exacerbated the problem on his return to Dublin by showing more interest in ethnology than fisheries development. The consequences played out in public as proceedings at the Royal Dublin Society were reported in the press.

The Society made its contribution towards the cost of the survey 'conditional upon the results being published by the Society' (RDS 127 [1890–91]: 28), yet the terms of that decision make it clear that this was Balfour's project. Green sent regular progress reports from the field, and these were published in the press. He presented the first results in November 1890, comprising a narrative account by Green and a scientific paper by Holt. Haddon, acting in his capacity as Naturalist appointed by the Society, submitted Holt's paper, describing it, according to a report the *Freeman's Journal* published on 20 November under the heading 'Royal Dublin Society', as 'a long and technical paper' that dealt with the eggs and larva of thirty-eight species (RDS 4,2 [1888–92]: 435–474). Asked if the report was purely scientific or related to fisheries development, Haddon replied, to applause, that 'it was now found to be impossible to draw the line between economic and pure science'. Unfortunately for Haddon, Balfour's sponsorship ensured that it was also impossible to draw the line between practical science and party politics, and Green's report was critical of Haddon on both grounds.

Haddon should have prepared a report for the meeting in November. Instead, he concentrated on his ethnological findings. He extracted the pages of his journal dealing with the Aran Islands and sent them, with sketches and photographs, to John Bettany of *Lippincott's Monthly Magazine* and pitched an illustrated article. He sent Dixon's photographs to Robert J. Welch, a professional photographer and member of Belfast Naturalists' Field Club, to be converted to slides and wrote a commentary for a slideshow on the islands, stating that:

> To a naturalist they are most interesting. The greater part of the surface of the island is composed of base limestone rock within the crevices of which many beautiful and rare plants and numerous ferns grow, the Maiden-hair fern being very abundant. . . . Aran is especially famous for its antiquities, pagan and Christian relics abounding, a considerable number of the former dating from many centuries before our era. No area of equal size in the British Islands contains so numerous and so varied remains of archaeological interest. (Haddon MS 1890, 'The Aran Islands')

Green took a different view in his report to the RDS:

> There were so many things about Aran of interest that I feel it difficult to pass on. But the pasturages gay with the bright blue gentians and other flowers, and the hoary ruins, have no connection with fishing. (RDS 127 [1890–91]: 53)

Green's frustration with Haddon's lack of political focus and practical application is apparent when the sarcasm of 'pasturages gay' and 'hoary ruins' is compared to the blunt statement that the business of the survey was 'fishing'. Compare this with a letter Green sent to the council of the Society from Killybegs on

21 June, which the *Irish Times* published on 28 June under the heading 'Royal Dublin Society'. Green informed the members that 'Mr. Holt is working very hard with his microscope'.

Green knew Holt from his 'publication on Fishes' (RDS 127 [1890–91]: 30) and met him when he consulted with Prof. W. C. M'Intosh at St Andrew's University prior to the commencement of the survey. M'Intosh worked with Huxley in 1883 and was instrumental in establishing a Fisheries Laboratory in 1884 with funding from the Fisheries Board for Scotland, and Adams (1996: 103) considered this 'the foundation of research on the biology of food fishes of British waters'. In his report, Green praised the work Holt did during the survey and the 'valuable' paper of scientific results he prepared for the meeting. It was a pointed comment. Haddon used the fact that the survey was ongoing as an excuse to delay publishing his results, despite a deadline that the RDS set in relation to funding.

Haddon and Green also disagreed on the politics behind the survey. Haddon's description of housing on North Inishkea was hardly sympathetic to the islanders, but the tone of his commentary changed dramatically in Connemara. 'South Connemara', he reflected, 'will henceforth have for me a distinct impression of sterility, stones & starvation'. Haddon discussed fisheries development over dinner with Fr Flannery, a parish priest supportive of Balfour's project, in the company of 'another fat priest & a local landowner & a land agent'. He concluded:

> It is impossible to give a description of the whole affair. I enjoyed it immensely as it was a peep into another world & many of the modes of thought & ways of looking at things were very different from what I have been accustomed to. It is becoming more & more evident to me that the ordinary 'Saxon' is incapable of understanding the typical Irish how much less is he capable of governing him! (SS *Fingal* Journal, 1890: 35)

Haddon left Connemara on 21 July and after a refuelling stop in Galway headed for the Aran Islands, where the practical differences between him and Green became very political. Haddon included the following statement in his slideshow commentary:

> The Aran Islands have from time to time come into notice on account of the failure of the potato crop, and it is possible that again this winter the inhabitants will require assistance. (Haddon MS 1890, 'The Aran Islands')

Haddon, unlike Banim, did not refer to political unrest in the islands, but this statement differs little from a warning Michael Davitt issued in 1888 as an appeal for assistance on behalf of 'The Starving Islanders in Arran'. Davitt, it should be noted, was a Fenian and cofounder of the Land League, although he was not actively involved in the land war at the time he issued this appeal.

Balfour thought such threats were exaggerated for political advantage and Green put the government case in his report to the RDS. He acknowledged that:

> when the bream fishing fails and the con-acre potato gardens are blighted, as unfortunately they are this year, the outlook would indeed be dismal only for the hope, always cherished, that the outside public will take pity on them and send relief. (RDS 127 [1890–91]: 52)

He did not use the word famine, emphasizing instead the habitual recourse to pity that was 'utterly subversive to the laying of a foundation of progress, manliness, and self-reliance' (ibid.). He asked his readers what could be done. Letting starvation and famine-fever take its course was not an option, so action was needed to 'prevent the people being satisfied to multiply and live on the brink of starvation' (ibid.). He rejected the idea of 'relief without *real* work' (ibid., original emphasis) and recommended, despite past difficulties, education and a sustainable fishery as a way out of the mess. Green did not refer to Haddon in person but, given the context – two months aboard a boat with a contrarian like Haddon – it is reasonable to take this criticism as being aimed at him.

Haddon's lack of political awareness combined with his neglect of his microscope and deferred report-writing were to prove disastrous. Green also gave a slideshow after the survey and the best account is a report in *The Graphic* dated 27 February 1892. *The Graphic* reprinted Green's account of the survey and recreated his slideshow with fifteen engravings based on photographs taken during the survey and illustrative of the more 'picturesque side' of the ichthyological research conducted by Holt. The photographs date from 1890 and include some that Haddon filed in his own collection, including the photograph of three men in a currach coming alongside the SS *Fingal*. Green did not refer to Haddon and an engraving of 'The Professor dissecting fish' showed Holt rather than Haddon at work. Green, in a manner of speaking, had thrown Haddon overboard and all that remained of his career as a marine biologist was his part-time Professorship at the Royal College of Science.

CONCLUSION

To summarize, Haddon travelled to the periphery of the United Kingdom of Great Britain and Ireland in June 1890 and began an extended tour of outlying districts and islands off the west coast. He went as an agent of the Tory government and worked on a fisheries development project designed to undermine electoral support for Home Rule. He intended to combine marine biology with anthropological 'researches' and thought of measuring the people he met, but Flower advised against it. He also expected to collect folklore, and Gomme was expecting a masterclass in scientific story collection. Haddon 'discovered' the Aran Islands in July, and everything changed. Here was an undisturbed ethnological field a day away from Dublin and, in his excitement, he made a decision that cost him his job as a government scientist. Mary Banim mythologized the Aran Islanders as fisherfolk who braved savage seas in frail canoes and fought a battle for survival against rack-renting landowners who claimed dominion over the small pastures they had made on limestone barrens. This struggle – elemental and political – captured the public imagination and a renewed threat of famine forced the Tory government to mobilize practical science in preparation for the 1892 general election. Balfour asked Green to save the Union by showing that the Tories were capable of saving the islanders from starvation, and Green began searching for new fishing grounds off the west coast of Ireland.

Haddon joined him in June and quickly realized that he had entered the ethnological zone that Kropotkin mapped and Elié Reclus and Gomme described for Ellis in the Contemporary Science Series. He imagined what an extended stay in the district might produce by way of ancient customs, but Inishbofin disappointed him, although he came away with a haul of stolen skulls, thereby filling a gap highlighted by Beddoe. Connemara left an abiding impression of 'sterility, stones & starvation' and forced a realization of the absurdity of British rule in Ireland. The Aran Islands, on the other hand, were remarkable! Here was an intact village community of ancient origin that demonstrated the ethnological potential of 'folk' communities that Haddon later outlined in the 'The Study of Anthropology' in 1895. Haddon took a week off from the survey, choosing ethnology over the political business of fisheries development, and Green sarcastically characterized the act as a choice of 'hoary ruins' over 'fishing'. Haddon's lack of political savvy and practical application clearly antagonized Green, who threw him overboard in November 1890, thereby ending an involvement in practical fisheries research that began when Huxley recruited Haddon in 1880.

In effect, Haddon's journey into the west of Ireland triggered some dramatic changes in direction and circumstances. Most notable, in historiographical terms, are the circumstance of the abrupt end of his career as a marine biologist, because they cancel out the well-worn narrative of a gradual and incomplete transition from zoology to anthropology between 1888 and 1898. More importantly, in terms of the 'ancestral' thrust of this monograph, themes emerge in Haddon's account that inform 'The Study of Anthropology', which Ellis and Haddon were working on at this time. I have given the example of the ethnological potential of 'folk' communities within developed societies, and this was further developed by them in a claim that

> There is no need to travel to the uttermost parts of the earth; we can prosecute researches or find food for reflection in our own nurseries, in the playground, on the village green – even in our cities. (Haddon 1895a: 25)

The discovery of the Aran Islands, I propose, triggered a pivot from Oceania to Ireland and the UK in search of a model of ethnography that was a practical fit for the reconstructed version of anthropology Haddon set out in 'The Study of Anthropology'. Haddon resumed his 'researches' in the islands in April 1891, when 'Holt Lane & I had a great day ruin hunting & photographing, we had a lot of walking & finished off with dinner at the 'P.Ps' (Parish priest) Father O'Donoghue' (Haddon 1891 *SS Harlequin* Journal: 4), who, incidentally, was associated with the Land League. Haddon returned to the Aran Islands in September 1892 and took photographs of himself and Browne measuring Tom Connelly's skull and recording the data on a schedule designed by Galton. The problem here is that, apart from the theft of the skulls on Inishbofin, there was nothing to indicate a pivot from the far left of ethnology to the far right of anthropology. Quite the opposite, in fact, so why did Haddon get involved with Galton and Cunningham in the establishment of the Anthropometric Laboratory of Ireland?

CHAPTER 5

THE LABORATORY

● ● ●

> It has therefore occurred to us that we might employ the anthropometric methods for the purpose of giving some assistance to the anthropologist in his endeavours to unravel the tangled skein of the so-called "Irish Race".
> —Cunningham and Haddon,
> 'The Anthropometric Laboratory of Ireland'

Haddon, Cunningham and Galton formed an unlikely alliance in 1891 when they agreed to establish in Dublin a branch of Galton's anthropometric laboratory. Galton used his laboratory to collect data on the physical and sensory capacity of individuals as a measure of whether British society was evolving in a positive or negative direction, the methodological foundation of his theory of managed evolution known more generally as eugenics. Galton's scientific authority and a general fascination with statistics ensured that anthropometry became synonymous with anthropology in the 1880s. Cunningham was an anatomist whose contributions to anthropology had, up to that point, been limited to comparative anatomy. He was, however, an early adopter of anthropometry and his experiments in comparative anatomy set a methodological standard for physical anthropology. That makes Haddon the odd man out, unless we treat Haddon as a former zoologist in thrall to Huxley and his biological version of anthropology. If that was true, then evolution would provide a common ground of sorts, and that is the common sense of the evolutionist tradition in the historiography of anthropology. For instance, Kuklick described the alliance in one sentence:

> Cunningham had worked with Haddon in Ireland collecting anthropometric data for the British Association, and he collaborated with him in an effort to set up an anthropometric laboratory there that replicated Galton's London establishment. (Kuklick 1991: 152)

Stocking (1995: 104) repeated the same line from Haddon's perspective, adding that 'coming from zoology Haddon naturally found physical anthropology congenial'. Jones (1998) went into more detail and was more attuned to the social and cultural spaces in which the Dublin laboratory operated. Nevertheless, she mistakenly attributed the ethnographic programme of the laboratory to a general survey of the UK instituted by the BAAS in 1892 (ibid.: 198) and placed it under the control of Cunningham's anatomy department, which she described as 'a redoubt of evolutionary thought and Darwinism' (ibid.: 205–6). More recently, Tanya O'Sullivan (2015: 144) incorporated Jones's treatment of the social and cultural space into an assessment of Cunningham's anthropometric work in the overlapping space of science and politics and argued that he used his anthropological laboratory to bolster opposition to Home Rule.

In this chapter I offer an alternative scenario. The rise of anthropometry in the 1880s registered a shift towards hard science values in the 1890s, which transformed dissection rooms into anthropological laboratories and allowed Macalister to claim that physical anthropology was becoming a *real* science (BAAS 1893: 886). That might explain Cunningham's partnership with Galton except that Cunningham dismissed eugenics during an investigation of physical degeneration among potential army recruits launched in 1903. He subsequently cited Cowles Prichard and Tylor as his inspiration for his form of sociologically oriented, practical anthropology (*JAI* 38 [1908]: 10–35) in defiance of Topinard's doctrine. Furthermore, Haddon had just been sacked from his job on Balfour's survey of fisheries because of his Home

Rule sympathies and Geddes, who campaigned against Galton, warned Haddon against getting involved with old-school anatomists associated with the skull-measuring business. These differences are striking, yet Haddon, Cunningham and Galton managed to open a laboratory in Dublin on 25 June 1891, and I propose that their desire to create a foothold for practical anthropology in universities was strong enough to forge a common purpose. It did not last. Establishing a laboratory required funding and the partnership between Cunningham, Galton and Haddon was subsumed into an institutional consortium that constituted a microcosm of the political conflict that transformed anthropology in Ireland into a practical science of political utility.

ANTHROPOMETRY

Anthropometry developed in the field of medicine as a system of bodily measurement that anthropologists adopted and applied to comparative anatomy (the study of differences between humans and other primates) and variation (characteristic differences within the human species). The functional unit of anthropometry was an index that Haddon (Haddon and Quiggin 1910: 33, 46) explained as the ratio between two measurements of a physical characteristic expressed as a percentage. The cephalic index was of most interest to anthropologists. Devised by Anders Retzius in 1840, it expressed the ratio of the breadth of a cranium – the part of the skull that contains the brain – to its length and was used to classify skull form as round (brachycephalic), long (dolichocephalic) or intermediate (mesaticephalic). This system was incorporated into the study of the racial origins of modern European populations, the baselines being set by long-headed Africans, round-headed Mongols and not-so-long and not-so-round Aryans. This became the organizing logic of the skull-measuring business and Tylor's dismissal of craniology as an 'imperfect science' defined the terms of the power struggle between 'physicals' and 'culturals' until Galton's adoption of anthropometry set a new standard for *scientific* anthropology.

Haddon (Haddon and Quiggin 1910: 47) credited Galton as 'being the first in this country to realize the importance of applying mathematical methods to anthropological measurements and observations', although Cunningham adopted a strictly anthropometric approach to his 1886 investigation of structural (form) and physiological (function) differences between humans and anthropoid apes. This set a new standard for comparative anatomy, but Galton's work had far more impact because it tapped into a post-evolutionist zeitgeist within the general public and the three hundred or so individuals active in organized anthropology. Galton, operating in a public laboratory, investigated inherited traits and the formation of observable 'types' in the context of the ongoing evolution of the British population and used anthropological problems to illustrate the efficacy of statistical models. Victorians, according to Pyenson and Sheets Pyenson (1999: 192–94), were obsessed with measurement and statistics, and a combination of the two became synonymous with scientific authority: measurement demanded precision and standardization; correlation and probability contributed to the construction of theories; error analysis converted precision into accuracy and contributed to the formulation of laws. Darwin's theory of selective adaptation 'excited the imagination' (ibid.: 276) of mathematicians like Galton and he pioneered the development of 'sophisticated statistical machinery to transform and thoroughly mathematise the biological sciences' (ibid.: 278).

This had a very particular impact on the escalating culture war in organized anthropology. Galton replaced Tylor as president of Section H – Anthropology in 1885 and presented his lecture on 'Types and Their Inheritance'. He extolled the 'beautiful regularity in the stature of a population, whenever they are statistically marshalled' (BAAS 1886: 1208) and claimed that this proved the existence of a 'law that governs hereditary transmission' (ibid.: 1206). He connected this to anthropology in his opening statement:

The object of the anthropologist is plain. He seeks to learn what mankind really *are* in body and mind, how they came to what they are, and *whither their races are tending*; but the methods by which this definite inquiry has to be pursued are extremely diverse. Those of the geologist, the antiquarian, the jurist, the historian, the philologist, the traveller, the artist, and *the statistician*, are all employed; and *the science of man progresses* through the help of *specialists*. (BAAS 1885: 1206, emphasis added)

Galton was generally more proscriptive than the last sentence suggests. He argued elsewhere that unless 'the phenomena of any branch of knowledge have been submitted to measurement and number it cannot assume the status and dignity of a science' (Galton 1879: 149). Galton was referring in this instance to psychometric experiments, but Karl Pearson (1924: 334) claimed that the statement applied more to 'that branch of [anthropometry] which deals with craniometry'.

The full impact of Galton's project becomes visible in debates about the definition and function of anthropology in the mid-1890s. Macalister and Flower surveyed the field of anthropology at meetings of Section H – Anthropology in 1892 and 1894, the latter already highlighted as marking the tenth anniversary of the establishment of the section. Macalister (BAAS 1893: 886–87) took as his theme the scientific status of anthropology and proposed that the heterodox nature of organized anthropology created two problems. First, the lack of clear boundaries between ethnology, philology, archaeology, folklore and other 'diverse' areas of enquiry undermined the claim that anthropology was an independent branch of knowledge and so constituted 'a real science' (ibid.: 886). Second, this lack of definition limited the development of anthropology within universities. To solve both problems and bring anthropology 'into range with the true sciences' (ibid.: 889) required the provision of training in exact methods of ascertaining, accumulating and verifying facts as a proper foundation for theoretical work, a point reiterated by Rudler in 1899 (*JAI* 28 3,2 [1899]: 314). Macalister then turned his attention to the emerging role of anthropometric laboratories as research facilities for anthropologists. He noted that anthropologists traditionally concentrated on skulls and contrasted the statistical results being produced in these laboratories with the speculative nature of descriptive craniology, declaring that the descriptive phase was over; that anthropology, unlike ethnology, was becoming a real science. Macalister was not interested in craniology as such. The point of his speech was that the object of change was the development of a practical science that employed 'true scientific knowledge' to direct the 'progress of the race' (BAAS 1893: 895). Thus, Macalister shifted the focus of the debate from a traditional study of race characteristics to Galton's sociological project for measuring people to determine 'whither their races are tending', thereby defining anthropology as anthropometry and anthropometry as the primary methodology of eugenics.

Flower developed the theme of practical science in 1894 and reviewed the beginning of disciplinary anthropology in universities in Ireland, England and Scotland. Again, the basic argument was that 'physical or Anatomical Anthropology' (BAAS 1894: 768–69) had 'submitted to a rigorous and, therefore, strictly scientific method of treatment' and replaced generalities with results conveyed with almost mathematical precision. He called this branch of anthropology 'Anthropometry' and it signalled the professionalization of the field: taking anthropology out of the hands of unorganized amateurs, introducing standardized methods of measurement and comparison by trained individuals who produced data that could be relied upon. The real value of anthropometry, Flower argued, was not to be found in the traditional field of race comparison – research carried out for its own sake – but in the capacity of anthropometry to 'elucidate various social problems' (ibid.). He named Roberts and Galton as pioneers in this field. Charles Roberts was a surgeon and academic who classified anthropometry as a branch of human anatomy and his role in elucidating 'social problems' can be illustrated by a report he prepared for the Statistical Society in 1876 that set the physical threshold for the employment of children in factories (Tanner 1981: 169–77). Flower did not refer to this or any of Roberts's other work. Instead, he gave an account of Galton's work on the identification of criminals and reported in detail on efforts by the council of the BAAS to have the method adopted by the British government.

Cunningham's involvement in comparative anatomy did not rule him out of this new departure. On the contrary. Flower relayed Cunningham's account of the establishment of the Dublin Anthropometric Laboratory in 1891 and its mobilization for ethnographical surveys in the west of Ireland. The overall thrust of Flower's arguments placed this project at the core of the changes taking place in organized anthropology: the professionalization of anthropology within the discipline of anatomy and the reorientation of practical anthropology in a sociological direction. Galton's theory of eugenics influenced the basic methodology, but the theory itself, though popular, was contested by Cunningham among others. That makes Cunningham a person of some interest in terms of understanding what happened in the Aran Islands in 1892.

CUNNINGHAM

Cunningham entered the history of anthropology as a comparative anatomist who set up an anthropometric laboratory in association with Galton and Haddon, a project ostensibly defined by a mutual interest in physical anthropology and scientific racism. The problem with this scenario is that Cunningham wrote to Haddon in February 1903 looking for help with a series of lectures on physical anthropology and admitted that his 'knowledge in this department [was] very fragmentary *as you know*' (emphasis added). Cunningham, it seems, did not think of himself as a physical anthropologist and, as the letter suggests, he was aware that Haddon was of the same opinion. That fact alone is enough to warrant a review of Cunningham's involvement in the Anthropometric Laboratory of Ireland project, especially the almost automatic assumption that an involvement in comparative anatomy was predicated on an evolutionist understanding of race and a methodology based on classification and ordering.

The evidence for an alternative interpretation can be found in Cunningham's earliest investigations of human variation and racial discrimination. These alerted him to the possibility that factors other than biology could explain observable differences between Europeans and other races and, in time, he tapped into the philosophical concerns of an earlier generation of comparative anatomists like Petrus Camper and ethnologists like Prichard. This claim is based mainly on Cunningham's 1908 Presidential Address to the Anthropological Institute in which he described his search for a practical, faith-based and sociologically purposeful form of anthropology, although the underlying philosophy can be detected in his 1886 study of the lumbar curve in humans and apes, a case study in anthropometry as much as a masterclass in comparative anatomy as a component of anthropology.

Cunningham measured the lower vertebrae of spines removed from 132 humans and generated a lumbovertebral index that could be compared to corresponding values in apes. He was testing the theory that the lumbar curve was a physiological effect of bipedalism and a marker of the separation between humans and anthropoid apes. On the human side, his specimens included seventy-six Europeans, 'twenty-three Andamans, seventeen Australians, ten Negroes, three Tasmanians, and three Bushmen' (RIA 1886: 15). He dissected thirty-one apes, and these included gorillas, chimpanzees, orangutans, gibbons, baboons, macaques, a colobus and a grey langur. There were not enough non-European human specimens at TCD, so he drew on collections in the Museum of Science and Art in Dublin (Haddon), the Royal College of Surgeons in London (Garson) and anatomy departments in Aberdeen (Struthers) and Cambridge (Macalister). Macalister and Garson, the leading advocates of anthropometry in the Anthropological Institute and the BAAS, assisted and made many suggestions as to procedure. Cunningham presented preliminary results at a meeting of Section H – Anthropology in 1885 when he exhibited 'some plates of frozen sections of the chimpanzee, which brought out several important points of comparison between it and man' (BAAS 1886: 1226). He read 'The Lumbar Curve in Man and the Apes' into the record of the Royal Irish

Academy in February 1886 and the academy published the paper in July.

Cunningham (1886: 52–54) reported a 'very remarkable' difference between the lumbovertebral index in Europeans and other races, especially the Andamans. He argued that this did not constitute evidence of speciation, but could be explained by 'the difference in their habits'. The literature on race – he cited Duchenne (1867), Pruner Bey (1885) and Topinard (1885) – was inconclusive, so Cunningham supplemented his lab work with the measurement of live subjects. He measured four San people whom, according to an advertisement in the *Freeman's Journal*, William Hunt, trading as Guillermo Farini, exhibited as a troupe of 'African Earthmen' on six occasions in Dan Lowry's Theatre in Dublin. Cunningham compared these data with corresponding measurements from 'two young, adult and finely built Irishmen' (1886: 57). The full spectrum of data indicated that variations in spinal form were the result of age, sex and occupation, and he supported his argument with ethnographical accounts provided by travellers. He found that it would be untenable 'to argue that the European had assumed the erect attitude at a period antecedent to the low races'.

In summary, Cunningham argued that there was a clear separation between humans and apes, variation within the species was superficial and observable racial differences could be explained by sex, age and occupation. In effect, research that met the scientific standard of precise measurement and mathematical certainty showed that, biologically speaking, the Europeans, Andamans, Australians, Negroes, Tasmanians and Bushmen were the same.

Cunningham reflected on this at the Anthropological Institute in 1908. He devoted part of his Presidential Address on 'Anthropology in the Eighteenth Century' to an assessment of Camper's contribution to anthropology and Prichard's to ethnology (*JAI* 38 [1908]: 19) and shifted the basis of the discussion from scientific practice to a philosophy of science. Camper was a Dutch physician who contrasted 'the structure of the negro with that of the European' (ibid.: 16) in a lecture delivered in 1764, and this resonated with Cunningham's study of the lumbar curve in one important respect. Camper claimed that skin colour was a matter of climate and that, given enough time, it would 'be possible to turn a white race black or a black race white'. Han F. Vermeulen reviewed Camper's ideas in 2015 and suggested that this was not just about biology. Drawing on earlier scholarship, Vermeulen argued that Camper

> insisted that racial differences were superficial. They were always a matter of degree in shape or skin hue. He exhorted Europeans to "hold out a fraternal hand to the Negroes and to recognise them as the descendants of the first man to whom we all look to as a common father" (Poliakov 1974: 162; Meijer 1999: 73). (Vermeulen 2015b: 370–71)

The last sentence points to a fundamental aspect of Cunningham's search for meaning in anthropology: religion. Cunningham did not refer to this aspect of Camper's thought, but the theme is explicitly treated in his account of Prichard's contribution to ethnology.

Prichard, according to Cunningham, was overshadowed by Blumenbach, and his assessment is very telling in terms of his ranking of anthropology and ethnology:

> Blumenbach was essentially a physical anthropologist, and in this department I think we may say he was unexcelled. Prichard had a much broader grasp of the subject. *An accomplished anatomist*, he was, at the same time, one of the most learned philologists of his day and also a noted psychologist, and he brought his extensive knowledge in each of these branches to bear upon his *ethnological* work. (*JAI* 38 [1908]: 27, emphasis added)

It was, according to Cunningham, possible to be an anatomist and an ethnologist, the contemporaneous separation of these fields being philosophical rather than practical. Cunningham (ibid.) believed that the Society of Friends endowed Prichard and Tylor with an interest in 'the progress and well-being of mankind', which cultivated an interest in a 'wider scientific knowledge of mankind' and, especially, 'anthropological pursuits'. Prichard, according to Cunningham, was warned by his father not to offend constituted authority by challenging the 'literal interpretation ... of the Scriptural account of the origins of man' (ibid.: 28), and, in a heavily hedged account, Cunningham celebrated Prichard's capacity to reconcile his advanced thinking on human origin with his faith. Cunningham was well known as a 'son-of-the-manse' (see Carpenter 1909: 231) and his paper was a manifesto for a faith-based practice that contributed to 'the progress and well being' (*JAI* 38 [1908]: 27) of humankind.

This is the least acknowledged aspect of his contribution to anthropology. Cunningham's identification with Prichard and Tylor, however retrospective, was consistent with the humanitarian attitude of his 1886 study of racial difference. Furthermore, Kuklick (1991: 153) argues that Cunningham refused to take the arguments of eugenicists seriously at hearings of a government-appointed Inter-Departmental Committee on Physical Degeneration (1903–4) and countered evolutionist explanations for an observed decline in the physical condition of sections of the population with a sociological explanation.

Why then did he enter a partnership with Galton and establish a branch of his Anthropometric Laboratory in Dublin?

A LABORATORY IN DUBLIN

Cunningham's partnership with Galton seems to have been, on the balance of the evidence considered here, grounded in practical science rather than a commitment to eugenics. Cunningham and Haddon (*JAI* 21 [1892]: 35) acknowledged the encouragement and assistance of Galton in their proposal to establish a laboratory in Dublin and Galton, in a review of work done at his own laboratory, confirmed that he had been shown proofs of forms to be used in Dublin (ibid.: 32). Unfortunately, the discovery of laboratory records in 2014 shed no light on these preparations.

Whatever correspondence passed between Galton, Cunningham and Haddon is not held in TCD, but there was enough evidence in the laboratory's records to deal with the substantive issue of eugenics. Galton's *Anthropometric Laboratory: Notes and Memoirs* (1890) served as a manual in the laboratory when it opened in 1891, but schedules of measurement used in the field in 1892 show an immediate shift from physical and sensory efficiency to head form and stature in data fields. The same shift is reflected in the range of instruments used when the laboratory transferred to the Aran Islands in 1892. These included Beddoe's cards for recording hair and eye colour, Flower's craniometer and Cunningham's modification of Busk's craniometer. I will develop this argument in the next chapter and, for now, the point is made that the orthodox study of racial characteristics rather than eugenics determined the methodology employed in the field. That points to an early divergence between the ethnographic programme and the laboratory.

Galton's original idea can be traced back to the Anthropometric Laboratory he set up during the International Health Exhibition in London in 1884, where he collected data on fourteen physical and sensory characteristics from 9,337 people at a cost of three pennies each (*JAI* 14 [1885]: 205–21). The main objectives, Galton informed the Anthropological Institute, were (a) to publicly demonstrate the simplicity of anthropometric measurement and (b) to promote a system of periodic measurement that could be used to show 'the progress of the individual ... or of the nation as a whole' (ibid.). Galton continued to operate the laboratory on a disused backlot on the exhibition grounds until 1888, when building work started on the Imperial Institute. The *Pall Mall Gazette* published an interview with Galton on 16 November 1888 under the heading 'A Morning with the Anthropometric Detectives', which is the best description I have found to date of the laboratory. The reporter asked Galton if there were other laboratories and Galton referred to John Venn's laboratory in Cambridge, adding that 'he talked about it at Oxford and elsewhere' but his efforts were hampered by difficulty in creating the right conditions. It required, Galton said, that 'some capable man must really interest himself and there must be a convenient locality'. That person turned out to be Cunningham and the locality TCD.

Their paths crossed at a BAAS meeting in 1889, when Cunningham attended the opening session of Section H – Anthropology, and presented examples of the research he was doing in his dissection room. Galton attended the same session and presented two papers on the measurement of physical efficiency as a condition for public service and a requirement in education. Earlier in the year, Galton and John Venn attended the Anthropological Institute and reported on measurements taken at a branch of Galton's laboratory that Venn (*JAI* 18 [1889]: 140–53) set up in Cambridge. Galton then analysed the data in a paper entitled 'On Head Growth in Students at the University of Cambridge' (*JAI* 18 [1889]: 155–56). Galton wanted to replicate the project in other universities and he may have attempted to recruit Cunningham when they met at Section H. Either way, their interests converged on the hereditary condition of gigantism and the role spinal anatomy played in determining the overall stature of an individual. Galton studied the skeleton of 'O'Brien, the Irish giant' (BAAS 1886: 1208) and Cunningham had custody of the skeleton of Cornelius Magrath, another Irish giant. Cunningham informed Macalister in December 1890 that he had commenced a demonstrably rigorous anthropometric investigation of Magrath's skeleton to settle a dispute over the exact height of the giant while living (see RIA 29 [1887–92]: 553–61). Six months prior to that the Royal Irish Academy granted

> £100 to Committee, consisting of Prof. Cunningham, M.D., Rev. Dr. Haughton, F.R.S., and Prof. Haddon, M.A., to assist in the purchase of Anthropometrical Instruments. (RIA 1887–93: 64)

Cunningham presented his results to the Royal Irish Academy in January 1891 and, one month later, he joined Haddon and Galton in a carefully choreographed announcement of their plans for an anthropometric laboratory in Dublin.

The reporter for the *Pall Mall Gazette* noted the difficulties Galton encountered in building his network of laboratories, but Dublin was different because Cunningham had a backer. The Revd Dr Samuel Haughton came from a Quaker background, was an evolution sceptic (Praeger 1949: 99), an unrelenting critic of Darwin (Bowler 2009: 412) and a Home Rule sympathizer (Whyte 1999: 37). He worked with Cunningham to professionalize medical education at TCD and as a Senior Fellow of TCD and President of the Royal Irish Academy (1886–90) he was in a position to broker a deal on funding and accommodation. The *Irish Times* included Haughton's account of that deal in an article about the opening of 'The Anthropometry Laboratory, Trinity College':

> The laboratory had received from Trinity College free quarters in a handsome room, and what was of much more value than any endowment, the cordial co-operation of their professor of anatomy, (Applause). The Royal Irish Academy, having heard of what Trinity College proposed to do, gave them a grant of £600 to provide the delicate and costly instruments necessary for carrying out their observations, and it was an open secret that if they conducted themselves as he (Dr. Haughton) hoped, they should receive next year another £100 or perhaps more – (applause) – to carry a travelling anthropometric laboratory around Ireland. (*Irish Times* 26 June 1891: 4–5)

The grant, according to the academy's minutes of 23 June 1890, was in fact £100, which would be worth just under €11,750 at current rates (March 2023). Some of the 'costly instruments' were designed by Galton and manufactured by his company Cambridge Scientific Instrument Company. Others were drawn from the standard anthropometric toolkit used by anthropologists.

Haughton's comment on funding was aimed at the Academy and, possibly, John Kells Ingram, an influential Senior Fellow of TCD who served on the Academy's governing body for forty-three years and took over as president in 1892 (Barret 1999: 13), having served as vice president for twelve years. That suggests that he was a party to Haughton's deal, and could influence future funding. Haughton would have known that Ingram clashed with Galton in 1876 in a row that threatened entire spectrum of social sciences (see Renwick 2012: 38–42), especially as this controversy came to a head at a meeting of the BAAS at TCD in 1878. It was resolved when Ingram proposed a new subject called sociology, although he remained a staunch opponent of Galton and recruited Geddes in his effort to discredit eugenics. Haddon's close association with Geddes should have made Ingram sympathetic to the ethnographic programme. Indeed, Ingram visited Geddes in Edinburgh in 1892, while Haddon was preparing for his study of the Aran Islands. Ingram, however, was a unionist (Collinson Black 2008) and Haddon had been outed by Green in 1890 as a Home Rule sympathizer. Cunningham, on the other hand, was a unionist and the laboratory was his project. He set the opening for 25 June and arranged for Queen Victoria's favourite, Prince Edward of Saxe-Weimar (Vibart and Falkner 2004), and Garnet Wolseley, an extreme loyalist who replaced the prince as head of the armed forces in Ireland (Beckett 2004), to attend as patrons.

The *Irish Times* article on the opening (26 June 1891: 4–5) recorded that 'Many medical men of high standing who hold high rank as scientists' gathered in the Anatomy Department and Haughton delivered an 'address explanatory of the nature of the laboratory and the uses which it would confer upon the public services of the country'. Most of the practical references in his speech corresponded with highlighted sections of a copy of Galton's manual that remains in TCD, and Haughton concluded the proceedings by using Haddon as his subject in a demonstration of 'the manner of measuring the skull, testing the strength of grasp, breathing capacity, &C.' In September 1892, Haddon and Browne, acting as a proxy for Cunningham, mobilized the laboratory and launched a programme of ethnographic surveys in the Aran Islands. They set up their laboratory outside a cottage and Haddon took a selfie of them at work (Figure 6.1).

CONCLUSION

To summarize, Galton reconfigured anthropometry to determine patterns of stature and test theories of heredity, generating a hard science dogma that Macalister and Flower espoused to claim that anatomical anthropology alone was scientific. Cunningham demonstrated the practical merit of anthropometry in his dissection room and adopted Galton's anthropometric laboratory as a model of practical anthropology. Haughton brokered a deal with the Royal Irish Academy, which provided funding to equip the laboratory. The laboratory opened in June 1891 as the cornerstone of a small, part-time Anthropology Department in the university. In September 1892, Haddon and Browne mobilized the laboratory and commenced a programme of ethnographic surveys in Home Rule heartlands in the west of Ireland.

I have sequenced these events as a progression from comparative anatomy to anthropometry and practical anthropology, a methodological progression propelled by a determination to establish anthropology as a 'real' science and demonstrate its efficacy in the field. Macalister saw anthropometry as an opportunity to provide the scientific community with the practical tools needed to understand and direct the influences that affect the progress of the race, thereby aligning anthropology in Cambridge with Galton's eugenics movement. Cunningham was equally alert to the social utility of physical anthropology, and the ethnographic programme Haddon devised provided an opportunity to test it under very different political circumstances.

Haddon's removal from the Survey of Fishing Grounds, West Coast illustrates just how seriously Balfour and his agents in the scientific community viewed the threat posed by Home Rule in the context of the 1892 general election. The decision to ask Queen Victoria's favourite prince and a commander of British forces in Ireland to act as patrons of the laboratory showed that TCD was determined to demonstrate 'a firm commitment to the Union' (Whyte 1999: 10) and deploy the laboratory as a public service in opposition to Home Rule. Haughton was sympathetic to Home Rule but must have put that to one side out of loyalty to

Cunningham. His deal with the Academy ensured that Galton got his laboratory in Dublin, but Cunningham quickly reconfigured the function of the laboratory as a means to study the 'ethnical islands' that were fuelling anti-government sentiment among sections of the English electorate. Accordingly, it was a mix of hard science dogmas, colonial imperatives and party politics rather than conventional evolutionism or eugenics that influenced the operation of the laboratory and that put Haddon and Cunningham on a collision course when fieldwork commenced in 1892.

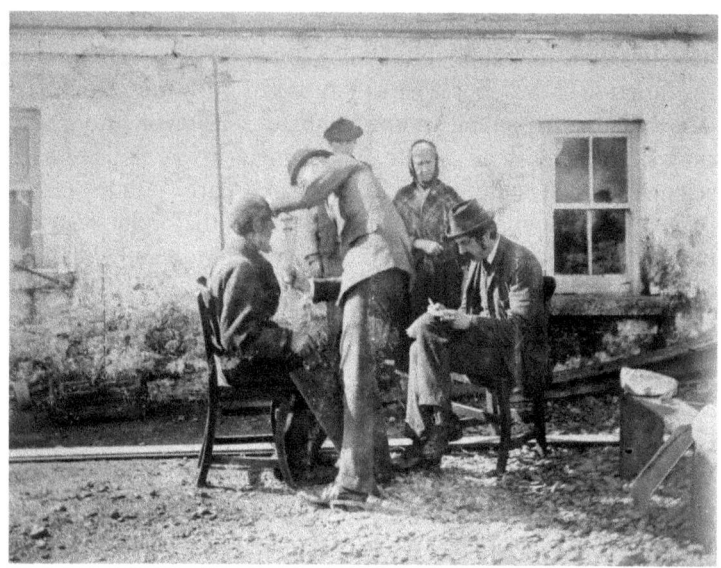

Figure 6.1. A. C. Haddon and C. R. Browne, *Anthropometry in Aran*, 1892. Digital scan and print of silver gelatine print (Timothy Keefe, Sharon Sutton, Ciarán Walsh, Ciarán Rooney, 2011). Courtesy of the Board of Trinity College, University of Dublin.

Aranmore

23 - Photo.

THE DUBLIN ANTHROPOMETRIC LABORATORY.

The Laboratory is in the Museum of Comparative Anatomy, Trinity College, Dublin. The Laboratory is open to the Public from 2 to 4 p.m., on Tuesdays, Thursdays, and Saturdays.

Date of Measurement: Day	Month	Year	Initials	Sex	Birthday: Day	Month	Year	Eye Colour	Hair Colour	Page of Register
24	Sept	1892	Tom Connelly		Kilronan		75	grey	grizzled brown	

Cranial length	Cranial breadth	Cranial height	Auriculo-alveolar length	Auriculo-nasal length	Face length	Face breadth	Height standing, less heels of boots	Height sitting above seat of chair	Tip of mid-finger to styloid	Tip of mid-finger from centre of patella	Styloid to Epicondyle	Epicondyle to Acromion	Acromion from ground, less heels of boots	Span of arms
202	152	126	103	95	133	135	1660		201		255			1742

Weight in ordinary clothing (in lbs.)	Strength of grasp (in lbs.): Right hand	Left hand	Greatest speed of blow	Breathing capacity (in Cubic inches)	Colour sense	Keenness of Eyesight: Right eye	Left eye	Is the Sense of Hearing normal?	Highest audible note by whistle (Vibrations per second)	Reaction time, in hundredths of a second: To sight	To sound
	60	35	34	90	105	573			,000		

Left Thumb | Right Thumb

ANTHROPOLOGICAL LABORATORY TRINITY COLLEGE, DUBLIN

One page of the Register is assigned to each person, in which his measurements at successive periods are entered in successive lines. A copy of these made at any specified date may be obtained on application by the person measured, or by his or her representative, on receipt of a stamped envelope.

N.B.—In the case of Students, it is very desirable that their measurements should be recorded every six months, so that they may thereby have an accurate means of estimating their physical as well as their mental development.

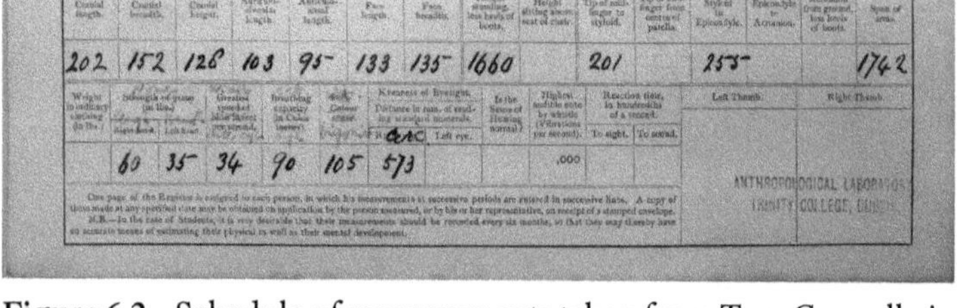

Figure 6.2. Schedule of measurements taken from Tom Connelly in 1892. Permission of the School of Medicine, Board of Trinity College, University of Dublin.

CHAPTER 6

FIELDWORK

● ● ●

It will, however, be noticed that we have in the present study far exceeded the lines of research which the Committee at first proposed for itself. We have done so in the belief that the ethnical characteristics of a people are to be found in their arts, habits, language, and beliefs as well as in their physical characters.

—Haddon and Browne, 'The Ethnography of the Aran Islands, County Galway'

Haddon travelled to the Aran Islands for the third time in September 1892. On this occasion he was accompanied by Browne and the trip represents the activation of a plan to assist anthropologists unravel the origins of the 'so-called "Irish Race"' that Haddon and Cunningham presented to the Royal Irish Academy and the Anthropological Institute in February 1891:

it is our intention when once we have fairly started to take excursions during the Long Vacation into the country, and with our apparatus, [to] pitch our tent in different districts until at last we or our successors shall have traversed the entire extent of Ireland. (*JAI* 21 [1892]: 36)

Cunningham briefed Flower in advance of his Presidential Address to Section H in 1894 and described Browne as his 'able assistant' (BAAS 1895: 767) who had taken charge of the Anthropological Laboratory, Trinity College Dublin and its programme of ethnographic surveys. Browne entered TCD in 1885 and studied medicine under Cunningham. He graduated with degrees in Medicine, Surgery and Obstetrics in 1890 and as Doctor of Medicine in 1893. He began measuring people when the Dublin Anthropometric Laboratory opened for business on 27 June 1891. He was elected a Member of the Royal Irish Academy (MRIA) on 13 June 1892 and registered his main disciplines as Medicine and Anthropology. As such, Browne was the first graduate of a new system of academic anthropology that Cunningham developed around the laboratory at TCD, which Macalister replicated in Cambridge in 1893 and Flower presented to the 1894 meeting of Section H as the beginning of disciplinary anthropology. Five years later, Macalister formalized the system when he created the first University Lectureship in Anthropology in his Anatomy Department.

Browne, suitably trained as an anatomist and certified as an anthropologist by way of a MRIA, was in charge when Haddon and he pitched their tent in the Aran Islands and set up their laboratory – two chairs and a satchel full of anthropometric instruments – outside the courthouse in Kilronan on 21 September 1892. They began collecting data on the physical characteristics of islanders. Browne took seventeen head, face and body measurements (RIA 3,2 [1891–93]: 774–75) and Haddon entered the data into a modified version of the form Galton designed (Figure 6.2). Three days later, they took a photograph of the laboratory in action (Figure 6.1), a carefully arranged illustration of an ethnologist assisting an anthropologist.

Browne filed the photograph with the caption 'Anthropometry in Aran' in an album he compiled in or around 1897, one of two albums that hold what survives of the photographic archive of the Irish Ethnographical Survey (figure 6.3), the precursor of the Ethnographical Survey of the United Kingdom; Haddon, operating from his base in the Folk-Lore Society, proposed the UK survey to the Anthropological Institute and Society of Antiquarians in April 1892, and the BAAS agreed to manage it when it met in September. Gwendolen Browne donated her father's albums to his alma mater in 1995 but the archive remained out of

Figure 6.3. C. R. Browne, *The People*, c.1897. Digital scan and print of silver gelatine photographic prints pasted into an album (Timothy Keefe, Sharon Sutton, Ciarán Walsh, Ciarán Rooney, 2011). Courtesy of the Board of Trinity College, University of Dublin.

sight in the Manuscripts Library at TCD until 2012, when Daithí de Mórdha and I curated an exhibition of fifty photographs and showed them in the communities Haddon and Browne surveyed between 1892 and 1900 (de Mórdha and Walsh 2012). This project triggered a wider review of the Irish Ethnographical Survey in the context of the development of anthropology in Ireland, which is more generally associated with the arrival of the Harvard Anthropological Survey of the Irish Free State in the 1930s.

Haddon's involvement in the first Irish survey has ensured that the Aran Islands have remained the most visible of the eight communities surveyed, and that visibility was guaranteed by an eye-catching introductory note stating that the ethnographers had far exceeded the anthropometric scope set out in 1891, placed equal emphasis on race and ethnicity and, in effect, written a report that promised a demonstration of anthropology in its widest aspect. In the absence of a manuscript or otherwise definitive paper record, uncertainty over the authorship of this note has complicated assessments of whether fieldwork in the islands made Haddon an evolutionist in a classic Darwinian sense (Kuklick 1991; Adams 1993; Stocking 1995; Jones 1998; Kuper 2001; de Mórdha and Walsh 2012; Walsh 2013; Ó Giolláin 2017) or an ethnologist who, as Greta Jones put it in 2008, extended anthropological inquiry into the sociocultural sphere (Forrest 1986; Jones 2008; Ashley 2001; Walsh 2022). There is also a body of work that engages with Haddon's fieldwork in the islands in the context of the rise of cultural nationalism and a literary engagement with the idea of the western isles as pre-conquest cultural reserves (Jones 1998; Kiberd 2000; Castle 2001; Carville 2007; Beiner 2012; Brannigan 2014; Ó Giolláin 2017; Walsh 2021c). The overlap in citations from Jones, Ó Giolláin and myself illustrates the ambiguous and, indeed, contradictory nature of some of the evidence, as illustrated here by the photograph of Haddon and Browne measuring Tom Connelly's skull and the seemingly contradictory statement that 'the ethnical characteristics of a people are to be found in their arts, habits, language, and beliefs'. However, all three strands of scholarship converge on the same question: why was Haddon measuring skulls in the Aran Islands?

We know from Geddes and Quiggin that Haddon was fascinated with skulls, and I have argued that his involvement in the consortium that set up the laboratory in Dublin was motivated by the need to gain a foothold in academic anthropology as it took shape in 1891. Beddoe identified the lack of craniological data from Ireland as a gap and Haddon seized upon Galton and Cunningham's plan for an anthropometric laboratory as an opportunity to fill it, although the decision to exceed the original lines of research suggests that he had not given up on his plan to reconstruct or socialize anthropology. Haddon was also involved in a parallel process in the UK and his need for alternative employment after Green terminated his involvement in fisheries research hums along in the background. In this context, the ethnographical surveys constituted a strategy to build a practical case for the bureau of ethnology Haddon proposed in 1891 with due deference to Beddoe and the 'physicals'. Likewise,

Cunningham's desire for a social science of political utility and the rapid erasure of Galton's influence raises the possibility that Cunningham was responsible for the sociocultural reorientation of the research. Political differences over Home Rule override any suggestion of a common purpose, however. Cunningham was focussed on establishing a social science discipline directed at the elucidation of various social problems and the ever-present threat to the political integrity of the United Kingdom of Great Britain and Ireland focussed his research on the immediate problem of famine in the Aran Islands, the very issue that cost Haddon his job as a government-sponsored marine biologist. Each of these back stories complicates the question posed above, and attempting to answer it involved reconstructing a chronology from institutional records that served as an armature for scraps of intelligence gleaned from the Haddon Papers, field reports, institutional records and other sources, Browne's albums especially.

In this chapter, I let the photograph of the laboratory in action do its work in terms of describing what happened in the field and focus instead on what happened after Haddon and Browne returned to Dublin. Haddon executed another, extraordinary pivot with the publication of his 'Studies in Irish Craniology – The Aran Islands' (RIA 3,2 [1891–93]: 749–67), thereby announcing that he had formally entered the skull-measuring business. The search for an explanation focussed on an exchange he had with Huxley in 1892 as he attempted to make the case for a bureau of ethnology and Huxley advised him to concentrate on the collection of anthropological information within the limits of organized anthropology in Britain. Haddon pitched the model he developed in Ireland and launched a project that set about defining fieldwork under the banner of an ethnographic survey of the UK. That project got caught up in the culture war between 'physicals' and 'culturals' and ultimately failed. That failure reveals a lot about Haddon's decision to publish his 'Studies in Irish Craniology', and the story switches back to Dublin, where the laboratory became the site of a three-way split between eugenics, craniology and sociology, and, as complicated as it was, the situation was exacerbated by a deepening sense of political crisis caused by the passage of the second Home Rule bill through the Imperial Parliament in London. In summary, everything to do with the Aran Islands was political, even the act of measuring Tom Connelly's skull.

THE SKULL-MEASURING BUSINESS

This section pulls back from the field and looks at what happened after Haddon and Browne returned to Dublin and wrote up their research. The focus here is on Haddon's decision to get involved in craniology and use the Aran Islands as an example of his capacity to fill the information gap Beddoe identified in 1890. Given the consensus between Geddes, Haddon and Ellis that anthropology needed to move beyond the skull-measuring business, this seems like a U-turn that would make nonsense of the declaration that ethnical characteristics matter as much as racial characteristics were it not for the fact that everything Haddon did in this period was influenced by his efforts to position himself as an ethnologist operating in a system dominated by anthropologists. His decision to publish 'Studies in Irish Craniology – The Aran Islands' is analysed accordingly.

Haddon and Browne measured the last islander on 28 September and reported to the Royal Irish Academy on 12 December 1892. Ingram presided over the meeting and the *Irish Times* reported that there was a good attendance. The reporter wrote that Haddon read 'The Ethnography of the Aran Islands, County Galway' and summarized the reading as follows:

> He enumerated numerous traits in the character of the people and gave an interesting account of several of their customs. They were a distinctly non-musical people, as evidenced by the fact that there was not a fiddler or a piper found amongst them. They were a courteous and rather good-looking people; their stature, however, was below that of the inhabitants of the mainland. When a father made over his property of holding to his married son the father was badly treated and badly fed by the young people. In

> this respect of the population of these islands presented a remarkable contrast to those of the mainland. During the summertime they frequently suffered from a water famine, and in that period their cattle are sent to Connemara. The opening of the islands to tourists had tended to benefit them greatly. (*Irish Times*, 13 December 1892: 7)

The reporter added that Mr Browne also spoke on the subject but gave no details. Haddon read a second paper on the craniology of the islands and, again, the reporter did not give any details. The report finished with a note that both papers were referred to the council of the Academy for publication.

Haddon reacted to the reference to mistreatment. He wrote a letter to the editor stating that 'the meaning of my remarks has been unintentionally altered' and continued:

> It is true it is stated in the paper that cases of this were known, but on citing the exceptions we desired to emphasise thereby the high morality of these interesting and friendly people, to which we bear strong and willing testimony in our paper. ('Letters to the Editor', *Irish Times*, 14 December 1892: 6)

Haddon's 'remarks' read as follows:

> Occasionally old people are badly treated; when an old man had made over his farm to his married son, the young people have been known to half starve him, and give him the small potatoes reserved for the pigs. (RIA 3,2 [1891–93]: 800)

The exchange illustrated Haddon's sympathy for the islanders, and this was fundamental to his identity as an ethnologist who, from the outset, showed no interest in physical anthropology and argued against restricting the study of anthropology to the natural history of humans on the basis that ethnographic knowledge bridged the extremes of humankind thereby promoted solidarity between complex and simple societies in the context of colonialism. The decision to extend the remit of 'The Ethnography of the Aran Islands' to include the islanders' 'arts, habits, language, and beliefs' makes sense in this context, and that makes his decision to compile and present his 'Studies in Irish Craniology – The Aran Islands' in the same session all the more remarkable.

Haddon introduced the published version of this study as follows:

> The following is the first of a series of communications which I propose to make to the Academy on Irish Craniology. It is a remarkable fact that there is scarcely an obscure people on the face of the globe about whom we have less anthropographical information than we have of the Irish. (RIA 3,2 [1891–93]: 759)

'Anthropographical' is a compound of anthropology and geography, and Haddon sourced some of his anthropological information in texts like Davis and Thurnam's *Crania Britannica* (1856–65), research notes Beddoe made on his visit to the Aran Islands while working on his study *The Races of Britain* (1885), and especially the work John Grattan did in the 1840s in Belfast. Haddon described Grattan as 'a pioneer investigator of the craniology of Ireland ... whose labours appear to have been almost entirely overlooked' (RIA 3,2 [1891–93]: 759–60). This grounded the study in the old and imperfect science Tylor dismissed in 1884, although Haddon gets around that problem by stating his preference for an up-to-date combination of French and German methods, which he applied using instruments developed by Cunningham and Flower (ibid.: 762). He measured skulls in various collections, and these included a skull from Aranmore, one of twenty-four skulls he stole from burial grounds during the fishing survey in 1890 and presented to the Anthropological Museum in Trinity College, Dublin at the time of the reading. Haddon emphasized the anthropological value of the Aran Islands by quoting Barnard Davis's description of two skulls Beddoe collected there:

> These graveyards of the Aran Isles are regarded by Sir W. E. Wilde, the distinguished Irish antiquary, as 'very early', and the crania derived from them 'as very ancient skulls'. (RIA 3,2 [1891–93]: 761)

Finally, Haddon included data from three fragmentary crania measured in 'Tempul Brecain, Onaght ('Seven Churches')' (ibid.) in the Aran Islands during the 1892 survey.

The difference between the ethnography and study in craniology is lessened somewhat by the emphasis on the measurement of physical characteristics in the published version of the ethnography, which, at twenty-one pages, is the largest of eleven sections in a sixty-five-page document including three pages of photographic plates. The ethnography opened with an account of the physical geography of the islands and the section on 'Physical Characteristics' was included under Anthropography. One of the more notable aspects of this section is the social aspect of the geographical half of that compound, which emerges when the focus switches to 'Vital Statistics (General and Economic)' on page 793. Over the next fourteen pages various social topics are considered under 'Acreage and Rental', 'Language and Literacy' and 'Health' before moving into the non-material domain with 'Psychology' and 'Folk Names'. Sociology replaces Anthropography on page 808 and the next eight pages cover 'Occupations', 'Family-Life Customs', 'Clothing', 'Dwellings' and 'Transport'. This is followed by shorter sections on 'Folk-Lore', 'Archaeology', 'History' and 'Ethnology', the last closing the report with the following finding:

> To what race or races the Aranites belong, we do not pretend to say, but it is evident that they cannot be Firbolgs, if the latter are correctly described as 'small, dark-haired, and swarthy.' (RIA 3,2 [1891–93]: 826)

'Firbolgs' were a pre-Celtic colony who were, by legend, a small, dark-haired, swarthy and longer-headed people of southern European origin (see Frazer 1891), credited with building a complex of stone forts in the islands. The main question for anthropologists like Beddoe was whether the 'existing Aranites' (RIA 3,2 [1891–93]: 825–26) were descendants of this colony. Running to a single page in length, the analysis of racial origins is a minor component of the report and the segregation of craniological data into a separate report is one of many splits, the most notable being the shift from Anthropography to Sociology on page 808.

In an effort to distinguish contributions from Haddon, Browne and Cunningham, I undertook an extensive search for a manuscript or associated papers in Dublin and Cambridge, and the only manuscript material located to date is held in a file in the Haddon Papers listed as 'Ethnographic Survey – Ireland'. The document consists of nineteen pages of mainly anthropometric information and political economy data that correspond to pages 782–98 of the published version. It also includes data on folk (family) names that corresponds to pages 805–7, all within the section on anthropography. The file also contains galley proofs of Plates xxii and xxiii. Accordingly, I have assigned authorship of the section on anthropography to Haddon and, moreover, the structure of the 'social' half of that section closely resembles the sociological approach Haddon outlined in 'The Study of Anthropology' in 1895:

> Sociology is the study of human communities, both simple and complex and an attempt is now being made to trace the rise of simple communities and their gradual and *diverse* evolution to the complex civilisations of ancient and modern times. (Haddon 1895a: 25, emphasis added)

'Diverse' is emphasized here because it was a signpost to a later argument that cultures cannot be classified according to 'a rigorously defined order of evolution', which I have interpreted as an unequivocal rejection of the comparative method employed by social evolutionists. Given Haddon's fascination with the topography of the Aran Islands, it is hardly surprising that he highlighted geography as a component of sociology:

The physical conditions of a country ... affect the human inhabitants of that country; in other words, the mode of life of a primitive people is conditioned by its environment. The method of living affects family life, and so we find that certain types of family organisation are related to definite habits of life. As civilisation advances, the state acquires powers and regulates families as well as individuals, but the characteristics of different forms of government are themselves due to the type of family organisation which obtain among those various people. According to this method of investigation, we start with physical geography and find ourselves drawn into statecraft and political economy. (Haddon 1895a: 25)

As such, anthropography represents a synthesis of geography, physical anthropology and political economy. Given the conversations Haddon had with Geddes and Ellis between 1889 and 1891, this corresponds with the Le Playist model Geddes formulated as the synthetic study of 'place-work-folk' (Renwick 2012: 92–93), and the section on anthropography illustrates how anthropology 'in its widest aspect' worked in practice.

'Studies in Irish Craniology', on the other hand, illustrates how Haddon tried to breathe new life into a methodology that emerged in the 1840s and had no place in 'The Study of Anthropology'. Haddon acknowledged as much when he referred readers of 'Studies in Irish Craniology' to 'The Ethnography of the Aran Islands' for 'a fairly complete account ... from an ethnographical point of view' (RIA 3,2 [1891–93]: 760). This echoed the statement that the ethnical characteristics of a people mattered as much as their physical characters, and the question arises of why he went to such lengths to promote the skull-measuring business.

In effect, Haddon's decision to launch his craniological studies after reading the ethnography of the Aran Islands reversed the trajectory of the plan to reconstruct anthropology agreed with Geddes and Ellis two years earlier. So why did he attempt to revive and perfect the imperfect science of craniology? The obvious temptation, historiographically speaking, was to go back to the letter Geddes wrote in December 1889 and argue from there that Haddon's desire to measure skulls had overwhelmed his commitment to reconstruction and that he had become a craniologist. An alternative explanation is that Haddon presented two essentially contradictory ethnographic philosophies in the hope of reconciling the methodological differences between old-fashioned 'physicals' and a new generation of post-evolutionist 'sociologicals'. In this scenario, Haddon's strategy was little different to the reconstructionist agenda he agreed with Ellis in most respects but one. Both constituted attempts to define the scope of anthropological investigations as the site of operation moved from the dissection room to the field, and the main difference is that Haddon's craniological studies were travelling in the opposite direction to various attempts to reconfigure anthropology as a modern, sociologically oriented and practical science. The effect is an epistemic tension that borders on outright contradiction, and resolving this involved retracing every step of Haddon's short journey to the Royal Irish Academy in December 1892 and his reading of two very different versions of anthropology.

DEFINING FIELDWORK

In January 1891, Frazer inquired how Haddon's 'many schemes progress?' and listed them as follows:

> I hope you have not given up the idea of writing an article for one of the Monthlies on the application of the Imperial Institute to anthropology? The idea is too good to be lost. Then about Irish anthropology, have you been digging up any more bodies at the risk of your life? . . . I hope your book on anthropology is getting on. (Frazer to Haddon, 29 January 1891)

Haddon's article for 'the Monthlies' referred to his critique of the Imperial Institute and his proposal for a bureau of ethnology.

The 'book on anthropology' is clearly a reference to his collaboration with Ellis. Sandwiched in between was the risky business of 'digging up' bodies in Ireland, almost certainly a reference to the grave-robbing incident in Inishbofin in 1890, which set a pattern of grave-robbing for craniological purposes. Holt informed Haddon in 1891 that he 'found a great skull place in Sligo' but he 'could not bring any away as we had no cloaks or anything and the place is in the middle of a town' (see Walsh 2021a). Other notes in Haddon's handwriting identified abbeys in Burrishoole, Cong and Askeaton as sources of skulls. In this context his proposal in February 1891 to assist anthropologists in their 'endeavours to unravel the tangled skein of the so-called "Irish Race"' was consistent with the task Beddoe identified in 1890 and indicates that Haddon was already involved in craniology.

Correspondence between Haddon and John George Garson corroborates this. In March 1891, Garson alerted Haddon to the fact that Cunningham had visited Galton and was looking for advice on craniometers. Garson informed Haddon that

> since Cunningham was over here an arrangement has been come to whereby I am to be associated with Mr Francis Galton at his Laboratory at South Kensington. I hope that we may be reasonably of use to each other. (Garson to Haddon, 30 March 1891)

It is not clear if they had the opportunity to be 'of use to each other' in 1891, but 'Studies in Irish Craniology – The Aran Islands' endorsed criticism Garson made of the Frankfort Craniometric Agreement (RIA 3,2 [1891–93]: 762; *JAI* 14 [1885]: 64–83), an attempt to standardize craniometric methods. Haddon had been reading the literature under supervision from Garson but was more preoccupied with his article for 'the Monthlies' and his book on anthropology. Haddon and Ellis reached an impasse in May 1891 and agreed instead on a book on 'the earliest origins of art among savages'. Haddon also wrote to Foster in May seeking funding to cover the cost of illustrating a monograph he had been planning since the exhibition in the British Museum and stated:

> I brought home a number of skulls & others exist in various museums so these are material for a craniological study of the people which I would include in the proposed monograph. (Haddon to Foster, 7 May 1891)

This correspondence will be considered in more detail in Part III and I introduce it here because Haddon's offer of 'a craniological study' is so phrased that it confirms that craniology was secondary to art, dance, folklore and photography, while acknowledging that a study of the craniology of the Torres Islanders would be expected in a monograph of this type, just as Boas included a section on skull form in the 1889 introduction to the Indians of British Columbia he wrote for Tylor. Nevertheless, Haddon clearly thought of it as a requirement rather than an interest, and it would take one last intervention from Huxley before Haddon and Garson got the opportunity to 'be reasonably of use to each other'.

Haddon spent most of 1891 trying to get his article for 'the Monthlies' published. The editor of the *Fortnightly Review* rejected it in February, the *New Review* in October and *The Nineteenth Century* in November. Haddon sent the manuscript to Galton and Macalister. Galton replied on 2 December and recommended that Haddon rethink it thoroughly from a business point of view. Macalister replied on 18 December and suggested that Haddon seek help from Flower and Huxley. Huxley replied on 1 January 1892 and warned Haddon that his scheme to establish an Imperial Bureau of Ethnology 'would not have the slightest chance of being taken in hand by the Government'. Huxley advised him to:

> bring the subject of collecting anthropological information systematically before [the] Anthropological section of the meeting of the British Association in a general form, and to get a strong committee appointed to consider in what way existing Agencies e.g., British Museum[,] Oxford, Anthropological Society can be combined, utilised and supplemented. (Huxley to Haddon, 1 January 1892)

Haddon took Huxley's advice and pitched an ethnographical survey of the UK to the Folk-Lore Society and the Anthropological Institute. Cuthbert E. Peek, Secretary of the Institute, and F. A. Milne, Secretary of the Society, both replied in March, stating that their organizations would consider cooperating. Milne, in a letter dated 13 March, clarified that the aim was to work with the the Institute and the Society of Antiquaries in collecting 'all the facts concerning Prehistoric Remains, Physical Types of the people, and Folk Lore' in selected districts. He wrote to Haddon on 14 April informing him that he had been elected as delegate to the BAAS to secure a place for 'Folk Lore' on the agenda of the Anthropological Section. Haddon attended a meeting of the council of the Institute in May 1892. Tylor chaired the meeting and Galton, Brabrook, Garson, Read and Rudler, among others, participated. The minute book records that:

> a letter was rec.d from the Folk Lore Society inviting co-operation of the Council with a view to obtaining a complete ethnographic survey of each county or district in the United Kingdom. Mr. Brabrook, Mr Galton & Dr. Garson were appointed Delegates to confer with representatives of the Society Antiquaries & the Folk-Lore Society on the subject. (A10 RAI Council minutes, 10 May 1892, f. 239)

Tylor signed off on the decision and Brabrook read 'On the Organisation of Local Anthropological Research' at the BAAS meeting in August 1892. He reported

> that an analysis of two hundred or more papers published by [corresponding] societies in connection with the subjects of Section H recorded during the last seven years shows that as many as twenty nine local societies have been engaged in valuable original anthropological work. (BAAS 1893: 896)

'Anthropological work' included studies of 'ancient remains, the local customs, and the physical characters of the people' (ibid.). Brabrook identified two immediate tasks. The first was to agree a uniform plan for fieldwork and the second was to publish 'a simple code of instructions' (ibid.) for researchers.

The council of the BAAS established a committee 'To Organise an Ethnographical Survey of the United Kingdom', with Galton in the chair, Brabrook acting as secretary, and Garson (anthropology), Haddon (folklore) and Anderson (archaeology) serving as ordinary members (BAAS 1893: lxxxix). Gomme was among three representatives from the Folk-Lore Society subsequently invited to join, along with representatives of the Antiquaries, Statistical and Dialect societies, the last introducing a linguistic component that aligned the project more closely with the model used by Tylor and Boas (BAAS 1890: 797–900). Brabrook wrote to Haddon in January 1893 informing him that the BAAS had received

> through the Folklore society an instruction that Professor Cunningham, Mr Charles R. Browne, and yourself have been appointed delegates of [the] Royal Irish Academy to the Ethnographic Survey Committee and, at the last meeting of the academy, were elected Members of it accordingly. (Brabrook to Haddon, 18 January 1893)

The committee also resolved that they act as a subcommittee for Ireland, and Brabrook requested that Haddon act as secretary. Incidentally, this letter coincided with Haddon's first slideshow at the Belfast Naturalists' Field Club, in which he explained that an ethnographic survey of Ulster would come under the remit of the Irish committee in Dublin and report through it to the BAAS in London.

The BAAS committee set about drawing up a 'simple code of instructions' (BAAS 1893: 896) and Garson assumed responsibility for the anthropometric component in association with Haddon. Brabrook replaced Galton in the chair in 1894 and reported that:

> the form of schedule *has occupied much time*, especially the portion of the form relating to physical observations, which

differs to some extent from that given in the first report.
The Committee have to thank Dr. Garson and Professor
Haddon for the attention they have given to this matter....
*The form of the schedule of physical types of the inhabitants as
now settled for England* is given at the end of this report. The
other schedules have not been altered from the forms given
in the first report. (BAAS 1894: 423, emphasis added)

The 'form relating to physical observations' had proven so problematic it set the whole project back by two years. Correspondence between Haddon, Garson and Browne reveals why. Garson wrote to Haddon in February 1893 reporting that 'our schedule ... was criticised a good deal', adding that they may have had 'too few measurements for the body'. Browne wrote to Haddon in June 1894 stating that he had consulted with Cunningham and challenged many aspects of Haddon and Garson's 'skull schedule'. In this context, Haddon's decision to supplement the ethnographic study of the Aran Islands with a study in craniology becomes the opening event in a row that rumbled on for two years and manifested a split between craniology and anthropometry as components of ethnographic fieldwork. Macalister (*JAI* 23 [1894]: 400–17) and Flower (BAAS 1894: 762–74) defined the split as a shift from an amateur pursuit of knowledge about racial origins to an academic, sociologically oriented and practical science. Flower cited Cunningham's project and ethnographic memoirs by Haddon and Browne as examples of a new methodology and so defined the nature of fieldwork associated with academic anthropology. In 1893, Haddon had been dropped from fieldwork associated with the project and was working with naturalists in Belfast instead.

THE SPLIT

Brabrook's attempt to agree a common plan of action expressed a more fundamental desire for an end to the divisions that split anthropology. He saw the survey as an opportunity to create a form of reciprocal accommodation – to borrow a biosocial term from Geddes – that combined physical anthropology, ethnology and folklore, archaeology, and philology into a unified science. 'The Ethnography of the Aran Islands' provided grounds for optimism with its declaration of a parity of esteem between anthropology and ethnology, but the row between Cunningham and Browne on the one hand and Garson and Haddon on the other was a setback, and that was only one of the problems that doomed the Ethnographic Survey of the UK to failure.

The problem in Ireland was of a different order. In 1891, Haddon and Cunningham were able to agree on an anthropometric exploration of racial origins, but that unity of purpose disappeared in 1892. The decision to extend the brief to include the study of ethnicity was unprecedented, but Haddon, a son of nonconformists, and Cunningham, a son of the manse, shared a desire to transcend the limits of physical anthropology and develop a faith-based, practical science that contributed to the well-being and progress of humanity. That was not enough to sustain the partnership in a politically charged environment like the Aran Islands in 1892, and they parted company in 1893.

Brabrook shut down the UK survey in 1899 (BAAS 1900: 493–95). He remained convinced of the importance of the work, but the committee lacked the resources to survey between three hundred and four hundred sites identified in the UK. He also cited difficulties with the usefulness of the information collected by amateurs and the lack of funding for professional researchers like Haddon and Browne (ibid.). In January 1896, Brabrook identified 'the doctrine of my valued friend Dr. Topinard' (*JAI* 25 [1896]: 399) as a barrier to progress in his address to the Anthropological Institute, in which he rallied the 'cultural' faction in the wake of events in Ipswich six months earlier. He reviewed the differences between 'physicals' and 'culturals' and declared:

> That it is right to study man as a whole, function as well as structure, thought as well as action, is the doctrine taught by the Ethnographic survey in which this Institute has taken

so much interest. This was laid down as the principle of its procedure by Professor Haddon, when he first suggested it, and is, I think, unquestionably right. (ibid.)

'Thought' included superstitions, modes of thought and customs, and if you substitute beliefs for superstitions, this statement becomes a reiteration of the principle 'that the ethnical characteristics of a people are to be found in their arts, habits, language as well as in their physical characters'. Brabrook also argued that it was time to abandon Topinard's 'insistence' that

> anthropology is a pure and not an applied science, a concrete and not an abstract science; and that, therefore, psychology and ethnography are not branches of anthropology but separate sciences. (ibid.)

The combination of 'psychology and ethnography' encapsulates the epistemological and methodological arguments Haddon advanced in 'The Study of Anthropology' and attempted to demonstrate in the Aran Islands by combining a study of physical characteristics with a synthesis of geography (place), political economy (work) and ethnology (folk). The sociological components were of interest to Cunningham in terms of the elucidation of the various social problems that were fuelling demands for Home Rule, and one of the most striking features of the period between the opening of the laboratory and the first survey was the slow erasure of Galton's input.

The forms used to register people submitting to measurement in the Dublin Anthropometric Laboratory are particularly revealing in this context. Galton measured 9,337 individuals during the six-month run of the International Health Exhibition in 1884 while Browne measured a mere 266 individuals in the first year of operation in Dublin. More revealing still is the fact that there were very few repeat measurements, despite Cunningham and Haddon stating the objective of measuring every student 'every six months during his University career' (*JAI* 21 [1892]: 36) in their plan in 1891. The registration forms merely confirm what Cunningham told Flower in 1894: the laboratory was used to give 'demonstrations in anthropological methods to any student who are interested in the subject' (BAAS 1894: 767). The change in function is even more visible in the schedules used in the Aran Islands (Figure 6.2). Each completed schedule was validated with the stamp of the Anthropological Laboratory, Trinity College Dublin. Even more remarkable still was the decision to use the fingerprint fields to comment on nasal profiles designed by Topinard (1885: 298), despite (a) Galton's research into fingerprinting as a scientific method for the identification of criminals and (b) his campaign to present this as evidence of the value of anthropology as a practical science, both of which Haughton highlighted in his speech at the opening of the laboratory in 1891. Furthermore, a general comparison of lab and field schedules reveals that head form, facial structure, complexion and stature replaced mental, sensory and physical capacity in the data fields. Thus, the schedules record how the lines of research Galton laid down in print in 1891 were overwritten in 1892 and more general data on physical characteristics collected instead.

This data was intrinsically political in 1892 because differences between 'the Anglo-Saxon' and 'the Celt' were a feature of Home Rule debates in anthropology. Lubbock, a banker, politician and first president of the Anthropological Institute, wrote a series of letters to *The Times* in which he described the United Kingdom as a synthesis of Celtic and Anglo-Saxon elements that, territorially speaking, consisted of a Celtic periphery and an Anglo-Saxon core centred on London. The Institute published the letters in its journal in 1887 (*JAI* 16 [1887]: 418–22) and Unionist anthropologists argued that this was the natural consequence of a necessary process of civilization by conquest and assimilation (see Walsh 2021c). Haddon was more interested in resemblances than differences and stood on the other side of that debate, regarding conquest and assimilation as the greatest threat to other civilizations. That placed him in opposition to Cunningham and Ingram, and there is an arguable case that the political application of data from the islands split Haddon and Browne's report into antagonistic treatments of anthropography and sociology, the latter by representing the islands as a well-governed colony of ethnically distinct and unassimilated natives.

That claim is based on the refusal of the ethnography to engage with the threat of famine and the related issues of eviction and anti-landlord agitation described by Mary Banim in her column in 1890. Haddon acknowledged the threat of famine in the slideshow he presented after the survey of fishing grounds in 1890. The ethnography, however, included a benign description of the landlord Digby that John T. O'Flaherty wrote in 1824 (RIA 3,2 [1891–93]: 795), almost seventy years before Haddon and Browne set foot on the islands. There is no reference to the formation of a branch of the Land League in the islands in the wake of the 1879 to 1880 famine and a brief but violent uprising against the small community of colonists that followed. Instead, the ethnography states that the land courts were dealing effectively with financial difficulties created by the lack of arable land in the islands (ibid.: 796). To put this in context, the islands were owned by the Digby sisters and managed by their agents Thomas Thompson and Henry Robinson. The Digbys hired Robinson in 1890 and he served as their manager until 1895. His father George managed an estate in Connemara and Henry inherited the agency in 1890. They were unpopular because they engaged in large-scale evictions during the Land War in the 1880s; George wore body armour and was accompanied by heavily armed bodyguards (Robinson 2006: 216–23). Henry took over the management of the Aran Islands at the end of a decade of conflict between Thompson and the islanders. The lack of employment, combined with severe pressure on land (Haddon and Browne quoted in Harvey 1991: 239) meant that the Digbys were compelled by Land Courts convened by the Irish Land Commission (established in 1881) to reduce rents by 40 per cent between 1885 and 1891 although evictions continued throughout this period. The fragile economy collapsed in 1894 and, as Lee Perry Curtis

(2011: 281, 284–86) put it, 'a rash of evictions' followed, accompanied by outrage in the nationalist camp. Haddon and Browne wrote 'The Ethnography of the Aran Islands' against this background but famine, eviction and anti-landlord agitation do not feature, and the reasons why are found in politics rather than science or, rather, the politics of science.

The Royal Irish Academy published the ethnography in 1893 as Gladstone's second Home Rule bill made its way through the Imperial Parliament and the sense of political crisis deepened with each step. As stated earlier, Ingram was a unionist, and Tanya O'Sullivan (2015: 145) has compiled a record of Cunningham's anti-Home Rule activism. For instance, he addressed a meeting at TCD of the Irish Unionist Alliance, a small but influential propagandist organization founded in 1891 to resist the imposition of self-government in Ireland (Hickey and Doherty 2005: 241). He assured Unionists, to applause, that they were better fitted for survival. The Alliance subsequently published an essay Cunningham wrote in which he described the uneducated and unassimilated 'Irishman' as 'excitable, emotional, superstitious, and I am sorry to say, in some cases a dangerous member of society' (Cunningham 1903: 163–67). It was a stunning reversal of the anti-racism of his 1886 study of human variation, but Cunningham, according to O'Sullivan, used his lab work to bolster opposition to Home Rule, and science served politics in a way that recalls Huxley's anti-socialist activism in the 1850s. It is likely then that Browne, his able assistant, followed suit when it came to writing 'The Ethnography of the Aran Islands', although the loss of almost all the records associated with it means that this claim relies on circumstantial evidence.

Haddon's sympathy for the islanders had no place in this mix of science and politics and Browne informed the Academy on 30 November 1893 that he *alone* had 'made the second local inquiry, the field chosen being the islands of Inishbofin and Inishshark, Co. Galway' (RIA 3,3 [1893–96]: 317). The only documentary evidence of a split is a fragment of a letter from Cunningham that confirms that the decision to send Browne *alone* to Inishbofin was made in Haddon's absence. Haddon remained on the Academy's management committee but took no part in ethnographic surveys of Inishbofin and Inishshark (1893), the Mullet, Inishkea Islands and Portnacloy (1894), Ballycroy (1895), Clare Island and Inishturk (1896), Dunquin and the Great Blasket Island (1897), Garumna and Lettermullen (1899) or Carna and Mweenish (1900). It's an interesting list. Browne covered the same territory that Arthur 'Bloody' Balfour and Alice 'Blanche' Balfour, his sister, campaign manager and publicist, covered in 1889, 1890 and 1891 in preparation for the 1892 general election. They inspected the roll-out of railways, telegraphs and fishing infrastructure that he later assigned to the Congested Districts Board. His brother Gerald was appointed Chief Secretary of Ireland after Gladstone and his Home Rule project were defeated in the 1895 general election, and Gerald Balfour told a post-election constituency event in Leeds that their opponents had dubbed their strategy a policy of killing Home Rule with kindness. The fields of anti-Home Rule activism and practical anthropology were, it seems, one and the same.

CONCLUSION

To summarize, Haddon and Browne (acting for Cunningham) arrived in the Aran Islands in September 1892, measured the skulls of twenty-seven islanders and presented their report at the Royal Irish Academy in December. Haddon then read a supplementary study of the craniology of the islands and the Academy published both documents in 1893, during a political crisis caused by the passage of Gladstone's second Home Rule bill through the Imperial Parliament in London. Haddon was dropped from a second survey of Inishbofin, and Browne alone carried out seven other surveys. In a parallel development, Huxley advised Haddon to abandon his advocacy for a bureau of ethnology and focus instead on the collection of anthropological information using the committee structure of the BAAS. Haddon, operating through the Folk-Lore Society, persuaded the Anthropological Institute to cooperate in a multi-agency ethnographic survey of the UK. Brabrook launched the project in August 1892 and the BAAS agreed to manage it. The priority was to agree a common plan of action for four separate fields of study and Haddon and Garson set about drawing up a manual for the measurement of physical characteristics, which Browne, in consultation with Cunningham, challenged because it was too focussed on skulls. Brabrook shut the UK project down five years later, citing practical difficulties while making it clear that the differences between 'physical' and 'cultural' factions were insurmountable due largely to the exclusively anatomical doctrine of Dr Topinard. He acknowledged that Haddon had always insisted that ethnicity and race formed equally legitimate fields of enquiry and, in doing so, reiterated a principle explicitly stated in the introduction to 'The Ethnographic Survey of the Aran Islands, County Galway'.

The temptation, historiographically speaking, has always been to credit one or other of the authors with extending the scope of anthropological investigations in the field or, the converse, to use the ethnography as evidence of involvement in the skull-measuring business in a colonial context, and either way, to situate Haddon at various points in a methodological transition from evolutionist scholarship to social science. Thinking in such binary terms is, however, hopelessly inadequate when it comes to the task of unravelling a document that maps the battleground between competing versions of a sociologically oriented anthropology and, in an Irish context, between pro- and anti-Home Rule factions within an emerging discipline. That task is complicated by the fact that the text is a historiographical orphan. Its origins can be traced to Galton's Laboratory, Cunningham's Anatomy Department, Haughton and Ingram's Academy and Haddon, who, as an ethnologist, lacked an academic home but operated out of the Folk-Lore Society and ran with the field club movement. The full manuscript and related papers have disappeared and all that remains are scraps of correspondence, a partial manuscript in the Haddon Papers and a thread running through the records of the organizations involved in the Irish and UK surveys. That is enough to piece together a story about a sustained attempt to define the nature of anthropology by agreeing a common approach to ethnographic investigations in the field. However, scientific ambitions and political differences – to borrow a phrase from Flower – intervened and the resulting conflicts are all too evident in the structure and silences of 'The Ethnographic Survey of the Aran Islands, County Galway'.

Cunningham's deal with Galton may have opened the way to eugenics research in Dublin, but he transformed the Irish Ethnographic Survey into a new form of politically relevant, field-based investigation of problematic social and economic conditions in the west of Ireland in response to a threat to the political integrity of the United Kingdom of Great Britain and Ireland. The absence of any reference to the threat of famine, eviction or antilandlord agitation made this a blatantly political text, and the picture of a well-governed island community further aligns the section on sociology with Unionist arguments.

Haddon's collaboration with Garson and, by association, Galton, was a tactical move into craniology that, at first glance, contradicts his earlier adoption of elements of anarchist geography, ethnology and Le Playist sociology. His formulation of anthropography was a compromise that was never going to placate the followers of Topinard and his partnership with Garson alienated Cunningham. That situation was made worse by Haddon's Home Rule sympathies as declared in public by his acknowledgement of the threat of famine in his first ethnographic account of the islands.

In the finish, Haddon, despite his epistemic pragmatism and institutional positioning, ended up in a sort of political no man's land with Galton on one side and Cunningham on the other, in much the same way as he ended up on the wrong side of Green, and with the same result, although his removal from fieldwork in 1893 was announced with a little more subtlety. Nevertheless, Haddon's route to a job in academic anthropology in Ireland was blocked and he redirected his effort towards the members of the field club who had availed of his extramural lectures in Belfast. He salvaged the more progressive components of the Irish Ethnographic Survey and set about creating a fifth field in the study of anthropology.

PART III

• • •

THE FIFTH FIELD

Figure 7.1. A. C. Haddon, *Michael Faherty, and two women, Inishmaan, Faherty refused to be measured, and the women would not even tell us their names*, 1892. Digital scan of silver gelatine print (Timothy Keefe, Sharon Sutton, Ciarán Walsh, Ciarán Rooney, 2011). Courtesy of the Board of Trinity College, University of Dublin.

CHAPTER 7

TEDIOUS TEXTS

● ● ●

I can't tell you all the excursions we made in Aran it would be as tedious for you to read as for me to write suffice it to say that Dixon & I left very little unseen & what with sketches & photographs we have a good deal on paper.
—Haddon, SS *Fingal* Journal

'The Ethnography of the Aran Islands, County Galway' closed with three plates of nine photographs Haddon took while in the field between 1890 and 1892. At first glance, they conform to Flower's advice on using photography to record the physical features of people who refused to submit to measurement:

> Photography of course, if for scientific comparison, should be <u>exact</u> profiles or <u>exact</u> full faces & sufficiently large to view details. (Flower to Haddon, 17 May 1890, original emphasis)

Haddon and Browne incorporated his advice into their ethnographic survey of the Aran Island in 1892:

> Photography – a considerable number of photographs were obtained of the people. In some cases groups were taken, but full face and side-view portraits were secured of thirteen of the subjects we measured. We found that the promise of a copy of their photograph was usually a sufficient

reward for undergoing the trouble of being measured and photographed. (RIA 3,2 [1891–93]: 778)

It would seem like a straightforward exercise in collecting anthropometric data were it not for Haddon's captions on page 830. They tell a different story. Haddon used the photograph of Colman Thomas Faherty and Michael John O'Donnell to explain:

When there is more than one man of the same name in the Aran Islands, the individuals are distinguished by the addition of their father's Christian name, as in the foregoing cases. Faherty, who is a thirteenth child, is a very typical Aranite. O'Donnell's ancestor came from Ulster. They are standing in front of St. Sournick's thorn. (RIA 3,2 [1891–93]: 830)

'St. Sournick' was a misspelling of Sourney, the anglicized version of Sairnait, a holy woman who lived in the sixth century and

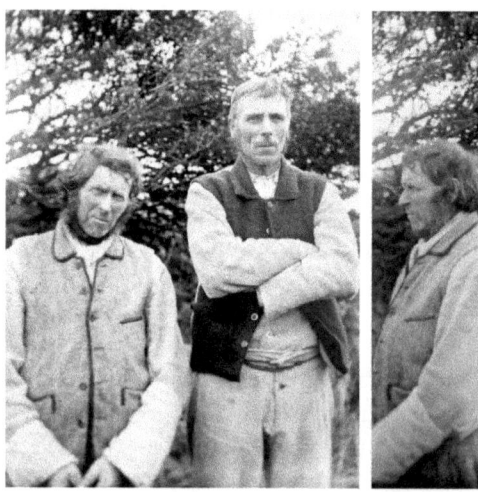

Figure 7.2. A. C. Haddon, *Colman Faherty, Thomas, aged about sixty years, Oghil. Michael O'Donnell, John, No. 25, Oghil*, 1892. Digital scan of silver gelatine print (Timothy Keefe, Sharon Sutton, Ciarán Walsh, Ciarán Rooney, 2011). Courtesy of the Board of Trinity College, University of Dublin.

is associated with Teampall Asurnaí (the mediaeval church of Sarnait), a tiny oratory located in Eochaill on the main island. The 'thorn' refers to *An Sceach Mór* (the Big Thorn-Bush), an old hawthorn which, according to folklore, marked Sourney's burial place. Haddon used the photograph to illustrate the folklore of trees in slideshows presented at the Folk-Lore Society and Section H in 1895. Thus, Haddon covered physical characteristics, racial types, migration, folk-name conventions, archaeology and folklore in a single image. The least typical photograph reproduced was that of Michael Faherty and two women on Inishmaan (Figure 7.1) whom Haddon met on the foreshore of the middle island. The caption reads:

> Michael Faherty, and two women, Inishmaan. Faherty refused to be measured, and the women would not even tell us their names. (RIA 3,2 [1891–93]: 830)

Haddon simultaneously explained the low sample – twenty-seven islanders out of a total population of 2,907 – and illustrated another 'little war' in the daily life of the colony. More significant is the fact that the informality of the composition and the agency of the sitters provide a striking contrast to the anthropometric portraits, however multivalent they are. The full spectrum of nine images and their captions represents a significant advance in the development of sketches and photographs as ethnographic forms in their own right.

It's a curious fact that Haddon is better known as a former zoologist than a photographer, yet his colleagues chose a monumental task of photographic archiving to mark his contribution to anthropology on the occasion of his eightieth birthday. Quiggin (1942: 148) tells us that Louis Clarke, curator at the Museum of Archaeology and Ethnology in Cambridge, suggested that ten thousand photographic images Haddon donated to the museum in 1925 be copied and presented to him as a special collection. It constituted, Quiggin and Fegan (1940: 100) wrote in an obituary in *Man* five years later, 'a permanent record of his life's work'. It would take another half century almost before anthropologists began to investigate the photographic legacy of their discipline and, even then, the relationship between photography and anthropology was generally regarded as problematic. In 1992, Jonathan Benthall, Director of the Royal Anthropological Institute, wrote a foreword to *Anthropology and Photography 1860–1920* (1992) in which he described opposition to such a project from influential individuals who argued that the photographic archive materialized the discreditable

> Victorian past of anthropology ... that had nothing to do with the humanist tradition established by Malinowski and Boas; or even that the project was not really anthropology and hence was no concern of the Institute. (Benthall 1992: vii–viii)

The reference to Boas is particularly interesting in this context. I have already discussed how illustration provided one of the more striking contrasts between a report on the Indians of British Columbia that Boas prepared for the BAAS in 1889 and 'The Ethnography of the Western Tribe of Torres Straits' that Haddon presented at a later meeting of the Anthropological Institute. To recap, Boas provided illustrations of twelve skulls while Haddon provided thirty-five of his own drawings of the people and their artefacts, some based on photographs he had taken.

Shortly afterwards, he included some of the same photographs in a magic lantern show designed to activate Kropotkin's theory that sympathetic knowledge was the best way to dispel atavistic and ethnocentric racism in an era of colonial expansion. Haddon rephrased it in the first article of a column he started writing for the *Irish Daily Independent* in 1893. He summed up the difference between old-school biologists and modern ethnologists in two words: the first looked for differences, the second for resemblances, a saying Haddon borrowed from his grandfather John Haddon, an anti-slavery activist. The photograph of Martin Faherty and the two women materialized a long tradition of humanist engagement with other people and cultures and Haddon's adoption of the photographic slideshow in 1890 signalled a new phase in humanitarian activism as a function of ethnology. This marks the beginning of a decade-long and long-forgotten experiment with photo-ethnography as an alternative to 'tedious' texts.

In 1975, Margaret Mead (1995: 3–10) described the refusal of an earlier generation of anthropologists to exploit new audiovisual technologies as a wanton act of criminal neglect by a discipline that had become trapped in its own traditions and created 'a Discipline of Words' that, however poetic, was incapable of conveying the full meaning of a ritual danced for the last time. This is important because it situates the problem of photography and cinematography in the perceived value of text and image as forms of ethnographic information capable of generating anthropological knowledge. That brings us back to Clarke's project. Quiggin (1942: 146) recalled how, ten years earlier, the same people decided to forego the traditional volume of essays to mark Haddon's retirement as Reader in Ethnology, and the logic of both actions can be traced back to Haddon's choice of image over text in his first ethnographic account of the Aran Islands in 1890.

This chapter deals with that choice, taking as a starting point a letter Haddon wrote to his son Ernest in 1885 in which the making of meaning is assigned primarily to images. Ernest may have been a child, but a similar bias becomes apparent in Haddon's ethnographic experiments in the Torres Strait, New Guinea, and the Aran Islands between 1888 and 1890. This preference for the visual, I propose, recapitulated childhood experiences of art in family life and business, and the 'tedium' of writing emerges as the trigger for the development of an alternative ethnographic practice built around images.

A LETTER TO ERNEST

Haddon took part in fisheries research off the south-west coast of Ireland in 1885 and wrote to his son Ernest explaining that:

Dada goes
in a boat on the sea [drawing]

and catches fish [drawing]
and sea stars [drawing]
and sea flowers [drawing]
and sea snails [drawing]
and shells and many funny things [drawing].
(A. C. Haddon to Ernest Haddon, 12 August 1885)

The text functions primarily as an armature for sketches and the burden of representation, to borrow a phrase coined by John Tagg (1988), is carried by the images. Descriptive taxonomy was a big part of Haddon's training and required considerable skill as an illustrator (RDS 4,2 [1889]: 297–98). His interest in sketching was not merely a function of his training as a biologist, however. Quiggin (1942: 132) noted that Haddon was interested in art in his youth and claimed that 'his work as an artist would have attracted attention apart from his service to Zoology and Anthropology'. Charles Seligman (1940: 848–50), a physician who accompanied Haddon to the Torres Strait in 1898, also recalled Haddon's early interest in decorative art in an obituary he wrote for *Nature*. He cited an illustrated letter that Haddon, aged 25, wrote to *Nature* on the subject of 'Greek Fret' in Central American architecture in response to an earlier article on 'the development of ornament as illustrated by General Pitt Rivers' Anthropological Collection' (Haddon 1880: 9–10). Seligman recalled how the first expedition to the Torres Strait 'triggered an alteration … in the man himself', which manifested as a transfer of interest from marine zoology to the study of the beliefs, language, arts and crafts of the islanders, adding that his 'persistent interest in decorative art' intensified after retirement in 1925. Haddon, by my reading of Seligman, discovered that ethnology, rather than marine biology, offered greater scope to pursue his interest in art. Furthermore, his correspondence with McFarlane prior to the expedition tells us that he considered art an essential part of an ethnologist's skill set, and his interview in *The Colonies and India* on his return puts art and photography at the centre of ethnographic representation in exhibition and in print.

Art, according to Quiggin, was part and parcel of family life. Elizabeth Cort, Haddon's grandmother, was an artist who studied under Richard Parkes Bonington (Cruft 1915: 55), a leading landscape painter based in France. His grandfather John Haddon was a singer and published several collections of religious and secular music (ibid.). His mother Caroline Waterman published under the pen name Caroline Hadley, and *Woodside Or, Look, Listen, and Learn* (1887) is an illustrated account of her children's home-schooling in the study of nature. His father John was a talented illustrator and, although the sketches in *Woodside* are signed with the initials A. R., the possibility of a connection tantalizes because the illustration of 'Jack and the Thrush's Nest' on page 36 could be a portrait of Haddon as a 10-year-old boy. When he was 19, Haddon took over the family publishing business (Quiggin 1942: 10–14) and spent a year in the drawing office, during which he attended evening classes in drawing, design and copperplate etching. Fegan and Pickles (1978) catalogued a folder in the Haddon Papers as 'Albums of drawings by Haddon (original) dating from early years', and it contains a drawing from a cast of a classical sculpture – typical of arts education at the time – as well as an imagined landscape full of dinosaurs. Haddon continued drawing and painting during expeditions in the southwest of Ireland in 1885 and 1886 and, as discussed, informed Geddes and McFarlane that he planned to bring an artist – his friend William Thomas – to the Torres Strait in 1888. Haddon's younger brother Arthur enrolled in the Slade School of Art in 1883 and subsequently established himself as a traditionalist painter and illustrator specializing in landscape and genre, including orientalist treatments of Middle Eastern subjects.

Haddon included Arthur in his plans to publish his research, which he outlined in his journal in September 1888. This entry concludes an extended reflection on his life in Mabuiag and the information he collected about the people he lived with. He did not, he wrote, have sufficient 'time or brain energy' to rewrite the rough notes he had taken during his 'yarns with the people' and added that:

Those who want information must wait until I return and then they can see my notes and sketches which illustrate them. I think of offering two or three articles to the Century Magazine so as to have the benefit of good and copious illustrations and I hope, in that case, that Arthur will be my artist. I intend making that one of my stipulations provided he cares to tackle it. (Haddon 1888–89 Torres Strait and New Guinea Journal: 50)

Haddon revisited that plan in the interview he gave to a journalist during the exhibition in the British Museum in October 1889. The journalist quoted Haddon telling of negotiating in pidgin for ethnological material with the aid of sketches and photographs and added:

some of these photographs may now be seen in the collection, recording features and decorations which, in a few years will have utterly died out.... It is understood that the British Museum authorities will select from this collection such objects as they desire to add to their permanent ethnographical collection. We shall look with much interest to the appearance of Professor Haddon's full journal and observations, especially as he made a large number of coloured drawings on the spot. (*The Colonies and India*, 23 October 1889: 29)

The British Museum has an online collection of fifty-nine photographs that may be those acquired during the exhibition. Haddon's journal also contains many entries in which he describes how he took these photographs and made his 'drawings on the spot'.

On 13 August 1888, five days after landfall in the Torres Strait, Haddon and Hugh Milman, acting magistrate, boarded the government steamship *Albatross* and set out on a week-long tour of islands in the Western Strait. They reached Nagir on the first afternoon and Haddon made a detailed sketch of a house. He then met some islanders and, with the aid of a sketch, acquired a decorated skull. He also acquired masks, amulets, bangles, breast ornaments, and bows and arrows, some used in the performance of a 'native dance or koppa-koppa' (Haddon 1888–89 Torres Strait and New Guinea Journal: 7) and some from New Guinea that the islanders used in hunting birds and 'possibly other bipeds' (ibid.). He visited other islands and 'as usual, made enquiries for ethnological specimens'. When they reached Tud (Warrior) island they persuaded the islanders to perform a dance and Haddon illustrated his account with a rough sketch that would 'give a better idea than words only.' To complete the picture, he bought

> a lot of the koppa-koppa toggery including a man's entire rig-out – so that you can gain some idea at home as to the appearance of the natives, that is so far as dress is concerned during a dance. (ibid.: 11)

They set off for New Guinea and landed in Mowatta, where Haddon used an assembly of villagers and bush people as an opportunity to take photographs using six photographic plates he had held in reserve after the main supply had been misplaced in transit. He also obtained thirteen skulls of 'bushmen ... killed in battle by Mowatta men' (Haddon 1888–89 Torres Strait and New Guinea Journal: 20) and more bows and arrows. He returned to Thursday Island on Sunday, 19 August and wrote that he had 'been fortunate enough to acquire a really valuable collection of anthropological specimens in a very short space of time and at an extremely moderate price' (ibid.: 23).

To conclude, the exhibition in the British Museum and interview in *The Colonies and India* both confirm the primacy of visual and material evidence over text, and Haddon's reliance on both while communicating his experience in the field constituted a new form of ethnography. Taking his first letter to Ernest as a template, one could summarize his tour of the islands by selecting ten of the images he created and sequencing them with a series of verbal cues: Haddon went in a boat and visited islands, where he met people, watched dances, made sketches, took photographs and collected masks, ornaments, bows and many other interesting things. It may be a little difficult to visualize this in word form alone, but substitute photographs for sketches and imagine it as a slideshow. That is exactly what Haddon did after he discovered the ethnographic potential of instantaneous photography during his first visit to the Aran Islands in 1890. That might have marked the beginning of visual anthropology had anthropology not begun its migration, guided by Galton, from the humanities into 'hard' science and its subsequent transformation into what Mead called a 'discipline of words'.

INSTANTANEOUS PHOTOGRAPHS

Paul Hockings used Mead's essay 'Visual Anthropology in a Discipline of Words' as the introduction to a collection of essays drawn from papers presented at a conference on visual anthropology convened during the 1973 World Congress of Anthropological and Ethnological Scientists. Hockings (1995a: vii) hoped that the first edition of *Principles of Visual Anthropology* (1975) would 'put visual anthropology in its proper perspective as a legitimate subdiscipline of anthropology'. Hockings might have been describing a task Haddon attempted in a series of slideshows presented between 1890 and 1895, which he followed with a major revision of the third edition of *Notes and Queries on Anthropology* in 1899. There is one significant difference between Hockings and Haddon. Haddon never thought of art and photography as a subdiscipline but as a form of anthropology in its own right. Nevertheless, David MacDougall, a maker of documentary and ethnographic films, described the period between Haddon and Mead as 'the "dark age" of visual anthropology' (2009: 57). Mead (1995: 4–5) was dismayed that anthropologists and ethnologists had not responded to the rapid disappearance of behaviours with methods made possible by advances in audiovisual technologies. They were, she argued, stuck in a scientist mindset and too reliant on the traditional instruments of questionnaire, pencil and notebook. Anthropology, Mead argued, had become a discipline of words and, as such, was incapable of conveying the full sense of a ritual danced for the last time (ibid.: 4). This adds a twist to Malinowski's criticism of Haddon as the personification of an earlier generation of anthropologists who went into the field 'armed with pencil and notebook' (Malinowski 1954: 122–23; Langham 1981: 174) and operated from the comfort of the colonist's veranda, a twist made even more ironic given the status anthropologists attach to Malinowski's *Argonauts of the Western Pacific* as a foundational text.

Mead did not refer to Haddon. Her argument suggests a time frame beginning in the 1920s, and de Brigard (1995: 16) provides an answer as to why Haddon wasn't considered relevant. She acknowledges that Haddon's 1898 film of 'three men's dances' was 'the earliest known to have been made in the field' but prefaces this by describing Haddon as a former zoologist who applied standards of evidence developed in the natural sciences to 'systematic salvage ethnography'. As such, Haddon's innovation was incidental to the development of ethnographic film as a medium in its own right. De Brigard hedges her assessment, but she fails to recognize that Haddon had lost interest in zoology and was fascinated by the meaning and materialism of dance performance. Furthermore, as the above quotations from his journal indicate, he grappled with the very problem Mead identified in 1975: the impossibility of conveying in 'words only' the full sense of islanders performing a dance.

Part of the problem was that the photographic technology available to Haddon in 1888 was incapable of dealing with movement, and this is evident in the 'freeze-frame' attitude of the people he photographed performing a circular dance on Mowatta (Mowat) in August 1888, which makes them look more like objectified anthropological specimens than the living ethnological subjects he described in his journals. Photography was, however, undergoing a technological revolution, and the expedition coincided with the launch in May of the Eastman Kodak box camera. This transformed the availability and utility of photography, but Haddon departed for the Torres Strait in April and, in any event, it would take another six years for Browne to begin experimenting with handheld cameras in his ethnographic surveys in the west of Ireland. Nevertheless, the encounter between Haddon, Michael Faherty and the two women from Inishmaan, whose refusal to cooperate produced an informality that epitomized instantaneous, social documentary photography, and Haddon's decision to publish the photograph in 'The Ethnography of the Aran Islands' signalled the introduction of instantaneous photography as an innovative ethnographic method prior to the widespread adoption of box cameras in fieldwork.

'Instantaneous' entered the lexicon of photography in the 1850s, when photographers attempted to replicate the fast exposure times Gustave Le Gray achieved in 1856. Three years later, the secretary of the Dublin Photographic Society reported to the Fine Arts Section of the Royal Dublin Society that the photographers were discussing instantaneous pictures (Chandler 2001: 120–21). However, the complex chemical processes involved in taking a photograph militated against instantaneous photography until the introduction of industrially produced, ready-to-use glass-plate negatives in 1878. Camera manufacturer J. Lancaster & Son exploited this development with a range of 'Instantograph' cameras that registered fifteen thousand sales in 1888. The company marketed the camera as 'the sine qua non of the Amateur Photographer' (Lancaster 1890: 10) because of its efficacy in making 'instantaneous pictures of moving objects, Portraits, Groups, Landscapes, Architectural and Engineering Subjects etc.' (ibid.). This type of camera was widely used in the 1890s and Dixon had one with him when he and Haddon discovered the Aran Islands in the 1890s. Watching Dixon operate his instantaneous camera became a turning point for Haddon in terms of his understanding the ethnographic potential of photography.

Haddon seems to have become interested in photography in the mid-1880s. Photography was taught at the Royal College of Science, although most of the evidence points to his association with Robert John Welch, a professional photographer who was active in the Belfast Naturalists' Field Club. Members of the club attended Haddon's university extension lectures and Haddon reciprocated by founding a field club in Dublin in 1885. There are numerous letters from Welch in the Haddon Papers relating to a photo-ethnographic partnership they established after Haddon went into anthropology in 1889, and these give an insight into how Haddon went about building a library of ten thousand images. There isn't enough space to develop that topic here, and what matters is how they combined their interest in fieldwork and photography. One letter confirms that Welch advised Haddon on photographic equipment prior to the 1892 ethnographic survey of the Aran Islands and it is likely that he did the same prior to the expedition to the Torres Strait. Furthermore, Welch processed the photographs Dixon took under Haddon's direction in 1890. Dixon kept fifty-one glass-plate negatives in a slotted wooden box that I found in a search of the 'Old' Anatomy Department at TCD in 2014. The label reads:

> A. F. Dixon, BA, /Dublin /per Professor Haddon / From R. Welch, publisher of Welch's Irish Views, 19, Lonsdale Street, BELFAST.

A further search uncovered positive slides of photographs taken by Haddon, and Welch's role in this project provides an interesting backdrop to Haddon's discovery of instantaneous photography.

Welch preferred large format cameras (Evans 1977: 16–18) and Haddon brought one to the Aran Islands. He recorded in his journal what happened when he attempted to photograph a regatta on Monday, 3 August:

> It was too dull & sunless for instantaneous photography. Dixon did his best but his results were not satisfactory. The high wind also bothered him, even with his 1/4 plate camera. It was impossible for me to work mine. (Haddon, 1890, SS *Fingal* Journal: 48)

1/4 plate cameras used negatives measuring 3.25 by 4.25 inches while a whole plate negative measured 6.5 x 8.5 inches and required a much larger camera mounted on a stand (tripod). Haddon recorded the regatta in his sketchbook, although his drawings of 'matchstick' men carrying currachs were no match for Dixon's photographs, even if the results were unsatisfactory. Haddon realized this at the time. Earlier in the week, they visited 'Teampull Mhic Duagh at Kilmurray' (Kilmurvey) and Haddon made four sketches. He informed the reader of his journal that 'the collection of photographs which Dixon is taking will illustrate Aran better than my sketches or imperfect description' (ibid.: 46). He also informed readers that a written account of all that they had seen would 'be as tedious for you to read as for me to write' and offered sketches and photographs instead.

TEDIOUS TEXTS

Haddon left the Aran Islands on 7 August and arrived back in Dublin on the last day of the month. He extracted ten pages from his journal and sent them with photographs to Bettany, who replied on 6 September and rejected a pitch for an illustrated article. 'Your Journal is most interesting to me', Bettany wrote, 'but it vitally needs $\sqrt{\text{the}}$ illustrations, which as you know we don't give in Lippincott's'. American periodicals, he advised, offered the best field for illustrated articles, and noted with regret that Haddon had not submitted a full book on the Torres Strait. Shortly afterwards Haddon pitched a series of illustrated articles to Johann Schmeltz at the *Internationales Archiv für Ethnographie* and essays on 'Tugeri Head-Hunters' (1891) and 'Secular and Ceremonial Dances of the Torres Straits Islanders' (1893) went into production. Arthur Haddon translated his brother's artwork into a series of illustrations and, in June 1891, Schmeltz agreed that Haddon could incorporate 'the plates of the dances' into a book that Haddon had outlined in a letter to Foster the month before:

> I have already published an account of the Western Tribe (Journ Anthry Inst XIX 1890) and also numerous legends (Folklore Ist Ed) but I have still a considerable amount of material in hand together with an account of arts and crafts of the people. I also consider it would be desirable to pub-

lish a collection of my photos. The Anthrop Instit. cannot afford to publish many illustrations & it is in these that the main cost of ethnological publishing lies. (Haddon to Foster, 7 May 1891)

Foster agreed to subsidize the cost of illustration, but the monograph remained unpublished. Macalister drew the attention of the Anthropological Institute to 'the plates of the dances' in the 'beautifully illustrated monograph' (*JAI* 23 [1894]: 404) and regretted that the poverty of the institute 'precluded our publication of papers of this nature requiring expensive plates'.

The correspondence effectively illustrates what John Tagg (2009: 95–96) called the 'economy of meaning', and this was a major problem for Haddon, whose constant references to the inadequacy of written descriptions and the tedium of writing suggest that he struggled with writing. That may explain Bettany's disappointment that Haddon hadn't delivered a book on the Torres Strait. It is also supported by contemporaneous correspondence between Haddon and Ellis. As discussed earlier, they agreed on a study of anthropology in 1890 before Ellis reluctantly accepted that Haddon found it too difficult and, one year later, commissioned instead a study on 'the earliest origins of art among savages'. Haddon wrote *Evolution in Art* and Ellis included it in the Contemporary Science Series in 1895; this was the only book Haddon completed between *An Introduction to the Study of Embryology* in 1887 and *The Study of Man* in 1898, which hardly counts as it was a collection of previously published material. Haddon insisted that the book was not 'a treatise on anthropology, or its methods, but merely a collection of samples of the way in which parts of the subject are studied' (Haddon 1898: iii). One of the samples he embedded in the introduction was the text of 'The Study of Anthropology', and it could have set the intellectual tone for *The Study of Man* under an editor other than James McKeen Cattell. He commissioned *The Study of Man* as the first volume of the Progressive Science Series, the aim of which, according to a publisher's postscript, was to have 'an author of acknowledged authority' represent the societal importance of contemporary advances in anthropology in 'a form that is intelligible and attractive'.

That is more or less what Ellis looked for in 1890, but the two editors were on opposite ends of the political spectrum. Cattell worked briefly with Galton in London and subsequently applied a quantitative, hard-science logic to psychology, arguing that it needed to rest on a foundation of experiment and measurement to attain the credibility associated with 'the certainty and exactness of the physical sciences' (Cattell 1890: 373). Incidentally, if space allowed, this would form the basis of an investigation of Haddon's invitation to Rivers to join the 1898 expedition and the subsequent emphasis on experimental psychometrics in fieldwork. Leaving that aside, Haddon's involvement in the skull-measuring business provided Cattell with plenty of material along those lines and Haddon attempted to balance this with a series of chapters dealing with the ethnological significance of toys and games that first appeared in his column in the *Irish Daily Independent*. He also included articles on the evolution of carts, including the jaunting car, as examples of the role technology played in social evolution. This merely created an intellectual and practical confusion that the American ethnologist and anarchist D. G. Brinton (1898: 82) thought illustrated the extremes of anthropological thought in the 1890s. This suggests that Ellis, as editor, was responsible for the intellectual and structural coherence of *Evolution in Art*. Nonetheless, the inclusion of examples of Haddon's journalism in *The Study of Man* points to one of the most interesting and least considered aspects of his practice: his work as a newspaper columnist who wrote about politically sensitive subjects like race, gender and class.

As a youth, Haddon engaged in political debate at home. Cruft (1915: 55) related Mrs Bayne's account, now lost, of the Haddon household and described how John Haddon and Elizabeth Cort were active in the anti-slavery movement and named one of their sons Wilberforce after 'the great abolitionist'. Cruft added that 'many philanthropists and foreign missionaries found a ready and hospitable welcome in that enlightened home' in London.

Quiggin (1942: 13) took up the story in 1942 and recalled how, in 1874, Haddon read to his grandmother 'part of Prof Tyndall's opening speech of the Brit Ass.' On another occasion, he read Darwin's *Emotions* to his aunt Marianne (ibid.: 16), most likely a reference to *The Expression of the Emotions in Man and Animals* (1872). Jones (2008: 67) argued that the shock of Tyndall's 1874 address brought Darwin to the attention of the wider public, and a degree of notoriety attached to Tyndall for a period. Ten years later, Caroline Haddon introduced socialism onto the agenda of the Fabian Society and caused considerable controversy with her anonymous paper on 'The Future of Marriage' (Haddon 1884; Sloane 2018: 43). Caroline Haddon and her sisters moved in circles that regarded marriage as an oppressive institution and argued for sexual liberty (see Greenway 2009). She met Ellis when he helped her and sister Margaret Hinton edit the work of the latter's husband James Hinton, whose belief in polygamy was so controversial that Caroline advised Ellis that it was 'inadvisable to show his manuscripts except to a small circle of intimate admirers' (Clark 2017: 119 and fn. 143). Their influence is discernible in 'Incidents in the Life of a Torres Straits Islander', in which Haddon adopted the style of a Fabian tract and progressed from nakedness as a normal state in a civilized society to sex via male initiation and female agency in courtship. Haddon went further, politically speaking, in 1891 when he tried to publicize the link between structural racism and genocide in his critique of the Imperial Institute, and counteract it by proposing a humanitarian bureau of ethnology. This was a precursor of sorts for his column in the *Irish Daily Independent*, in which evolution became a thinly disguised pretext for an exploration of race, class and gender over ten instalments of 'Rambles in the Natural History Museum' and three dealing with 'Science and the Woman Question'.

He launched his column with a provocative study of evolution as a theme in the displays of the Natural History Department of the Museum of Science and Art in Dublin, a project completely in keeping with Huxley's plan to use museums as centres of public education in matters of evolution, but completely at odds with Huxley's political project. He described the old system of collecting and displaying specimens as a 'science of death' and informed his readers that the emphasis zoologists once placed on classification had been made redundant by new knowledge about the causes of variation; this is where the influence of his grandfather breaks through in his journalism. He summed up his argument as follows:

> The mental attitude of the older and the more modern schools may be expressed in two words – they looked for differences, we look for resemblances. (*Irish Daily Independent*, 26 December 1893: 5)

The punchline was a quotation from his grandfather John, whom Cruft described as follows:

> Though a strong Nonconformist, he was not narrow in his views. He constantly used to say 'I prefer to find points of contact, not difference, with my fellow Christians'. (Cruft 1915: 55)

Haddon then turned his attention to evolution and wrote:

> From the foregoing remarks it is apparent that in studying life evolution must be accepted as a working hypothesis. There is no biologist who has frankly faced the facts of life who can honestly deny that evolution has operated and is in force. There may be discussions as to the causes or the methods of its operation, there can be no doubt to its occurrence. (*Irish Daily Independent*, 26 December 1893: 5)

Haddon proceeded to engage his readers with a discussion of variation in other species and signalled his intention to tackle race in a second article using 'a very instructive collection of animal life and structure which teaches us the history of races'. This suggested a display case comparing the skeleton of a human to those of anthropoid apes, but the article featured instead a display of birds that Haddon used to illustrate a lecture on speciation and demonstrate 'how we may find two animals quite unlike in colour or size, only we refer to them as one species'. He then considered the question of 'the struggle for existence . . . a phrase that one constantly hears', and concluded that:

> It is not only by structures for offence and defence that success is attained in the battle of life. Instinct, intelligence and the moral qualities are of greater importance. The race is not to the swift nor the battle to the strong. . . . In some respects of still greater value in the struggle for existence is the development of the social instinct. There are many associations or partnerships between animals, and the study of these forms is one of the most interesting and suggestive occupations that anyone can take up. (*Irish Daily Independent*, 27 December 1893: 5)

The inclusion of 'moral qualities' makes it clear that he was using animals to illustrate the idea of race and the concept of human diversity. His biosocial treatment of 'the struggle for existence' clearly signalled his alignment with Geddes and Kropotkin in their row with Huxley. He finished the article with a remarkable statement:

> I know of no other case in any museum that I have visited in Europe, America, Australia where so much philosophy is presented in so clear and concise a manner. (*Irish Daily Independent*, 27 December 1893: 5)

Haddon followed 'Rambles in the Natural Science Museum' with an equally 'philosophical' exploration of gender in 'Science and the Woman Question'. Haddon may have found writing tedious but his journalism, inspired perhaps by Caroline Haddon's provocative tracts, was anything but.

CONCLUSION

Haddon's letter to Ernest recapitulated a childhood interest in art and anticipated a preference for pictures in his ethnographic experiments in the Torres Strait and New Guinea in 1888 and 1889. The journal he kept during that expedition is remarkable as a record of patterned behaviour, a routine of exploring, drawing, photographing and collecting that often revolved around *koppa koppa* or dance. On his return to London, he tackled the problem of making these experiences meaningful to the general public as much as to fellow naturalists. He exhibited his collections, wrote articles for popular journals and gave public slideshows. He continued the experiment in the Aran Islands, discovering that even the slowest photograph handled incidents in the lives of islanders better than the fastest sketch. He adopted instantaneous photography as a method and, although that may have alleviated the tedium of writing, the cost of printing pictures was prohibitive and many of his publishing projects unravelled. His capacity as a writer comes into question, with constant references to the tedium of writing, and the contrast between *Evolution in Art* and *The Study of Man* focusses attention on Ellis as editor and his determination to get a book out of Haddon.

His journalism is, historiographically speaking, the most productive body of written work Haddon produced in the early 1890s in terms of reading his understanding of ethnology as a reformist science, but it has been overlooked by historians of anthropology. The irony here is that Stocking (1995: 105–6) presented *Evolution in Art* – the only book Haddon managed to write in this period – as convincing evidence that Haddon was an old-school biologist operating in the guise of an anthropologist. If Haddon had completed the Ellis commission and their study of anthropology had lived up to the introduction Haddon published in response to the outrage he provoked in Ipswich, he would have provided a methodological and epistemological bridge from Tylor (1971) to Radcliffe-Brown (1922) and assured his place in the history of anthropology.

He didn't, and the availability of alternative ways of making meaning was, undoubtedly, a factor. Seligman, as stated, noted 'a change in the man himself' that manifested as a fascination with the art of Oceania, and I have argued that Haddon's family's involvement in art, literature and politics predisposed him to a creative engagement with the people he met and explains his fascination with the materiality and social function of their dances. Words failed him when he tried to express this and he adopted instantaneous photography as an alternative. However, the translation of visual ethnography into anthropological knowledge hit a snag when the cost of illustration became a barrier to a form of ethnological publishing that conveyed the full sense of what he had experienced in the field. This was a dilemma, but his commitment to visual ethnology was such that he overcame the barrier of cost by adopting the magic lantern slideshow as an effective and affective method of engaging the public in a conversation about the meaning of civilization.

CHAPTER 8

THE MAGIC LANTERN

• • •

> Proceeding, Professor Haddon had a series of views shown by aid of a lime light, illustrative of the habits and manners of the natives, the way in which they existed, and the houses in which they lived. When lads sprang up to manhood, they were formally initiated into the various mysteries of the tribe.
>
> —*Daily Express*, 22 February 1890

A lime light consisted of a block of calcium oxide (lime) heated in jets of burning gas to produce 1,000 candles of light. Invented in 1825, these lights powered 'magic' lanterns, slide projectors developed in the seventeenth and eighteenth centuries. They consisted of a light source in a box fitted with a focusing lens and, in between, a rack for holding a painted glass slide mounted in a wooden frame. Lime lights entered photography in the 1850s after the Langenheim brothers invented a system for printing photographs onto glass, and slideshows became a popular form of entertainment, education and agitation in the 1870s and 1880s (see Shepard 1987; Rockett and Rockett 2011). Haddon gave his first recorded slideshow at the Royal Dublin Society on 20 February 1890. He also exhibited dancing masks, grass petticoats and other material he collected in the Torres Strait and New Guinea and sold to the Museum of Science and Art in Dublin, reversing the curatorial order – objects plus photographs and sketches – of his exhibition in the British Museum in October 1889.

The problem here is that the public nature of this aspect of Haddon's practice meant that it left few traces in anthropological archives and, when it did, the performative nature of the medium meant that few accounts of the content of slideshows survive. For instance, the Anthropological Institute recorded the following event at its meeting on 10 April 1894:

> Prof. A. C. HADDON delivered an address on 'Ethnographical Studies in the West of Ireland', illustrated with the optical lantern. (*JAI* 24 [1895]: 105)

It is difficult to find this record on the online version of the journal because the digital object identifier relates to an article on the skull of a microcephalic Hindu by R. W. Reid, and it just so happens that Haddon presented his slideshow just before Reid read his paper, which of course was published in full. The BAAS report on the Transactions of Section H in 1894 recorded a slideshow on 13 August as follows:

> 14. On the People of Western Ireland and their Mode of Life. By A. C. Haddon. (BAAS 1894: 785)

The text of this slideshow may have been based on an illustrated lecture Haddon presented to the Belfast Naturalists' Field Club in January 1893 and the club published a detailed account in its 'Proceedings' (BNFC 2,3,vi [1892–93]: 538–39), which in turn corresponds with press reports of Haddon's reading of 'The Ethnography of the Aran Islands' in Dublin the previous December. Likewise, the Folklore Society published a summary of Haddon's 1895 lecture on 'Photography and Folklore' in the minutes of a meeting chaired by Gomme. The minute consists of a brief introduction and a list of slides exhibited under various headings. These resemble the captions Haddon wrote for his 1890 slideshow on the Aran Islands, and Haddon used the photograph of Colman Thomas Faherty and Michael John O'Donnell (figure 7.2) to illustrate folklore of trees. The record states:

Folklore of Trees: Fairy thorn at Holywood, Belfast; St. Sourney's thorn, Aran (P. R. I. A., 1893, p. 830); St. Croghans's sacred Ash, Kenmare River. (FLS 6,3 (Sept. 1895): 223)

These are the exceptions that prove the rule.

Haddon's slideshows go some way to explaining why he built a library of ten thousand photographs and lantern slides over a period of three decades, and the challenge of breaking this down into a series of events that help build a chronology in terms of a methodology is well illustrated by the difficulty of finding these records. This perhaps explains why they have almost disappeared from the history of anthropology, and that illustrates a secondary problem of a historiographical nature. Elizabeth Edwards and Christopher Morton (2009: 8) have argued that disciplinary histories are written from available archives, and I enlist their argument to claim that Haddon's slideshows have been invisible to historians of anthropology. The consequence is that Haddon's principal methodology has also been invisible. What gets lost in this scenario is the *magic* of the magic lantern: how Haddon created an engaged, humanitarian ethnology.

In this chapter, I track the development of Haddon's magic lantern method through a series of slideshows on the Aran Islands presented between 1890 and 1895. Then I examine the relationship between ethnological knowledge and philosophy in terms of the transformative function of his slideshows; the magic lantern as a meaning-making device in the context of colonialism and its consequences for other civilizations. The third part considers Haddon's photography manifesto of 1899 and its revision in 1912 and presents this as evidence of Haddon's principal innovation: his long engagement with the very modern problem of ethnographic representation in the colonial era.

A METHOD

Newspapers in Dublin announced in February 1890 that Haddon would present 'Life of A Savage', the first of two public lectures on New Guinea, as part of the Royal Dublin Society's programme of afternoon lectures. The press release promised that the lectures would provide the public with 'the opportunity of forming an acquaintance with that darkest of dark continents', where Haddon

> made a large number of observations on their habits and customs, past and present. If rumour speaks correctly some very strange facts have been brought to light all of which can hardly be narrated at a popular lecture. During his eight month's residence in the Straits, some 200 photographs were taken, a selection from which will illustrate the lectures. There are photographs of the houses, canoes, occupations, and appearance of the natives. Of the latter, some are Christianised natives, others are absolute savages destitute of the amenities of civilisations. (*Daily Express*, 18 February 1890: 5)

On 22 February, the *Irish Times* published an account of the lecture under the heading 'Royal Dublin Society', and the story carried a small but significant detail. The reporter recorded that Haddon introduced the lecture as 'Life of A Savage or Native Life in New Guinea', a title that qualified the racist sensationalism of the press release and connected the slideshow to themes explored in 'Incidents in the Life of a Torres Straits Islander'. The reporter also recorded how Haddon 'briefly sketched some of the native habits, giving lime light illustrations of the former and present system of dressing among the natives, the character of their dwellings, etc.'

The slideshow became Haddon's method of choice when he returned from the Aran Islands six months later. He sent Dixon's photographs to Welch in Belfast to be processed as lantern slides and wrote a commentary titled 'The Aran Islands'. This document is held in the Haddon Library, where Aidan Baker, the Haddon Librarian, found it in 2013. It consists of two pages of handwritten text and a list of ten lantern slides (figures 8.1–8.10) manufactured from 'photographs taken by Mr. A. F. Dixon of Dublin'.

Figures 8.1–8.10. A. F. Dixon, *Untitled*, 1890. Digital scan and print of silver gelatine, glass-plate negative (Ciarán Walsh and Ciarán Rooney, 2019). The original negatives are held in the School of Medicine, Trinity College, University of Dublin. © curator.ie.

The text that accompanied these slides comprised a short introduction to the islands and a series of short captions for the slides, 804 words in total. Haddon (1890 MS, 'The Aran Islands': 2) listed the captions as follows:

(1) a class from national school held in the open air,
(2) a group of two men and a boy on the top of the ancient stone fort at Inishmaan. The men are wearing pompooties and the boy the characteristic petticoat which the small boys wear as well as girls.
(3) Wayside monuments which were erected on the land of the deceased. The earliest inscription is as follows:
>   PRAY FOR THE SO
>   UL OF RICKARD F
>   ITZPATRICK WHO
>   DTHE 9 DAY OF
>   OCTOBER ANNO
>   D 1701.

These monuments are to be seen by the side various roads on Inishmore.
(4) Granite boulder resting on the limestone which constitutes the chief part of an Aran field.
(5) Tempall Benain a very ancient tiny church 10 feet 10 inches long by 6 feet 10 inches broad, inside measurement, situated on the top of Killeany hill.
(6) Killeany church which was for a long time buried by blown sand.
(7) ~~View in the church of St~~ E. Window & altar of the Church of St. Breckan Kilmurvy.
(8) Dun Aengus, a large pre-Christian fort in a very good state of preservation, the outermost wall is surrounded by a *chevaux-de-frise* of sharp upright stones.
(9) A Cloghaun or ancient bee-hive dwelling.
(10) a somewhat similar erection made of large stone slabs.

The teacher of the 'open air' class was David O'Callaghan, the master of a primary school in Oatquarter. The 'open air' nature of the class illustrates the limits of instantaneous photography. The blurring of some of the detail indicates the slow speed of the camera lens and photographic negative and this would have made an indoor shot impossible. 'Pompooties' referred to the *brogaí úrleathair* (rawhide footwear) the islanders wore and the 'erection made of large stone slabs' is a wedge tomb in Eochaill that dates from 2300 to 2000 BCE. It is known locally as *Leaba Dhiarmaide agus Ghrainne* (Diarmaid and Grainne's Bed) and Tim Robinson (1997: 226–35) wrote a description of the site that resonates with Haddon's own very minimalist description of 'ruin hunting and photographing' (SS *Harlequin* Journal: 4) in the islands in 1891, probably in the company of O'Callaghan.

The fact that Haddon opened this slideshow with a photograph of O'Callaghan teaching is interesting. O'Callaghan sent Haddon an account of the operation of the 'Evil Eye' curse in May 1891. Haddon also took a photograph of O'Callaghan and Browne standing beside the Church of the Four Comely Ones on Inishmore in 1892, which is close to the wedge tomb featured in the last slide. It would appear that O'Callaghan acted as Haddon's guide between 1890 and 1892, and this is important in relation to Haddon's warning about the threat of famine in his introduction, a sentence that I have argued marked Haddon as a Home Rule sympathizer. Tim Robinson included a brief biography of O'Callaghan in *Stones of Aran: Labyrinth* (1997: 280–84). He noted that O'Callaghan was involved with Patrick Pearse, one of the leaders of the uprising in 1916, in organizing the first meeting of the Gaelic League in the islands in 1898, and Robinson developed this theme by quoting a description (ibid.: 282) of the teacher that Tom O'Flaherty, one of his pupils, wrote in 1934:

> He was no cheap jingo nationalist of the type who froths at the mouth at the mention of an Englishman; but he hated British Imperialism with all its works and pomps. He was the first Sinn Féiner in the island and had no difficulty in making one of me. (Flaherty 1934: 158)

Arthur Griffith founded Sinn Féin in 1905, but the reference is relevant because it establishes that Haddon's guide to the Aran Islands was a cultural nationalist and anti-imperial activist.

Thus, the discovery of the commentary in 2013 utterly disrupted the common sense that Haddon had gone to the islands in 1892 merely to measure skulls, and this triggered a second review of Haddon's papers and photographic collections using Browne's photograph albums as a guide. The search switched to TCD and the negatives of Dixon's photographs were found in a box on a shelf in a storage space under the old anatomy theatre, in circumstances that suggested that they had been put there after Welch processed them in 1890. This made it possible to reconstruct the slideshow, although the circumstances of its performance remained unclear, and a search of institutional and online newspaper archives revealed that Haddon presented six slideshows on the Aran Islands between 1890 and 1895. There may have been more, but records have been found for the following:

- 1890 Date and venue unknown: 'The Aran Islands'.
  October: 'Aran Islands'. Conferring Day *Conversazione*, Royal College of Science, Dublin.
- 1893 January: 'Ethnographical Studies in the West of Ireland'. Belfast Naturalists' Field Club, Belfast.
- 1894 April: 'Ethnographical Studies in the West of Ireland'. Anthropological Institute, London.
  August: 'On the People of Western Ireland and their Mode of Life'. BAAS Section H – Anthropology, Oxford.
- 1895 March: 'The Western Isles of Ireland / On the People of Western Ireland and their Mode of Life'. Temperance Hall in Hexham, near Newcastle upon Tyne.

The reading of 'The Ethnography of Aran Islands, County Galway' at the Royal Irish Academy in December 1892 may have been illustrated by slides along the lines of the slideshow in Belfast the following month, but there was no reference to use of a lime light in press reports.

Before the discovery of Browne's albums in 2009, the plates in 'The Ethnography of the Aran Islands' were the only readily available record of Haddon's use of photography in an ethnographic setting in Ireland. They appeared at first glance to confirm a project of craniology through photography, the static representation of the 'motionless anthropometric body' that Alison Griffiths (1996: 32) identified as a general feature of photography in imperial anthropology and, specifically, the 'the repetitive, aesthetically dull pattern of the conventions of anthropological portraits' that Justin Carville (2011: 106) discerned in the 'The Ethnography of the Aran Islands'. The photograph of Martin Faherty and the two women reproduced in Plate XIII was exceptional and, working back from Haddon's revision of the section on photography in *Notes and Queries on Anthropology* in 1899, its inclusion was clearly intended to distinguish between instantaneous photography and the anatomical portraits required by physical anthropologists. The discovery of the 1890 slideshow material showed that this was more typical of the instantaneous photographs taken in 1890, and, therefore, the anthropometric framing of the other photographs became a greater anomaly in terms of Haddon's photo-ethnographic method in general.

This anomaly is even more obvious in newspaper reports of the reading of 'The Ethnography of the Aran Islands' in December 1892. The *Irish Times* published an article on 'Royal Irish Academy' on 13 December in which the correspondent glided past the part where Haddon 'enumerated numerous traits in the character of the people' and proceeded to give a snapshot of life on the islands. The emphasis on social and cultural aspects of life in the islands is even more evident in a report of the slideshow Haddon presented to members of the Belfast Naturalists' Field Club four weeks later. The *Irish News and Belfast Morning News* published a report on 'The Belfast Naturalists' Field Club' on 7 January 1893 in which the journalist describes how, 'With the aid of lime light illustrations' Haddon 'gave a very graphic and picturesque account of the islands and the interesting people who inhabit them, dwelling particularly on their folklore and ancient beliefs'. This report bears a strong similarity to Haddon's article on 'The Aran Islands, County Galway: A Study in Irish Ethnography', which the *Irish Naturalist* published in December 1893, and it could be that this was written as the commentary for the slideshow in Belfast. The second paragraph encouraged people to get involved in 'the study of our fellow-country men, whether from an *anthropological* or *sociological* point of view' (Haddon 1893a: 303, emphasis added), and that is precisely what the organizers of the meeting in Belfast had asked Haddon to do.

Reading these reports of the Dublin reading and Belfast slideshow clarified two things. One, Haddon's version of the ethnographic survey of the Aran Islands entered the public domain primarily as an ethnological account in the form of a slideshow. Two, this gap widened and became more obviously political in slideshows presented at the Anthropological Institute in April 1894 and Section H in August 1894, which Haddon repeated in Hexham in March 1895 against a backdrop of evictions in the Aran Islands. The political sensitivity of Haddon's slideshows is manifest in a change of title from 'Ethnographical Studies in the West of Ireland' in April to 'The Western Isles of Ireland: On the People of Western Ireland and their Mode of Life' in August, and a timeline for 1895 (Figure 8.11) places that change in a very political context.

In January and February, evictions in the Aran Islands and the threat of famine in the south-west generated a heated debate in

Figure 8.11. 1895: a timeline. © curator.ie.

	Jan	Feb	Mar	Apr	May	Jun	Jul	Aug	Sept	Oct	Nov	Dec
Anthrop.	Anthrop. Institute Brabrook v Topinard	Browne reads Ethnography of Mullet / Inishkea / describes hand camera						Huxley Dies		Browne Ethnographic survey Ballycroy hand camera used		
Haddon	Modern Relics Olden Time, Belfast; Evolution in Art Havelock Ellis (ed.)		Western Isles Hexham	Photography & Folklore FLS				Barley Survey; Invites Hyde to Aran	Union of Field Clubs Aran; RSAI Aran	Summer Meeting Edinburgh No. 9 Geddes Demolins Haddon & Reclus	BAAS Ipswich Race Debate; Survey Oceania	The Study of Anthropology (+ Ellis)
	47 evictions Aran Islands; Anarchist-Communism meeting Glasgow	Widespread newspaper reports of distress in west & southwest	French amnesty & anarchist "invasion" of London					General Election Home Rule parties defeated on Anarchy; Galway Clifden Raiway opens	Sixth Int Geographical Congress London Reclus lectures; Lumieres invent cinematograph	G. Balfour "Killing Home Rule with Kindness" Speech Leeds		First Lumiere cinema show

the press. Haddon presented his lecture on the 'Western Isles' in Hexham in March and the *Evening Herald* published a summary of 'The Ethnography of the Aran Islands' the day after. The *Freeman's Journal* reported that the evictions were suspended on 11 April, leaving 152 persons homeless. The *Kerry Weekly Reporter* reprinted the *Evening Herald* article in May. Huxley died in June and Haddon asked Douglas Hyde, one of the founders of the Gaelic League, to join him in an excursion to the Aran Islands. In July, a Conservative and Unionist alliance defeated the Liberal and Nationalist alliance in a general election that was, in effect, another referendum on Home Rule. Haddon returned to the Aran Islands with the Irish Field Club Union (see Praeger 1949: 190–91) and the Royal Society of Antiquaries of Ireland. In August, Haddon joined Geddes, Reclus and Demolin at the Summer Meeting of Art and Science in Edinburgh. In September, he attended Section H in Ipswich and opened his critique of British imperialism with a statement sympathetic to the cause of Home Rule in Ireland. Finally, two events in October and November captured the extremes of that debate. Haddon published 'The Study of Anthropology' in the *University Extension Journal* and Gerald Balfour coined the phrase 'killing Home Rule with kindness' at a post-election constituency event in Leeds.

Clearly, Haddon had become the go-to person for information on the islanders and their mode of life as evictions made the islands a focus of debate about Home Rule in the oldest colony in a general election year. His speech in Ipswich left no doubt as to where his sympathies lay. He was not a nationalist, however. He was an outspoken critic of imperialism and, as such, made common cause with nativists like Chalmers and nationalists like Banim and O'Callaghan. Also noteworthy in this context was his attempt to recruit Denny Lane as a folklore collector. Lane was a Young Irelander who was interned after an ill-fated attempt at revolution in 1848. Haddon met Lane's son Daniel during the fishing survey of 1890 and subsequent correspondence between them tells us that Haddon tried to recruit his father and settled for his son instead (FLS 4,3 [September 1893]: 349–64). Messrs Denny Lane were honourably mentioned in a report the *Cork Constitu-*

tion published on 30 November 1894 about a lecture Hyde gave on 'Irish Folk-lore'. The reporter quoted Hyde as saying that 'the natives of the wilder parts along the coast' had little contact with 'that rather grimy thing called civilisation [and] should have preserved among themselves the most important and interesting stock of folk-lore in Western Europe', a line of argument that could only have come from Haddon. All of these connections point to nationalism – political and cultural – as a factor in the roll-out of his slideshows, but Haddon's first slideshow on 'Native Life in New Guinea' suggests that he was more of an idealist, that his anti-imperialism was more philosophical than political.

A PHILOSOPHY

The Royal Dublin Society promised the public that 'Life of A Savage' would take them on a journey into the 'darkest of dark continents', guided by a scientist who had lived among absolute savages for eight months. It tantalized the reader with rumours of strange customs and habits and, even more so, with the fact that Haddon had taken some two hundred photographs. The tone of the press release resembled an advertisement in the *Freeman's Journal* in 1886 for an exhibition at Dan Lowry's Theatre of a small group of San people whom it described as 'African Earthmen. . . . The very lowest form of the human race, the appearance of these creatures is very interesting.' As stated, Haddon changed the title to 'Native Life in New Guinea' and set out to humanize the object of public curiosity, with the intention of forcing his audience to consider racism and its consequences. Kropotkin's influence has been discussed and the influence of Freemasonry mentioned in passing. The latter is considered here in more detail in the context of 'Papuan Dances', which Haddon wrote as a follow-up to 'Incidents in the Life of a Torres Strait Islander' and Bettany published in the July to December 1890 edition of *Lippincott's Monthly Magazine*.

'Papuan Dances' is the first iteration in a popular journal of Haddon's fascination with dance, which was such a striking feature of the journal he kept during the 1888 expedition and, ten years later, became the subject of an experiment in the new art of cinema. He opened 'Papuan Dances' with the statement that 'few human customs have so varied a history as dancing' and drew the reader's attention to a paradox that generated the purpose of the article:

> This old association of dancing with religion is well known, but as the spirit of reverence increased so the dancing diminished. (Haddon 1890c: 386)

'Diminished' meant that the connection between dance and religion was broken and modern dance had drifted into a simplicity and sensuous physicality that threatened older forms in country villages, which maintained a connection, however degraded, with seasonal festivals that once had a religious significance. Remembering that connection was the job of the folklorist and Haddon described their work as follows:

> There is an immense amount of information concerning past and present ceremonial and festive processions and dances scattered up and down in literature. But it is to savage people that we must turn for suggestion as to the probable significance of many of them. The conservatism of the savage is the sheet anchor of the inquirer into folk-lore. (Haddon 1890c: 386)

It bears repeating that turning to 'savage people' reiterates Kropotkin's proposition that the study of social organization proceeds from simple to complex societies, and Ellis used his introduction to *The New Spirit* to claim that simpler societies acted as lamps to reformists in relation to gender equality (Ellis 1890: 9). Accordingly, Haddon set out two changes in the orientation of the study of 'savage people' and their customs. The first was that 'conservatism' replaces primitivism, and that shifts the basis of inquiry into sociology where, according to my reading of the 'The Study of Anthropology', the place-work-folk formula that

Geddes adapted from Le Play provided a method. The second was a shift from 'literature' to an engagement with the 'savage people', and Haddon takes the reader into the field with his description of witnessing 'processions in connection with fishing expeditions, war dances to celebrate victory; and purely festival dances' performed and explained by the Papuans themselves. He noted that:

> When the history of the evolution of the quadrilles or country dances shall have been written, their origin will be found to be very little different from that of the savages, and both find their explanations in imitations of every-day life. (Haddon 1890c: 389)

Haddon closed the article with the following statement:

> Outsiders are too apt to think lightly of rites the meaning of which they are ignorant, and to jest at the trappings of a ritual when they do not possess a key to the symbolism intended to be thereby conveyed. Only those who have been brought up in a faith can feel the emotions of sanctity which an ancient ceremonial calls forth, hallowed as it is by the associations of past generations. It is doubtful whether there is a single race of men to whom such feelings are unknown and they may be found to be strongly developed where least expected, so great is the religious solidarity of the human race underlying all superficial differences. (Haddon 1890c: 391)

Reading this, it is impossible to avoid making a connection with Haddon's initiation into Freemasonry immediately prior to his departure for Oceania. Indeed, the journey from London to the Torres Strait re-enacted the symbolic journey in his initiation from West to East and, with the ritual removal of a blindfold in a secret, sacred space marked by the totem-like pillars of Boaz and Jachin, from ignorance into knowledge. Haddon completed this journey when he achieved the rank of Worshipful Master in 1918, and his initiation in 1888 may explain his fascination with ceremonies associated with the Malu cult that is such a feature of *Head-Hunters: Black, White, and Brown* (Haddon 1901a: 42–52). He described the general features of initiation ceremonies in *Head-Hunters*:

> The lads are secluded in a tabooed spot in the bush, access to which is strictly prohibited to any non-initiated person. Sacred emblems are frequently shown to the lads; these are often masked men who symbolise some legendary or mystical person or event.... whatever may be done, or shown, or told to the lads is to be kept secret by them ... they are instructed in the moral code, social customs, and sacred legends of the community, and, in fact, all that it behoves a 'man' to know. (ibid.: 42–43)

Space did not allow a description of initiation ceremonies in 'Papuan Dances' and Haddon returned to the topic in 1893 with 'Secular and Ceremonial Dances of the Torres Straits Islanders' in *Internationales Archiv für Ethnographie*. This time the article was illustrated with chromolithographic reproductions of paintings that Haddon's brother based on Haddon's sketches and photographs.

Dance and art were inseparable in this phase of Haddon's work. He was involved in a parallel investigation of art that was closely connected to dance through masks and other forms of ornament. He presented 'A Study of Savage Art' as a third afternoon lecture at the Royal Dublin Society in February 1891. He persuaded Ellis to run with a book on the savage origins of art in May, and, in June, three days before the Dublin Anthropometric Laboratory opened, the Royal Irish Academy provided a Science Grant of £50 to 'to assist him in preparing a Report on Savage Art' (RIA [1887–93]: 87). There was no reference to evolution in any of the records consulted. The *Freeman's Journal* published a short report and described the lecture on 'Savage Art' as follows:

The lecture, which was illustrated by limelight, traced the development of art amongst the inhabitants of British New Guinea from the earliest designs from human and animal models. (*Freeman's Journal*, 21 February 1891: 5)

That suggests to me that Ellis came up with the title *Evolution in Art* to fit in with other works in the Contemporary Science Series, in which evolution was a theme and the word itself functioned as a metonym for a zeitgeist of reconstruction. However, in 1891, Haddon told Alice Balfour about his 'new method of studying art from a biological standpoint of view' (SS *Harlequin* Journal: 7) and the organic logic of evolution – migration, adaptation, selection and variation – underpinned his theory of progression from mimesis to abstraction, a theory which was widely accepted until the 1940s.

Haddon's preoccupation with dance and art was problematic in terms of positioning himself within organised anthropology. Macalister described 'Secular and Ceremonial Dances of the Torres Straits Islanders' as a 'beautifully-illustrated monograph' (*JAI* 23 [1894]: 404) but thought Haddon's familiarity with savage people belonged to the domain of the philosophical anthropologist (ibid.: 412–14). He did not intend it as a compliment, although Haddon and his friends would have agreed with the label. Grenville Cole, a colleague at the Royal College of Science, wrote to Haddon on 8 July 1901 and informed his friend that he thought him irreplaceable in Dublin because of 'his enthusiasm for the moral side of the natural sciences'. Shortly before he left, Haddon admitted to Myers in 1901 that he had need 'for all my philosophy' after he failed to secure the University Lectureship in Anthropology in Cambridge and university managers offered him a poorly paid alternative:

> It as a truism but true – to have to have your life you must lose it. The reading of a book of ~~science~~ √ nature in this as in so many other points confirm the essential statements made by the religious teachers of all ages. The facts of existence are the same – the interpretation of them ~~may~~ varies. I cer-

tainly have need for all my philosophy as I have had many disappointments in life & now have so much to discourage me. (Haddon to Myers, 27 January 1901)

Starting at the end, the immediate disappointment was the loss of the aforementioned job, and I add to the list of 'many disappointments' the loss of his job on the fisheries survey, his removal from the role of lead ethnographer on the Irish Ethnographic Survey, Huxley's rejection of his scheme for a Bureau of Ethnology and, finally, the failure of the ethnographic survey of the UK because the idea behind it – anthropology in its widest aspect – was too dangerous to an anthropology shaped by the restrictive doctrine of Dr Topinard. It is hardly surprising that he confided in Quiggin (1942: 114) that he felt he was not wanted in Dublin or Cambridge.

Regarding the letter and what it tells us about the nature of his philosophy, the substitution of 'science' with 'nature' is far more interesting, and one must consider whether Haddon ever thought of anthropology as a science; whether he thought of anthropology as the study of human nature in action and in thought. His study of the materiality and meaning of dance was, in effect, the study of the 'essential statements made by the religious teachers of all ages', and that defined the job 'of the inquirer into folk-lore' as one of reconnecting attenuated modern forms with ancestral knowledges that revealed the original environmental impulse that shaped a motif or movement. Accordingly, anthropology in its widest aspect was not a methodological but a philosophical proposition, and that was the substance of the revelation described in the closing paragraph of 'Papuan Dances'. That brings us back to its textual twin, 'Incidents in the Life of a Torres Straits Islander', and the influence of Kropotkin. In his 1910 *History of Anthropology*, Haddon identified two elements that had modernized anthropology. The second was, as stated, religious and political controversies generated by dangerous ideas. The first, however, was geography, and I read that as an acknowledgement of the importance of (a) the anti-racism role Kropotkin assigned to geography and (b) the place-work-folk formula Geddes adapted from Le Play. That also makes one wonder whether

Haddon ever thought of himself as a scientist or, instead, thought of anthropology as the human half of geography, as opposed to Huxley's construction of anthropology as the human half of zoology (Huxley 1861: 198–99). After all, it was Haddon's fascination with the pasturages and hoary ruins of the Aran Islands that so antagonized Green (RDS 127 [1890]: 53) that he ended Haddon's career as a marine biologist.

The logical conclusion of this argument is that Haddon was, as Macalister stated in 1894, a philosopher rather than a scientist, and I propose that his philosophy may have been grounded in the spiritual journey he commenced with his initiation into Freemasonry in 1889, but also embraced his humanitarian heritage, anarchist geography and a reconstruction zeitgeist that came with his initiation into the anarcho-utopian network assembled by Geddes and Ellis. In this context, Haddon's early journalism becomes a serialized manifesto on the philosophy of anthropology, and this was matched step by step by a series of formal innovations that culminated in 1899 in a long-forgotten manifesto on photo-ethnography.

A MANIFESTO

Haddon translated the text of 'Incidents in the Life of a Torres Straits Islander' into the slideshow 'Native Life in New Guinea' in 1890 and, eight years later, repeated the exercise when he translated 'Secular and Ceremonial Dances of the Torres Straits Islanders' into two short films shot on location. The evolution of his philosophy and technical innovation were flipsides of the same process, which at its core was an evangelical approach to conversion through witness, revelation and, crucially, empathy with the victims of imperialism at a time of intense instability in the oldest colony. Public reaction to his speech in Ipswich reveals how disruptive of orthodox anthropology his philosophy was, and I now consider the other side of that process, the photo-ethnographic method that dominated his practice in the 1890s.

Haddon's decision to take a camera with him on his first expedition to the Torres Strait and New Guinea marked the beginning of a relentless experimentation in ethnographic form. Other milestones include the discovery of instantaneous photography in the Aran Islands in 1890, the performance of a slideshow as an alternative to a reading of 'The Ethnography of the Aran Islands' in 1893, and his experiments in colour photography and the art of cinema in the Torres Strait in 1898. At some stage in the process, he established a partnership with Charles Hercules Read, keeper of the ethnographic collections at the British Museum and editor of the ethnographic section of *Notes and Queries on Anthropology*. Haddon persuaded Read to include his photo-ethnographic method in a revised, third edition issued in 1899, and this, I propose, constitutes a long-forgotten manifesto that might have marked the beginning of the history of visual anthropology if more attention was paid to photography as a form of ethnography.

Notes and Queries on Anthropology appeared in six editions between 1874 and 1951, and the first four – 1874, 1892, 1899 and 1912 – have been used by historians as an index of the methodological and theoretical changes that led to the emergence of a recognizably 'modern' form of anthropology in the 1920s. The 1912 edition, according to Stocking (1995: 113, 121), constituted a new departure that was built around 'a general account of method' that Rivers wrote for Part III – Sociology (N&QA 1912: 108–80). Stocking represented this as a shift in power from the 'old guard' of organized science to the 'young Turks' of an emerging academic discipline, with a corresponding shift from (a) evolutionism to diffusionism as the primary logic of enquiry and (b) from systematic surveys by amateurs to empirical fieldwork by trained scientists. A slightly revised edition of Haddon's manifesto made the cut as an appendix, and this can best be explained by looking at its place in the 1899 edition.

Stocking (1995: 120) described this edition as 'little more than a reprint' of the 1892 edition, and that was a mistake. Granted, the editors Garson and Read (N&QA 1899: iii) stated that 'The alterations have not, however, required to be so extensive, especially in the first part, as on the previous occasion'. Haddon, however, rewrote the section on photography and, as the only major revision, this constituted the reason for a new edition, and it was much more than a methodological adjustment. Haddon anticipated the post-evolutionist trend in the 1912 edition by making the case for photography as form of anthropology in its widest aspect, in opposition to photography as an instrument of anthropology in its most restricted sense. Read wrote a prefatory note that set up Haddon's arguments as follows:

> The best plan seems to be to devote as much time as possible to the photographic camera or to making careful drawings, for by these means the traveller is dealing with facts about which there can be no question, and the record thus obtained may be elucidated by subsequent inquirers on the same spot. (N&QA 1899: 87)

Haddon developed this argument in the section on photography and, limited by space, offered a few hints on what that would mean in relation to the 'class of photographs' taken:

> A few views of characteristic scenery are sufficient, merely pretty bits need not be taken nor views that do not teach anything. Every photograph should be taken for a definite purpose, and it is generally possible to secure views that illustrate several points. ... With regard to portraits, a certain number of types should always be taken as large as possible full face and square side view; ... Some unarranged groups should be taken instantaneously so as to get perfectly natural attitudes, ... It is important to get photographs of various stages of a ceremony or the making of any object. Pictures of the way in which tools and implements are held, and of the stages of manufacture are more valuable than tedious verbal descriptions. The common actions of daily life should not be neglected ... (N&QA 1899: 238–40)

The reference to 'full face and square side view' effectively summarized the advice Haddon got from Flower in 1890. However, this was qualified by requiring 'views that illustrate several points', and, as argued earlier, Haddon demonstrated this in 'Photography and Folklore' with a photograph he took in the Aran Islands in 1892 using Flower's anthropometric formula, but framed it in a way that illustrated the folklore of trees.

Elsewhere he added hints as to the 'method of procedure', and these include the anthropometric procedure that Galton devised for the ethnographic survey of the UK (BAAS [1894]: 642–43). He finished the piece with the following advice: 'Always seize the first opportunity of photographing' (N&QA 1899: 240). Garson added additional technical notes and set out a much more rigorous version of Galton's technique in a section titled 'Photographing Natives' (ibid.: 244–46); this edition is remarkable for the addition of English and French measuring scales to the cover. Haddon, however, stated a preference for instantaneous rather than anthropometric portraits:

> Some portraits should be three-quarter view or in a position that gives a more pleasing picture than the stiff portraits required by the *student* (N&QA 1899: 239, emphasis added)

Haddon underscored the point with a warning that 'it must never be forgotten that when a native is posed for photography, he unconsciously becomes rigid and the delicate play of limbs is lost'. This sounds a little odd unless one considers the following instruction that Flinders Petrie issued to ethnographers in the 1892 edition:

> In photographing groups, always focus before the natives are placed in position; this can readily be done by placing an object where they will afterwards be made to stand. (N&QA 1892: 238)

Haddon's alternative method can be seen in an early form in the 1890 slideshow on the Aran Islands and in a more thorough ethnographic arrangement in the album Browne compiled of photographs taken in the Aran Islands between 1890 and 1892 (figure 6.3), which he organized under Coastline and Surface, The People, and Antiquities. This contrasted with the emphasis on anthropometric portraiture in the 'The Ethnography of the Aran Islands', even if some of these photographs illustrated several points of interest and the photograph of Michael Faherty and the two women was a masterclass in politically aware instantaneous photography.

Haddon was more explicit about the distinction between 'stiff' and 'instantaneous' portraits in the 1912 edition. He described Galton's procedure, although he did not name it as such, and this suggests that it had become standard practice. Haddon then advised readers as follows:

> For further details as to photographs intended for anthropometric purposes, or for precise comparison of racial characteristics, consult the Report of the British Association Anthropometric Committee on Investigation in the British Isles. (N&QA 1912: 270)

The manual of anthropometric methods that Garson wrote in 1899 had been removed and the revised edition of Haddon's entry contained a small but very significant change in the wording of his earlier recommendation:

> Besides the stiff portraits required by the *anatomist*, some portraits should be taken in three-quarter view or in any position that gives a more natural and characteristic pose. Some unarranged groups should be taken instantaneously ... (N&QA 1912: 270, emphasis added)

It is not clear how many of the changes were recommended by Haddon or inserted by editor J. Linton Myres, and in a sense, this is irrelevant because the overall effect replicates the separation between 'instantaneous' ethnology and 'stiff' anthropology in the 1899 edition.

Haddon's expedition to Papua in 1914 offers an interesting perspective on this aspect of his method, especially his adoption of new technologies that made instantaneous photography possible. The Percy Sladen Trust Expedition to Papua was a three-month exploration of a territory that Joshua Bell (2009: 152) described as 'widely regarded as one of the last vestiges of humanity's disappearing Stone Age'. Haddon employed his daughter Kathleen, a zoologist, as the expedition photographer. She was, according to Haddon, an experienced traveller who was prepared to 'rough it' (ibid.: 150). She used a Vest Pocket Kodak camera first introduced the year before to make an instantaneous record – often working alone – of daily actions in villages they visited, or, as she wrote in an article in *Life* in 1929, when it was inadvisable to use a stand camera for scientific purposes (ibid.: 44–45; Kathleen Haddon 1929). The hint of how dangerous such fieldwork could be is obvious, but it should also be noted that Haddon warned ethnographers that posing subjects and fumbling with camera equipment was fatal to the social documentary effect required by ethnographers (N&QA 1899: 240; N&QA 1912: 270). As such, Kathleen Haddon filled the role Dixon played in the Aran Islands in 1890 and Anthony Wilkins in the 1898 expedition to the Torres Strait. Thus, the Percy Sladen Trust Expedition illustrates how the lessons learned in 1890 influenced Haddon's practice thereafter, especially his preference for image over text. Haddon's original plan for the 1914 expedition resembles a reworked version of Anton Dohrn's 1885 model of a floating zoological laboratory, except that it was staffed by a photographer, an artist (if possible) and at least two stenographers or typists – a line-up designed to relieve the investigators of the tedium of writing up oral reports or rough fieldnotes (see Edwards 1910: 221–23; Haddon 1906: 157–58).

If there is little here that looks like a methodological innovation, let alone a theoretical breakthrough, then consider this. As stated, Read prefaced Haddon's manifesto with a recommendation that ethnographers prioritize sketches and photography. Margaret Mead made the same argument in 1975 and painted a picture of criminal neglect by a discipline that had become trapped in tradition and persevered with

> hopelessly inadequate note-taking of an earlier age, while the behaviour that film could have caught and preserved for centuries (preserved for the joy of the descendants of those who dance a ritual for the last time and for the illumination of future generations of human scientists) disappears – disappears right in front of everybody's eyes. (Mead 1995: 4–5)

Haddon would have appreciated the symbolism of 'illumination' and he witnessed the 'joy of descendants' when he presented a slideshow in the Torres Strait in 1898 of photographs taken ten years earlier (Haddon 1898–99 Torres Strait and New Guinea Journal: 64). Their agreement on the importance of recording a ritual danced for the last time has been discussed, and this is where the full effect of Haddon's formal innovation can be seen in the 1912 edition of *Notes and Queries on Anthropology*. Cecil Sharp, author of the section dealing with dance, recommended that ethnographers should take photographs and 'if possible use the cinematograph in conjunction with the phonograph [to] record the important movement of the dance, and the costumes' (N&QA 1912: 216, 226). Haddon repeated this advice in relation to the making of objects and performance of ceremonies (ibid.: 271) and this registers a shift from serial photography to cinematography with audio recording, which Haddon experimented with during the 1898 expedition, the most likely source of Sharp's recommendation.

Elizabeth Edwards, one of the most prolific writers on the relationship between photography and anthropology, argued that Mead's approach to ethnographic film was later characterized as a form of 'documentary certainty and representational nirvana'

(Edwards 2015: 236–39) that was swept aside in the 1980s and 1990s in a 'much-cited crisis of representation and the growing ferment of cultural politics'. That may undermine the value of the link between Haddon and Mead as a token of modernism and, to counter that, I propose that 'Native Life in New Guinea' and the slideshows that followed represent a critical engagement with the problem of ethnographic representation in a colonial context. It is difficult to see this in Haddon's manifesto alone, but there is a trail of epistemological breadcrumbs that begins with 'Incidents in the Life of a Torres Strait Islander' and runs through 'Native Life in New Guinea', all six slideshows about the Aran Islands and *Notes and Queries on Anthropology* in 1899 and 1912. Granted, Haddon's manifesto may lack theoretical density and the language may be a little odd by today's standards, but it stands as a statement of a theory of representation that survived the cull of evolutionist thought and practice – the biological doctrines of Huxley and Topinard – in the 1912 edition, fabled to be the version Malinowski took with him to the Trobriand Islands. It should be noted here that the idea of evolution continued to shape scientific thinking in the emerging fields of social science. The popularity of eugenics is a case in point (Renwick 2012: 174). The popularity of Haddon's theory of the evolution of art is another, and that orthodoxy makes Haddon's unorthodox photo-ethnographic experimentation all the more remarkable.

CONCLUSION

To summarize, Haddon developed a distinct methodology that can be tracked through slideshows presented between 1890 and 1895. These constituted a form of performed ethnography that visualized a philosophical quest for ethnological knowledge as part of more general anti-imperial and social reform movements. His investigation of secular and ceremonial dances pushed the study of humans beyond biology and into the realm of philosophy and art. New ways of generating ethnological knowledge required new forms of fieldwork, and Haddon summarized a decade of experimentation in the ethnographers' manual in 1899, addressing problems of representation that Mead revived in 1975.

The magic lantern is employed here as a conspicuous metaphor for transformation through enlightenment, and my reading of Haddon suggests that this is why he liked the medium, as much as he disliked writing. Haddon may have started out reading Kropotkin, but Freemasonry was an overriding influence, and both shaped his formation as a philosophical anthropologist. The closing statement in 'Papuan Dances' resonates with Ellis's (1890: 9) claim that the light shed by 'survivals' illuminated the path of social progress. Add to this the reconstruction zeitgeist that Haddon noted in the Contemporary Science Series, and the line-up at the Summer Meeting of Art and Science in 1895 indicates that anarchism and reconstructionism were interwoven influences that meshed with a family tradition of religious nonconformism and humanitarian activism. His speech in Ipswich one month later manifested in unequivocal terms a commitment to human rights overseas, which I have described as a heritage on the basis of John Haddon and Elizabeth Cort's involvement in the movement to abolish slavery in the 1830s.

Haddon's experience of Papuan dances forced him to consider the nature and function of his own faith, and that triggered a switch, influenced by his grandfather's latitudinarian attitude, from an old-school preoccupation with differences to a philosophical quest for resemblances that drew on art and dance as reservoirs of ancestral knowledge. To understand the symbolism of dance he had to discover the savage within, and to become an ethnologist he had to become that savage, albeit a very modern and English version of that savage. Being an ethnologist meant capturing the actions, ideas and things that manifested ancestral knowledges in the common actions of daily life and using this knowledge to engage the public with the essential unity of humankind and the dreadful consequences of colonialism. As an ethnographer he strove to capture the full *affect* of a ritual danced for the last time using a range of representational strategies. His adoption of cinematography and phonography in 1898 marked the culmination of a relentless programme of formal experimentation, and that is sufficient to consider Haddon a modernizer, if not a modernist, despite his rough words and an obvious lack of theoretical density in his texts. None of this earned him a place in the history of 'modern' anthropology, and the next chapter considers that conundrum.

Figure 9.1. A. C. Haddon, *The Dance of the Zogo Le*, 1898. Digital scan of a still from the short film that Haddon made of the dance of the Malu Zogo-Le on the island of Mer (Murray), Torres Strait. Permission of National Film and Sound Archive of Australia.

CHAPTER 9

THE LAST DANCE

● ● ●

A phonograph record was played simultaneously with the exhibition of a dance by means of a cinematograph, and the result was a very successful and vivid representation of a custom of savagery. With life-like fidelity three natives in palm-leaf costumes, and disguised with hideous marks, were seen gyrating amid a luxuriant tropical growth, while the other machine supplied the rhythmic sinister sounds that seemed to be the fitting accompaniment of the menacing disguise with which the dancers disfigured themselves.
—*The Optical Lantern and Cinematograph Journal*, 15 January 1906

This anonymous review of Haddon's screening in Cambridge of his short film of the last dance of the Malu Zogo-Le appeared in the *Optical Lantern and Cinematograph Journal*, first published in London in November 1904 as a trade magazine for the emerging field of commercial cinema in Britain. A change of title to *Kinematograph and Lantern Weekly* in 1907 registered a shift from the optical lantern to cinema, and *Lantern Weekly* was dropped altogether in 1919. The British Newspaper Archive uploaded scans of the magazine in October 2020 and there are other reports of an earlier screening at the Anthropological Institute in February 1905. *The Field* ran this story on 18 February as 'The Anthropological Institute' and reported that it was 'the first instance moving pictures have been used to illustrate the customs of savage races before the members of a scientific society'. The

Daily Telegraph reported it as 'the first occasion on which the cinematograph has been employed for the purpose of anthropological research'. This journalist recorded that Haddon

> exhibited a series of secular and sacred dances by natives of the Torres Straits. Some dirges and songs which accompany these performances were contributed by Dr. Myers to the beating of a native drum. (*Daily Telegraph*, 18 February 1905: 10)

As with Haddon's slideshow, a record of the screening was harder to find in institutional archives.

The Anthropological Institute recorded the 1905 event under 'Miscellanea' and the minute states:

> Dr. A. C. HADDON, F.R.S., exhibited a number of lantern slides and cinematograph films illustrative of the ethnography and dances of New Guinea and the Torres Straits; and Dr. C. S. MYERS sang a number of native songs, accompanying himself on the drum. The exhibit was discussed by Messrs. DURAND, TABOR, GOMME and RAY, and Dr. HADDON replied. Mr. E. B. HADDON read a paper on 'The Dog-motive in Bornean Design' (p. 113), illustrated by lantern slides and specimens. Dr. HADDON added a few remarks. Questions were asked by Messrs. GOMME and KINGSTON. (*JAI* 35 [1905]: 435–37, original formatting)

The appearance of Ernest Haddon is noted, as is the topic of his paper, which recalls the early piece his father wrote on Greek Fret that Seligman thought registered the beginning of an interest in art. Likewise, the presence of Gomme attests to an enduring partnership in the modernization of the collection and study of folklore that began in the west of Ireland in 1890. That phase of Haddon's project culminated in the 'Photography and Folklore' slideshow in 1895 and, ten years later, Haddon's demonstration of the 'vivid representation of a custom' also registered a shift from the 'magic' lantern to the cinematograph, although, as the tone of the review in the *Optical Lantern and Cinematograph Journal* attests, it had lost none of its 'magic'.

The remarkable thing about the Institute's record, however, is the lack of reference to that 'magic' or the first use of a cinematograph in the context of ethnography or science in general; as recorded in the press. This oversight, along with the 'miscellanea' tag, contrasts sharply with the excitement in the emerging business of cinema reviewing one year later. This corroborates Mead's criticism in 1975 of the criminal neglect by anthropologists and ethnologists of these technologies as their disciplines took shape. That begs the following question: what did Haddon's use of strikingly modern technology mean within organized anthropology in the last decade of the nineteenth century and the first decade of the twentieth?

In previous chapters, I reconstructed Haddon's ethnology as a philosophical and formally innovative practice that was intended to demonstrate a modern 'cultural' alternative to orthodox 'physical' anthropology. I propose here that his adoption of the cinematograph in 1898 elevates it to a modernist enterprise. 'Modern' and 'Modernist' are not usually associated with late Victorian anthropology. On the contrary, the common sense is that modern anthropology becomes visible in the 1920s, on the far side of the First World War (1914–18), revolution in Russia (1917) and, given Haddon's interest in the meaning of art and dance, the invention of cinema (1895), cubism (1907), *The Rite of Spring* (1913), Dada (1916), surrealism (1917), Bauhaus (1919) and *Ulysses* (1922). Cubism is especially interesting, given that Picasso's encounter with ethnographic collections in Paris triggered an experiment in form that revolutionized the visual arts. These events have never been used to benchmark anthropology as an emerging science of culture, probably because it would be difficult to find anything in the history of anthropology that matches those milestones, even as we mark the centenary of the publication of foundational texts by Radcliffe-Brown and Malinowski. Furthermore, Haddon's interest in art and dance was regarded by those Tylor labelled 'physicals' and Haddon labelled 'anatomists' as belonging to the domain of philosophy rather than science and, therefore, considered it as being outside of the scope of disciplinary anthropology. Stocking and Jones flipped that equation by using Haddon's interest in art and folklore as evidence of a biological understanding of culture. Either way, the modernizing impulse that drove Haddon's adoption of instantaneous photography, the optical lantern and the cinematograph in combination with the phonograph went unnoticed.

In this chapter, I make the case that Haddon's filming of the last dance of the Malu Zogo-Le represents an encounter with performance art that generated an experiment in ethnographic form that constitutes a singular modernist achievement in an otherwise conservative field. I begin with a review of some critical thinking related to Haddon's enhanced sense of the importance of visual evidence. This shifts to Belfast in 1893 and a collaboration with Clara Patterson that situates this experiment within folklore collection operating as an instrument of cultural nationalism. The last section explores Haddon's reputation as a provocateur and asks if the point of his ethnology was to draw a blade across the bourgeois gaze in the oldest colony at a time of unprecedented racism and intensified political and cultural action for decolonization. In other words, does this experiment in ethnographic form—shaped by a disruptive, anticolonial attitude—qualify him as a modernist, and, as such, a discernible influence on the literary modernism of John Millington Synge?

AN EXPERIMENT

Haddon's field record of his experiment with cinematography and colour photography is brief. In the first week of September 1898, the members of the expedition were preparing to leave Mer when:

> some Australian natives came in a bêche-de-mer [sea cucumber] boat and I wanted to get a cinematograph of their dancing, and it was also only just at the last that we could get part of the Malu ceremony danced with the masks that

had been made for me, but the dance was worth waiting for. I tried to cinematograph it, but as so often happens the machine jams and the film is spoiled. I am afraid this part of my outfit will prove a failure and the colour-photography is I fear at present of little practical value. I have had many disappointments on this expedition perhaps I was too sanguine. (Haddon 1898–99 Torres Strait and New Guinea Journal: 210)

'Colour-photography' referred to a technique developed in 1894 by John Joly, Professor of Geology at TCD, and marketed commercially in 1895 before being abandoned because of its limited usefulness (Sachse 1896; Flueckiger 2016). It should be noted here that it took another decade almost for the Lumière brothers to market a viable colour system, which Albert Kahn used to document world cultures, despatching photographers Marguerite Mespoulet and Madeleine Mignon to the west of Ireland in 1913 (see Okuefuna 2008). The meaning of 'sanguine' becomes clear when one reads Haddon's entry on photography in the 1899 edition of *Notes and Queries on Anthropology*. He advised readers as follows:

Do not leave the purchase of photographic equipment to the last, but practice with the camera, the plates intended to be used, and the developer some time before starting, so as to be thoroughly conversant with the tools. If possible develop all the plates in the field so as to have the chance of replacing failures. (N&QA 1899: 237)

Welch prepared Haddon for his first experiments in photo-ethnography between 1888 and 1892 and, by 1898, Haddon was a very experienced photographer. 'Sanguine' suggests that he underestimated the scale of the technical adjustment required in adopting cinematography. Still the footage of the Malu ceremony was not 'spoiled', although Haddon did not find out until the camera was tested on return to London. This part of the story was well told by Chris Long and Pat Loughren in *Cinema Papers* in 1993, retold in more detail in 2002 by Alison Griffiths in *Wondrous Difference: Cinema, Anthropology, & Turn-of-the-Century Visual Culture* and told again on video in 2010 by Michael Eaton in his short film *Masks of Mer*.

Despite the problems and disappointments of 1898, Haddon encouraged Walter Baldwin Spencer to take a kinematograph (or equivalent) and a phonograph with him on a year-long expedition to Central Australia with Frank Gillen in 1901. Griffiths (2002: 152) described how Spencer filmed several Arrente ceremonies and quoted Arthur Cantrill's observation that given the limits of the equipment, Spencer's filming of spontaneous ceremonies improved dramatically during the expedition. This, combined with his experience of screening his own films in 1905 and 1906, may explain why Haddon endorsed Sharp's recommendation in the 1912 edition of *Notes and Queries on Anthropology* that the cinematograph and phonograph be used to record dances and, in his own section on photography, used to record the 'the making of an object, or of a ceremony' (N&QA 1912: 271). Yet Haddon never repeated the experiment and Griffiths (2002: 167) argued that cinema remained 'a decidedly ancillary method of *data collecting* within turn-of-the-century anthropology' (emphasis added), speculating that the greatest obstacle was the translation of a pictorial record of dance into *useful* anthropological knowledge in terms of legible scientific documents that could be studied by subsequent anthropologists. Griffiths (ibid.: 140), citing Edwards (1998), noted a disparity between affect in Haddon's account of the Malu ceremonies in *Head-Hunters* and data in the expedition's reports, arguing that it illustrated different modes of visuality – defined by John Berger (1972) as culturally determined ways of seeing and by Gillian Rose (2012: 2) as the way seeing is culturally constructed – in operation in cinema and science. The same 'disparity' can be detected between the popular, philosophical intent of 'Papuan Dances' in *Lippincott's Monthly Magazine* and the formal, ethnographic method of 'Secular and Ceremonial Dances of the Torres Straits Islanders' in *Internationales Archiv für Ethnographie*. It is repeated between the review in the *Optical Lantern and Cinematograph Journal* and the minute of the Anthropological Institute, and these examples establish that the disparity is a function of context rather than epistemology. Haddon explained the 'disparity' in *Head-Hunters* as follows:

> To give the reader a substantially accurate idea of the Malu ceremonies, I do not propose to describe exactly only what we saw, but I shall endeavour, as briefly as possible, to resuscitate the past. Full details will be published elsewhere. (Haddon 1901a: 47–48)

'Elsewhere' was the formal space of the expedition reports, and this sentence signals to specialist readers that Haddon had enacted a conventional separation between *Head-Hunters* as a narrative account intended for the general public and the *Reports* as scientific papers generated for specialist researchers, also illustrated by the different function of reports Green and Holt presented to the Royal Dublin Society in 1890.

In *Head-Hunters* Haddon described the action he filmed as follows:

> The grotesque masks worn by ruddled men, girt with leafy kilts, had a strange effect as they emerged from the jungle, and very weird was the dance in the mottled shade of the tropical foliage, a fantasy in red and green, lit up by spots of sunshine. (Haddon 1901a: 47)

This corresponded closely with the review in the *Optical Lantern and Cinematograph Journal* and points to the type of knowledge Haddon was trying to produce in terms of cinema's capacity to 'resuscitate the past'. The camera jammed at that point, and we must refer to the text to 'see' the rest of what he might have captured, if he had been able to work his way around tabu associated with the ceremony. He described the impact on the *kersi* (initiates) of a ceremony process that lasted eight months or so and:

> occurred at an impressionable age of life, when new ideas and sensations are surging up, and when the fuller life of

> adult manhood is looming in the immediate future. The emotions of the lads were quickened by the remarkable ceremonies in which they had recently participated, and their minds were kept more or less on the stretch by the knowledge of others yet to come.
>
> Part of the Malu ceremonies consisted in thoroughly frightening the *kersi* with the 'Devil belong Malu'. This was accomplished by men disguised by being completely covered with coconut leaves, who rushed about making noises by hitting or rubbing together two rough clam shells. (Haddon 1901a: 50)

Haddon was talking about adolescence, sex and boundaries, and the passage illustrates his interest in psychology as a route into the meaning of these ceremonies. He explained his method in 'The Study of Anthropology' and so registered a methodological shift from a comparative study of savage custom to an investigation of the social function of ritual. He introduced this innovation in his first account of 'Papuan Dances' in 1890 and reworked it in *Head-Hunters* with a closing reflection on the ethnological meaning of the Malu ceremonies:

> The paraphernalia of nearly every ceremony of all peoples are generally foolish, and often grotesque, to the outsider; but they awaken deep religious sentiment in the true believer, who, when duly instructed, beholds in them a symbolism that visualizes the sacred legends and aspirations of his community. There cannot be the least doubt that these sentiments exist among so-called savages, and those who scoff at their ceremonies thereby condemn themselves. (Haddon 1901a: 51–52)

The paraphernalia of apparently foolish ceremonies could be a reflection on the theatricality of Haddon's own initiation as a Freemason in 1889, and 'those who scoff' might include Macalister, who dismissed his familiarity with savage people and their ways in 1894 (*JAI* 23 [1894]: 412). That underlines the point made earlier in relation to his journalism. Haddon was engaged in a philosophical inquiry into the essential unity of humankind and the knowledge produced was the foundation for a public plea for solidarity with the victims of colonialism.

The problem for the historicists who rewrote the history of anthropology in the 1990s is that they focussed on data collecting in the context of Haddon's training as zoologist, and the filming of the last performance of a Malu dance became an instance of salvage anthropology that made sense in a context defined by evolution bracketed by race and colonialism. What gets lost in this scenario is the point of Haddon's description of the Malu ceremonies, namely that he understood the function of (a) ethnography as visualizing the sacred legends and aspirations of a community and (b) ethnology as a process of public enlightenment through engagement with the rituals of other civilizations. The result is a dichotomy between Haddon's aim of 'resuscitating the past' and de Brigard's (1995: 16) construction of Haddon's experimental use of film as 'systematic salvage ethnography' by 'a former zoologist'. Griffiths (1996: 19) developed this argument in a paper in *Visual Anthropology*, using Haddon and Spencer's ethnographic film to investigate the impact of visuality on 'knowledge production within anthropology'. She rationalized the subsequent lack of interest in motion pictures as an investment by nineteenth-century anthropologists in the

> motionless anthropometric body as a trustworthy indicator of evolutionary theory, of the idea that the static body of the 'ethnographic Other' was sufficiently rich in topographic detail to have made animation superfluous. This privileging of static representational strategies suggests anthropometry's ties to criminology and the inspectional regimes of nineteenth century medicine. (Griffiths 1996: 32)

The 'ethnographic Other' indexes Edward Said's orientalism in an argument in which Griffiths situates still photography as a function of imperial anthropology within a post-Foucault realm of instrumentality and surveillance that Sekula (1986) and Tagg

(1988) constructed as the other pillar of postcolonial studies of photography *and* anthropology. This provided the theoretical framework for a seminal critique of historical collections in *Anthropology and Photography 1860–1920* (1992), edited by Edwards, which Edwards and Morton then 'interrogated' in 2009 in *Photography, Anthropology and History*. Back in 1996, Griffiths listed the following as contributing factors in the alienation of ethnographic film in Haddon's time: the compelling realism of motion pictures; the agency they imparted on their subjects; and the concomitant capacity to undermine the authority of the 'ethnographer's mechanized gaze' (Griffiths 1996: 33). Ironically, Griffiths described the very qualities that animate Haddon's accounts of filming the Malu ceremony and his advocacy of instantaneous photography in *Notes and Queries on Anthropology*. Griffiths attempted to resolve this anomaly in 2002 in a detailed and sympathetic treatment of Haddon's experimental use of film. However, references to Haddon's zoological training and association with orthodox, physical anthropology meant that the logic of her 1996 analysis bubbled under the surface and this, in turn, reveals how orthodox an evolutionist mindset had become in academic writing about the relationship between anthropology, photography and film-making in the colonial era.

To conclude, Haddon has remained a former zoologist in disciplinary histories of anthropology and critical studies of photography in anthropology, despite readily available evidence that he was on a philosophical quest and was determined to bring everyone in touch with their inner savage through an investigation of the social meaning of dance across space and time. His attempt to mobilize a popular ethnographic movement in Belfast in 1893 is a case in point.

THE MOVEMENT

In November 1892, Robert Lloyd Praeger and Francis Joseph Bigger asked Haddon to present a slideshow on the Aran Islands to members of the Belfast Naturalists' Field Club with the aim of encouraging the collection of folklore on a more systematic basis. Over the next two years, Haddon tried to mobilize the members as ethnographers and recruited Clara Patterson as a fieldworker in his investigation of the relationship between Papuan dances and singing games in Ireland and the UK. Bigger's involvement makes the timing very interesting. The Conservatives lost the 1892 general election and Gladstone, the Liberal prime minister, drafted a second Government of Ireland (Home Rule) Bill which the House of Commons passed in April 1893, but the House of Lords rejected it in September, precipitating a general election in 1895 that became, in effect, another referendum on Home Rule. Bigger was a nationalist who promoted the revival of the Irish language and folk traditions and turned to Haddon for practical support in 1892. Praeger counted Haddon among his most valued friends and was familiar with his work in the west of Ireland (Praeger 1949: 24–27). They met in Belfast and, when Praeger took up a job at the National Library in Dublin in 1893, he took over the running of the field club Haddon founded in 1885 and joined him in a group of scholars and journalists who met daily in a teashop on Lincoln Place in Dublin.

Praeger shared the secretaryship of the Belfast club with Bigger, and their invitation to Haddon connected his field club experience with their folklore ambitions and the project became the catalyst for a wider mobilization of cultural nationalism in Ireland. However, historical and critical accounts of these events (Adams 1993; Jones 1998; Beiner 2012; Ó Giolláin 2017) represent this as a watershed between evolutionist anthropology on one side of the colonial divide and, on the other, cultural nationalism and literary modernism. This section deals with the question of cultural nationalism as a necessary precursor to the problem of Haddon's relationship to literary modernism in Ireland. It draws on research commissioned by Matthew Cheeseman and Carina Hart (Walsh 2021c) as a contribution to their exploration of the relationship between folklore and nationalism in the context of Brexit.

On 24 November 1892, the *Northern Whig* reported that Bigger informed members of the Belfast Naturalists' Field Club that the committee planned to include local ethnography in its activities and had arranged with 'Professor Haddon, of Dublin, a member of the British Association Ethnographical Committee' to deliver a lecture in January, adding that there was a lot of interest in the subject. The Club advertised the event on 17 January 1893 in the *Northern Whig* under the heading 'The Primitive Races of Ireland' and billed the lecture as 'The Aran Islands, a Study in Irish Ethnography'. The advertisement also served notice that steps would be taken to form a local committee to assist the British Association Ethnographical Committee. Haddon travelled to Belfast and presented a slideshow on the Aran Islands as an example of ethnography in practice. The Club's Annual Report and Records of Proceedings for the year 1892 to 1893 recorded a very large attendance of members and visitors' and minuted Haddon's introduction as follows:

> Professor Haddon said that there is even in Ireland considerable ignorance respecting its western isles. People have a hazy notion that they are extremely interesting, and that their scenery is fine; but few have any definitive knowledge about them. He had been invited by the Belfast Naturalists' Field Club to give an account, so far as he was able, by word and picture, of the Aran Islands, Co. Galway. He gladly embraced the opportunity thus afforded of suggesting to that energetic club a new kind of field work. Of late years, the study of Irish Natural History has received a fresh impetus, but the natural history of the Irish man is as yet unworked, and owing to various causes it is increasingly becoming more difficult to study, hence the necessity for prompt action in the matter. He proposed, then, illustrating the methods of this new study by limiting his remarks to a description of a very circumscribed area. This would necessitate the grouping of his facts into a more academic form than is customary in popular lectures. His remarks would be arranged under the following heads: ENVIRONMENT, THE PEOPLE THEMSELVES, MODE OF LIFE, FOLKLORE, ARCHAEOLOGY, and HISTORY. In other words,

in order to find out who people are and how they have become what they are, we must first study what they are, what they do, what they think, and what they have done. Analysis must precede synthesis. (BNFC 2,3,vi [1892-93]: 538–39, original formatting)

The Club reconvened the following day and Haddon switched to a conversational mode to explain the work of the British Association Ethnographical Committee and point out to them the ways in which they could assist its operations:

He dwelt on the pressing importance of the subject of British and Irish Ethnography. In this age of progress, the relics of the pre-historic past were passing with rapidity and, if not studied and gathered with all speed they would be lost to us for ever. In the endeavour to study the origin of the ancient races, we had to study them on a systematic scientific basis: he especially dwelt on the importance of beliefs and customs as affording important evidence on this point. Owing to the representations of scientists who recognized the necessity for immediate action in the direction of an ethnographical survey, the British Association was acting in concert with the Folk-Lore Society, the Anthropological Institute, and the Society of Antiquaries of London, as well as other kindred societies; and a committee, of which he had the honour of being a member, had been appointed for the purpose of carrying out this work. A committee had now been formed in Dublin to carry out the survey in Ireland, under direction of the central committee in London, and he now suggested that the Belfast Naturalists' Field Club should appoint a committee to undertake ethnographical work in Ulster, their results to pass through the Dublin committee to the central institution. (ibid.: 542–43)

The Club established an ethnographic committee for Ulster that met in October and reported to the members in November. William Hugh Patterson, an antiquarian, a member of the Royal

Irish Academy and a prominent member of the Club, reported that Haddon explained the delay in fieldwork instructions being drawn up by the BAAS, but, unfortunately, the report did not record the details. Patterson then reported on ethnographic work undertaken by members over the previous nine months, which comprised papers on folklore by Bigger, Lily S. Mollan and Mrs Blair. He also reported that:

> Clara Patterson has taken down, and made photographs of, several children's games, a branch of folk-lore that is of extreme interest. Lastly, the series of photographs, made by R. J. Welch, for the purpose of illustrating Irish peasant life and the survival of the past in the present, are of very great value in the Survey work which is now being started. (BNFC 2,4,i [1893–94]: 53)

Patterson noted that nothing had yet been achieved in England and, in the absence of an agreed methodology, Haddon pointed out 'the direction that future work might take'. He asked members to collect data on hair and eye colour using the method that Beddoe developed and the BAAS approved. The minute continues as follows:

> He also asked for volunteers to undertake the collection of physical measurements and the measurements of skulls. Amateur photographers could also help by photographing local forms of houses, vehicles, implements and the like, and especially full face and accurate side face, of types of the people, and he requested that copies of such photographs should be sent to him at the Royal College of Science, Dublin. (ibid.: 53–54)

Patterson concluded his report by referring members to 'The Ethnography of the Aran Islands' and printed instructions issued by the Folk-Lore Society.

Patterson's report clarifies two things. The first is that Haddon was relaying instructions from the BAAS. The second is that the club members were more interested in the study of folk lore and life. Patterson corresponded with Alice Gomme about children's games, and this may have been a factor in the decision to invite Haddon to Belfast, given her husband's unequivocal endorsement of Haddon's skill as a folklore collector and the work he was doing in Ireland (see FLS 2,1 [1891]: 13). Furthermore, Haddon published 'A Batch of Irish Folk-lore' in *Folk-Lore* in September 1893, in which he explained that for 'the past year or two I have been endeavouring [to] get people to collect Irish-folklore' (FLS 4,3 [1893]: 349). The collectors included Clara Patterson's brother Robert, although she had a more direct link to Haddon. She enrolled in lectures organized by the Society for the Extension of University Teaching in Belfast, winning a bronze medal in zoology in examinations conducted by Haddon in May 1892. In February 1893 she entered anthropology as her occupation and branch of study when she registered to be measured in the Dublin Anthropometric Laboratory, and was possibly the first woman to describe herself as anthropologist in Ireland. The following November, she exhibited her photographs at a meeting convened by the Ethnographic Committee. Ronnie Adams, librarian at the Linen Hall Library in Belfast, revisited the project in 1993 and wrote that Patterson informed Alice Gomme that she was unhappy with the photographs she had taken in one district because:

> the children were so anxious for their faces to show they would look around in a wooden manner, I am going up the hill to 'real' country children to try instantaneous photos. (Patterson quoted in Adams 1993: 4)

'Going up the hill' is a remarkable reference to the sectarian landscape of Northern Ireland. The uplands were the edge-lands of empire in Ireland, the bad land where displaced Irish natives lived in isolated folk communities that Haddon labelled 'ethnical islands' in 1891 and proposed as the basic operational unit of the Irish and UK ethnographic surveys. 'Instantaneous' is equally remarkable in that it registers Haddon's influence and reveals that

Haddon, despite the emphasis on anthropometry in his earlier contribution, was working on photo-ethnography with Patterson and Welch.

Patterson presented her findings at a special meeting in November 1893. William Butler Yeats opened the meeting with a talk on 'Irish Folk-Lore' (BNFC 2,4,i [1893–94]: 46–48) and Bigger then read a paper by Patterson. Guy Beiner (2012: 149) observed that papers by women members were read by men 'as was the practice in such Victorian clubs'. Haddon challenged such discrimination in 1890, when he arranged for Alice Shackleton to be the first woman to read a scientific paper (RDS 4,2 [1891]: 673–701) to the Royal Dublin Society. Shackleton and Patterson benefitted from improved access provided by the university extension movement and so personified the gender aspects of the 'reconstruction *zeitgeist*' that Haddon enthusiastically endorsed in a letter to Ellis in May 1890. The naturalists in Belfast, however, were clearly more resistant to reconstruction than their counterparts in Dublin, and Bigger's reading of Patterson's paper underscores the unorthodox and disruptive nature of Haddon's project in general. However, Patterson's paper exposes an evolutionist logic that Jones (1998: 195) thought defined Haddon as the 'Darwinist evolutionist par excellence'.

Patterson stated that the progression from simple to complex societies was best explained by reference to the theory of recapitulation in embryology, whereby a growing child 'repeats ... the savage state out of which civilised man has grown' (BNFC 2,4,i [1893–94]: 48). She fixed the relationship between savage and civilized people as the equivalent of that between children and adults, and, in this context, claimed that traces of savage ritual could be found in the games children played. The evidentiary finger points to Haddon, her zoology tutor whose first book was a study of embryology. Patterson's remarks also originated in an argument Haddon developed in his column in the *Irish Daily Independent* in 1894. He proposed that it was possible to 'trace degenerate and fragmentary survivals of the ceremonies and religious practices of our savage ancestors' (Haddon 1894c: 6) in a fading tradition of singing games in Britain. However, the reductive logic of Patterson's statement jarred with the subtlety of the argument Haddon developed in a subsequent lecture in Belfast. He returned to the subject of Papuan dances in December 1894 as part of a lecture on 'Modern Relics of Olden Time', and the BNFC minute is worth quoting at length:

> The lecturer pointed out the importance of dancing amongst savages. Different kinds of savage dances were described, more particularly the initiation ceremonies. This led to a description of the bull roarer, and two specimens of this ancient and sacred instrument were exhibited and swung; the one was obtained by the lecturer in Torres Straits, the other from England. Some Papuan death dances were described, the performers of which are covered with leaves and wear leafy masks. These were followed by representations of the costume of the Irish 'straw-boys', and the parallelism between the two was startling. The significance of a certain class of children's games was dealt with and it was shown that many of these illustrate the customs of our heathen ancestors, some being marriage games, others being funeral games, others again being reminiscent of well-worship. Some photographs of holy wells and the offerings at them were next shown, and lastly a fairy thorn at Hollywood. Professor Haddon emphasised the facts [*sic*] that these were not trivial subjects and that only by studying the customs of the folk and children's games and the like was it possible to form some idea as to the religious practices of our ancestors. (BNFC 2,4,ii [1894–95]: 216–17)

In this context, Haddon's collaboration with Patterson becomes a further step in his investigation of ancestral knowledges.

This was a key component of the sociological approach he proposed in 'The Study of Anthropology', and that disrupts the common sense that Haddon's lecture exposed a biological approach to the ethnological study of culture, thereby creating a dichotomy between Haddon's ethnology and Bigger's nationalism in the context of the mobilization of a popular folklore movement in Belfast between 1893 and 1895. I have not been able to establish if Bigger was aware of the political differences between Haddon, Green and Cunningham. Praeger, however, knew Haddon well and, in response to a request from Alison Hingston Quiggin (1942: 62), remembered his urgent and 'superabundant zeal' in engaging with the problem 'of rapidly changing conditions among savage tribes' (Praeger 1949: 26), that is, the impact of colonialism on other civilizations. So the very fact of the invitation suggests that Bigger saw Haddon as a potential ally at a time of intensified decolonization in Ireland. Add to that the modernizing objectives of 'The Study of Anthropology' and there is a case to be made for common ground with key players in cultural nationalism and literary modernism, Douglas Hyde and John Millington Synge especially.

A MODERNIST?

Adams (1993) and Beiner (2012) produced detailed accounts of events in Belfast using records held in the Linen Hall Library, and their readings of those records tell us that the tide of history was running against Haddon. That is hardly surprising. His request 'for volunteers to measure peasant skulls' (Adams 1993: 4–5) provided a basis to compare Haddon's combination of skull-measuring and salvage with the cultural effect of Hyde's lecture on 'Celtic Language and Literature' (BNFC 2,4,ii [1894–95]: 204–5) as illustrations of antagonistic movements. For instance, Haddon invoked the correspondence between singing games and savage dances and, as a finishing flourish, adopted the persona of a savage in a performance with a bullroarer. Hyde's lecture, on the other hand, prompted members to set up Irish classes before forming a breakaway branch of the Gaelic League. These events have an attractive symmetry in terms of a historiographical contest between ethnology and cultural nationalism: Prof. Haddon, the former zoologist and colonial scientist-turned-anthropologist, looks to a biological past, while Dr Hyde, the leader of a language-based cultural revival in Ireland, looks to a postcolonial future. However, the circumstances of Bigger's invitation and the purpose – methodological and epistemological – of Haddon's collaboration with Patterson renders that argument obsolete. This is considered in more detail in Hart and Cheeseman's volume (Walsh 2021c), and this section considers the possibility that Haddon was a modernist whom Synge, like Bigger before him, looked to as a guide to the life and lore of the people of the western isles. The problem here is that comparisons between Haddon's role in 'The Ethnographic Survey of the Aran Islands' and Synge's authorship of *The Aran Islands* have tended to replicate the logic of the split between Haddon and Hyde in Belfast, and so draw a firm line between Haddon's scientific racism and Synge's literary modernism.

There is a significant body of scholarship that has considered the ethnographic integrity of Synge's account of life in the Aran Islands and the ethnographic reliability of Haddon's survey (Messenger 1966; Kiberd 2000; Ashley 2001; Castle 2001; Kuper 2001; Carville 2007; Brannigan 2014; Ó Giolláin 2017; Ferriter 2018). For instance, Declan Kiberd (2000: 421) argued that Synge was the first person to attempt a sympathetic, left-wing documentation of the lives of the islanders. Adam Kuper (2001: 85), on the other hand, portrayed Haddon as 'a follower of Huxley' who was more concerned with Darwinian anxieties about 'inbreeding' among the islanders than 'the language, customs and ideas of the *volk*'. Gregory Castle (2001: 2) used the ethnographic component of both documents to set up a dichotomy between colonial anthropology and literary modernism, drawing on Terry Eagleton's argument that the conditions for modernism were created by a confrontation between disruptive new technologies and traditional cultures in the politically unstable edge-lands of *ancien régimes* and empires (Eagleton 1995: 274). By all accounts, Haddon was on the wrong side of this definition of modernism. However, if one applies Eagleton's formula to the events in Belfast, the situation becomes far less clear-cut.

I have argued that Haddon's contribution to the mobilization of a folklore movement in Belfast focussed on the problem of the representation of ethnicity during an intensification in campaigns to achieve the decolonization (political) and de-Anglicization (cultural) of the oldest colony. Whether that fits Eagleton's formula depends on whether we treat Haddon's photo-ethnographic practice as an instrument of anticolonial activism or as a form of salvage anthropology tainted by scientific racism. This is where Haddon's performance with a bullroarer becomes interesting. Praeger has been quoted already as describing his friend Haddon as an energetic and humorous provocateur who engaged with the problem 'of rapidly changing conditions among savage tribes'. With this in mind, picture the scene in Dublin in February 1890: the lecture room of the Royal Dublin Society was crowded as Haddon lit a lime light and threw photographs of native life in New Guinea onto a screen, allowing the audience to *see* a land that was still considered unsafe for white travellers and missionaries. He used tabu subjects like nakedness, female agency and sexual attraction in courtship to shock his audience and disrupt their common sense of civilization.

Haddon was familiar with advanced thinking on sex and sexuality, and, just as Caroline Haddon shocked her contemporaries with her 1884 anonymous tract on 'The Future of Marriage', her nephew used his photographs to draw a blade across the bourgeois gaze, just as vividly as Luis Buñuel would in *Un Chien Andalou* in 1929. That is a big claim, but Haddon, having engaged his audience with the lure of cannibalism and nudity, set about fascinating them with the subtlety and depth of savage thought – a task that was so subversive of bourgeois ethnocentricity that comparison with the disruptive aesthetic of Buñuel is merited. Haddon continued to play the trickster in Belfast in 1894, animating still images of dancers and the material evidence of a bullroarer by assuming the persona of a 'savage' performer and connecting his audience to a collective memory of childhood rituals, hoping, I propose, to provoke the sort of revelation he described in 'Papuan Dances'. The unveiling of cinema in Paris one year later provided him with the scope to revolutionize his model of performed ethnography, and his account of filming the Malu Zogo-Le recalls Dziga Vertov's declaration in his *Kinok* manifestos that revolutionary cinematographers decipher in new ways a world unknown to the viewer and so, he claimed, create 'a fresh perception of the world' (Vertov 1923 in Michelson and O'Brien 1984: 18). That is a fair summary of Haddon's intention as stated in the closing paragraph of 'Papuan Dancers' and his chapter on 'The Malu Ceremonies' in *Head-Hunters*. On that basis alone, Haddon is entitled to be considered a modernist.

Regarding literary modernism in Ireland, there is an attractive logic in having Haddon 'the head-hunter' and Synge 'the playboy' on opposites sides, yet there is convincing evidence that Synge followed Haddon to the Aran Islands. Haddon was no stranger to Irish modernists. He was connected to Yeats through Ellis and Symons as well as Bigger and Praeger. Synge, at the age of 14, joined the Dublin Naturalists' Field Club when Haddon set it up in 1885 (Stephens 1974: 38), and all one must do is read Haddon's letters to his children to appreciate how he would have treated a young boy keenly interested in natural science who showed up among a membership of 'distinguished scientists or elderly amateurs' (ibid.). Moreover, one can detect echoes of that contact in subsequent events. W. J. McCormack (2000: 253) acknowledged Haddon and Browne's 1892 survey as a factor in Synge's decision to go to the Aran Islands. We know from a description that John Masefield (1916: 13) published of Synge writing *The Aran Islands* that photography was integral to his method, and his insistence that Martín McDonagh discard his 'Sunday suit from Galway' (Stephens 1971: xii) for a photograph (figure 9.2) recapitulates Haddon's insistence on native dress in photographs taken in the Torres Strait and New Guinea ten years earlier.

That amounts to a shared act of de-Anglicization in Hyde's language. In addition, Synge's reference in *The Aran Islands* to 'the impulsive life of a savage' (1979: 122–23) in the context of the 'sexual instincts' of the Aran Islanders sounds uncannily like the script – as reported in the press – for the slideshow advertised as 'The Life of a Savage'. This is consistent with a seam of anthropological thought in *The Aran Islands* that Castle mined in 2001, and I propose that the source of that thought is revealed in *The Playboy of the Western World*, where Synge plays with the skull-measuring business in the opening scene of Act 3:

Figure 9.2. John Millington Synge, *An Islander of Inishmaan*, 1898. Digital scan and print from glass-plate negative (Timothy Keefe, Sharon Sutton, Ciarán Walsh, Ciarán Rooney, 2011). Courtesy of the Board of Trinity College, University of Dublin.

> Jimmy: ... Did you ever hear tell of the skulls they have in the city of Dublin, ranged out like blue jugs in a cabin of Connaught?
>
> Philly: And you believe that?
>
> Jimmy: [*Pugnaciously*] Didn't a lad see them and he after coming from harvesting in the Liverpool boat? 'They have them there' says he 'making a show of the great people there was one time walking the world. White skulls and black skulls and yellow skulls, and some with full teeth and some haven't only but one.' (Synge 1958: 147–48)

The last line seems too close to Haddon's title to be mere coincidence and that, I propose, firmly connects the dramatist to the ethnologist.

There is an interesting political dimension to this connection. Haddon read Kropotkin and Élie Reclus before he travelled through the west of Ireland in 1890, and Synge met Augustin Hamon, editor of the anarchist journal *L'Humanité Nouvelle*, before he went to the Aran Islands in 1898. Indeed, McCormack (2000: 143) tells us that Synge's mother Kathleen was worried after 'poor Johnnie' told her he was gone to Paris in 1896 'to study socialism' and she later 'tackled him about becoming "a rebel"' (ibid.). In addition, Kiberd (2000: 423, 27) noted that the narrative technique of *The Aran Islands* was in many ways photographic and that it could be 'read as a document in the history of anarchism'. One could say the same thing about Haddon's essays in *Lippincott's Monthly Magazine* and his first slideshow on the Aran Islands.

To summarize, the evidence supports the general view that Haddon and Synge's interests converged on the Aran Islands, but disrupts the logic of a divergence along colonial and modernist lines, just as Haddon and Hyde are said to have diverged on the question of nationalism. That places 'the head-hunter' and 'the playboy' in the same field, a field of anarchist political philosophy and experimentation in ethnographic form in which a radically reconstructed anthropology and literary modernism took hold; the first, briefly, and the story of its forgetting can be read between the lines of Mead's 1975 essay.

CONCLUSION

The anonymous review of the 1906 screening of Haddon's film of the last dance of the Malu Zogo-Le (figure 9.1) benchmarks the beginning of ethnographic cinema, but the making of the film was a problem for Griffiths, who, like de Brigard, recognized the innovation but could not see past the former zoologist behind the camera. The same logic transformed Haddon's collaboration with Bigger and Praeger into a denial of his contribution to the mobilization of cultural nationalism in 1893 and so undermined his status as an anti-imperial modernizer. Yet Patterson's ethnography of singing games provides a methodological and epistemological link between 'Papuan Dances' in 1890 and the filming of the last dance of the Malu Zogo-Le in 1898. That experiment shifts the focus of this analysis to the avant-garde cinema of Vertov and Buñuel, whose modernism was defined by the same mix of technical innovation, perceptual disruption and political intent that characterized Haddon's adoption of a savage persona. However, the critical comparator in an Irish context is Synge. They met when Synge was 14 years of age and the impression Haddon made is as manifest in references in *The Aran Islands* and *The Playboy of the Western World* as it is in Synge's adoption of a photo-ethnographic method.

Synge was, at the time of writing, unfinished business, although the evidence available is sufficient to reject the argument that Haddon and Synge represent antagonistic cultural forces in the context of Home Rule and decolonization. As stated, the very fact that Bigger turned to Haddon for help in 1892 establishes that Haddon was involved in mobilizing cultural nationalism at a very early stage in the movement. Haddon's Home Rule sympathies also bedevilled previous attempts to create work for himself in Ireland, as evidenced by his removal from the survey of fishing grounds in 1895 and the Irish Ethnographic Survey in 1892, among the many disappointments he referred to in his letter to Myers. The latter explains why he went to Belfast as a representative of the 'British Ethnographical Committee' and not as an associate of Cunningham, who, in 1893, assured Unionists that the natural law of survival of the fittest guaranteed the survival of British rule in Ireland. Furthermore, Bigger subsequently recruited Hyde and I have argued elsewhere (Walsh 2021c) that Haddon alerted Hyde to the survival of pre-conquest customs and beliefs in the west of Ireland.

I now apply that argument to Synge and go one step further, a step that makes Haddon's understanding of folk culture far more progressive than the language-based revival strategies of Hyde and his followers in an emerging Irish Ireland movement. Kathleen Synge could have been referring to Haddon when she wrote that her Johnnie had gone to Paris to study socialism, the act of which echoes Geddes's invitation to Haddon to come to Paris and join a great scientific movement led by revolutionaries. Synge and Haddon stepped back from the revolutionaries in their networks and, instead, found common ground in the philosophical implications of the survival of pre-conquest an-archic (self-governing) communities in the west of Ireland. Accordingly, the main finding here is that Synge followed Haddon to the Aran Islands, and Masefield's brief account of the writing of *The Aran Islands* is firm evidence that Synge replicated the photo-ethnographic methodology Haddon developed in 1890. It hardly needs to be stated that this finding challenges the common sense that Synge went to the Aran Islands because Yeats told him to. This releases Haddon from his traditional role as the bogeyman of cultural nationalism and literary modernism and places him in the vanguard of both movements. That fundamentally alters the grounds of any discussion of his contribution to the modernization of anthropology, and this study concludes with a reassessment of his legacy.

CONCLUSION
A LEGACY?

Haddon described the first task of his manifesto on 'The Study of Anthropology' as the removal of 'preconceived ideas' (Haddon 1895a: 25) about the scope and significance of anthropology. I followed suit in relation to his contribution to the modernization of anthropology, stepping outside of mainstream historiography and remembering key actions and ideas that have disappeared from the story of anthropology. To recap, I threw the former zoologist overboard and put in its place an artist and a philosopher in the guise of a very English 'savage', a play on Haddon's adoption in performance of the persona of a savage, which, I have argued, was the inner savage he connected with when initiated into Papuan dance in 1888. On that basis, I have interpreted Haddon's rendering of his own nickname as the white component of *Head-Hunters: Black, White, and Brown* (1901), and, as such, the title stands as a statement of solidarity with the savage peoples who lived at the edge of the British Empire and bore the brunt of the Anglo-Saxon will to dominate the world. Haddon's anticolonialism was inevitable given the anti-slavery heritage he inherited from his grandparents and his upbringing in a nonconformist family engaged in the arts, philosophy and politics. This provided a framework for an exploration of Haddon's attempt to reconstruct the institution of anthropology as part of a wider post-evolutionist movement that emerged out of interconnected networks of utopians, socialists, anarchists, third-way Fabians and solidarists in England and France, a project that was, by definition, a radical enterprise. The backlash that followed his performance in Ipswich in 1895 confirmed that it was perceived as such by powerful players in academic anthropology as it emerged from amateur scholarship and became a practical science of political utility in the last decade of the nineteenth century. We can tell from the letter he wrote to Myers in January 1901 that one of Haddon's many disappointments was the realization that he had become an outsider in this new order.

He was written out of the story of social anthropology as it took shape in the first two decades of the twentieth century, only to be reinstated in the 1990s as a former zoologist who opened a practical route to social anthropology for others very different to him. The memory of the time he spent in Ireland was that of a colonial scientist tainted by scientific racism. That was the Haddon I perceived when I found a photograph he took of himself and Browne measuring Tom Connelly's skull in the Aran Islands in 1892. That was a mistake. A closer reading of Haddon's involvement in the skull-measuring business revealed a long-forgotten struggle against reactionary forces who were determined to restrict the scope and function of anthropology, a practical struggle that became a philosophical quest that required new forms of ethnographic representation. On that basis I have argued that Haddon was a modernizer, if not a modernist. The main task now, by way of a conclusion, is to review his legacy in terms of the subsequent development of anthropology and to decide whether his ideas have any relevance to current debates about the nature of anthropology today – to decide, in effect, the question of ancestry.

With regards to legacy, I propose that the process of writing Haddon out of the history of anthropology began at a meeting of Section H in Portsmouth in 1911 when his friend William Halse Rivers read a paper that placed Haddon on the wrong side of a lab-based, theoretical model developed by Galton. That event became a watershed moment in terms of historiographical treatments of Haddon in the 1980s and 1990s, and I counter with a review of the state of anthropology that Radcliffe-Brown presented in 1931, the centenary of the foundation of the British

Association for the Advancement of Science (BAAS), whose annual meetings became the setting for many of the controversies that Haddon believed drove the modernization of anthropology. Radcliffe-Brown described Haddon's introduction of a field-based system of studying culture from a psychological and sociological perspective as so unorthodox that it 'came too soon in the history of anthropology' (BAAS 1932: 157), and I have interpreted this as a description of an avant-garde that Mead reinforced, incidentally, in 1973 when she lambasted the methodological conservatism of the anthropological and ethnological scientists who came after Haddon because they ignored the ethnographic potential of the art of film-making. Unfortunately for Haddon, he was by then cast in the role of zoologist-turned-anthropologist, and the full significance of his short film of the last dance of the Malu Zogo-Le was lost when anthropology slowly emerged from what David MacDougal (2009: 57) called its 'dark age' in the 1970s. Radcliffe-Brown's assessment, though hedged, contradicted this, and that provides a basis for revisiting the question of legacy in terms of the persistence of ideas.

Regarding relevance, I stated at the outset that Haddon was written out of the story of anthropology for the same reasons that make him interesting today. I have argued that Haddon chose images over text and so engaged with the problem of representation that became a major crisis for anthropologists and ethnologists in the postcolonial era. His search for *resemblances* rather than *differences* was manifest in an absolute refusal to objectify savage people, as illustrated in the change of the title of his first slideshow from 'Life of a Savage' to 'Native Life in New Guinea' and his adoption of a social documentary style in his first slideshow on the Aran Islands in 1890. The slideshow became his method of choice in a campaign to mobilize the public and organized anthropology to act in solidarity with the Papuans, Aranites and all the other civilizations under threat of extermination from Anglo-Saxon colonists. That connects with two contemporary movements. The first is the mobilization of Indigenous activists against land grabs and legislated genocide at fourteen or more flashpoints across the globe, a resemblance strengthened by the fact that Haddon's experiment in film constitutes an analogue of video-based campaigns on online platforms like the Tribal Voice project. Haddon thought genocide and racism inextricably linked, and the second movement that matters is the mobilization of civil society in opposition to structural racism in the wake of the murder of George Floyd in police custody on 25 May 2020.

In 1891, Haddon called out the executive and the Imperial Parliament for having legalized the murder of fellow *subjects* – it was the British Empire, after all – in the colonies, and in Ipswich in 1895 he staged a protest in an attempt to mobilize organized anthropology in support of his campaign against racism, genocide and the destruction of other civilizations. That event was forgotten for a long time, but my doctoral research has ensured that Haddon has become a person of interest as universities and other colonial-era institutions scramble to deal with the conjoined issues of racism and colonial legacies. That connects with a decade-long debate within the social sciences about current trends in knowledge-production and, specifically, the antagonism between a radical tradition of emancipatory practice and the restricted epistemology of a practical science of political utility in a neoliberal academy. That debate bears a strong resemblance to Haddon and Frazer's argument with Macalister in 1899 and thus brings this monograph full circle.

To summarize, the intertwined themes of engaged practice and formal innovation frame an extended, two-part assessment of Haddon's legacy. The first part considers some of the ideas Haddon developed in the early 1890s that have survived into the present as a sort of deep-seated disciplinary memory that constitutes, in Haddon's language, the ancestral knowledge of the original, contrary ethnologists associated with the Aborigines Protection Society. Despite the ascendancy of a 'hard' science culture advocated by Rivers in 1911, that memory persisted and (a) informed arguments that Radcliffe-Brown made in 1931, (b) influenced William Lloyd Warner's framing of Harvard's anthropological mission to Ireland in the same year, (c) resonated with arguments Geertz made in 1973 for 'an interpretive science in search of meaning' (Geertz 1973: 5) and (d) survived in a much-attenuated yet recognizable form in a 2001 assessment of Warner's project by Anne Byrne, Ricca Edmondson and Tony Varley (Arensberg and Kimball 2001). The second part revisits the conflict between Haddon's idealism and Cunningham's practicality in the context of current debates about racism and colonial legacies. I have argued that Cunningham's capture of Haddon's radical ethnological experiment in the Aran Islands marked the beginning of 'practical' anthropology in terms of a structural relation between party politics, government, social policy and academic social science. I propose that recent structural changes in universities have triggered a similar conflict that has split anthropology between an ascendant 'hard' science of political utility and a disciplinary tradition of engagement with contentious social, cultural, ethical and political issues.

THE PERSISTENCE OF MEMORY

The question of Haddon's legacy in terms of disciplinary anthropology depends, it seems, on which anthropology we are talking about, whether it is the humanitarian tradition revitalized by Haddon, the 'practical' tradition inaugurated by Cunningham or the 'hard science' tradition promoted by Rivers. We begin with the last. Rivers will be considered in a separate volume in this series of monographs, and his relationship with Haddon would have been beyond the scope of this study had he not edged his friend and colleague sideways in 1911 on the basis of a lack of theoretical development in line with Galton's demand for a 'hard' science that privileged precise measurement, exact processes of reasoning and the verification of definite laws (Galton 1877: 471; 1877a: 492). Rivers acknowledged that advances in ethnographic methods meant that anthropological facts 'rank[ed] in clearness and trustworthiness with the facts of other sciences' (BAAS 1912: 490) and thus met the first condition of Galton's demand. Rivers then challenged the psychological assumptions of Tylor's comparative method in terms that agree with Haddon in 'The Study of Anthropology' but deferred, perhaps out of loyalty to his friend, any discussion of the complicated combination of the ethnological and psychological analysis of culture. He focussed instead on the nature of facts required to advance the theoretical side of anthropology and stated the problem as the absence of a 'general agreement about the fundamental principles upon which the theoretical work of our science is to be conducted' (ibid.), the second and third conditions of Galton's demand. Rivers accepted the post-evolutionist and, essentially, geographical logic of the study of 'primitive decoration' but argued, without naming Haddon and Frazer, that the study of 'material objects' and 'magico-religious institutions' (ibid.: 494–96) was no match for the *precision* gained from an inductive study of social organization. In so doing, Rivers broke a long connection with geography and an equally long tradition of a philosophical engagement with the nature of difference across space and time.

The combined effect of these arguments leads me to conclude that Galton's 'hard' science doctrine rather than Darwinian evolutionism separated Haddon and Rivers in 1911. Radcliffe-Brown more or less confirmed this in his 1923 paper on 'The Methods of Ethnology and Social Anthropology'. He acknowledged that many scientists were 'very largely compelled to take up the evolutionary point of view in their study of culture' (Radcliffe-Brown 1923: 127) in the second half of the nineteenth century, neatly summarizing the conditions under which Haddon, on the 'advice' of Huxley, engaged with Garson, became a craniologist and incorporated physical anthropology into the programme of the 1898 expedition to the Torres Strait. Radcliffe-Brown developed his argument in his 1931 assessment of the position of anthropological studies on the centenary of the founding of the BAAS. He considered Haddon briefly, but concluded that his field-based, systematic investigation of culture favoured psychology, although the task belonged to sociology, and that this 'attempt came too soon in the history of anthropology' (BAAS 1932: 157). Thus, in two versions of the same paper, Radcliffe-Brown appears to exonerate Haddon's engagement with evolutionist anthropology while using his engagement with psychology and sociology to establish him as an avant-garde whose understanding of the importance of sociology Radcliffe-Brown shared. He then separated the old, psychology-based social anthropology of Rivers from a new form of anthropology he called comparative sociology.

Radcliffe-Brown did not dismantle the reputation of Rivers – his mentor – altogether. He agreed with the principle that 'the generalising method of the natural sciences be applied to the social and cultural phenomena' in a way that demonstrated that 'a particular phenomenon or event is an example of a general law' (BAAS 1932: 148–49) and that those laws 'explain' that phenomenon, slightly rephrasing an argument Rivers made in 1911 (BAAS 1912: 498). He went further, however, stating the need to examine specific forms of a phenomenon against universal trends and compare these with related forms in all cultures while understanding that the problem was one part or aspect of a much wider problem, which, in the case of totemism, was that 'of the nature and function of the ritual relations between human and animals and plants in general' (BAAS 1932: 151). There is a pattern of thought in his argument that can be detected in Haddon's study of the relationship between Papuan dances and singing games played by children in a village outside Belfast. Haddon used both as examples of a universal impulse to dance with the intent of engaging people in a conversation about the meaning and social function of ritualized behaviours at the extremes of humankind, a conversation that spilled over into male initiation and female sexual agency and, all the while, engaged with the wider problem of racism rooted in ethno-specific ideas about civilization.

This may seem like a stretch, but Radcliffe-Brown's explication of his innovation offers further evidence of the persistence of Haddon's ideas. Radcliffe-Brown described how this 'new anthropology *i.e.,* Comparative Sociology' (BAAS 1932: 149) emerged out of social anthropology over a number of decades, and cited Steinmetz, Westermarck and Durkheim especially as influences in the shift from origin to function in debates about totemism and religion. He did not mention Haddon. However, he noted that, with the exception of France, comparative sociology had failed to find a place in centres of study in Europe and the

US, mainly because it was left by anthropologists to sociologists and vice versa, adding that anthropologists generally focussed on the study of non-European people who were generally unknown to sociologists (ibid.: 166). That does not apply to Haddon. In December 1889, Geddes invited Haddon to join a movement developing around comparative sociology in France. Within a year, Haddon began work on 'The Study of Anthropology' which he modelled on Spencer's *The Study of Sociology* and included sociology as a component of an expanded anthropology: anthropology in its widest sense. He put these ideas into practice in the Aran Islands, demonstrating that the study of people under the name of anthropology was not confined to the uttermost parts of the world, but happened wherever people were. Haddon spent the remainder of the decade trying to blend anthropology, ethnology and sociology and this became the basis of his appointment as an ethnologist at Cambridge in 1901. Geddes wrote to Haddon on 10 May 1903 and reminded him that he had 'approached sociology through anthropology' while Geddes had approached 'anthropolo. through sociol.', a conversation that led to both becoming founding members of the Sociological Society.

Haddon addressed the issue of sociology three years later in a much revised second edition of the *History of Anthropology* that he wrote with Quiggin in 1910. He revisited a point made in the first edition to the effect that ethnology constituted 'the comparative and genetic study of human culture and man as a social animal' (Haddon and Quiggin 1910: 99). He clarified his intent in the second edition by stating that ethnologists had always fully appreciated the importance of contemporary sociology and declared that 'there is but an arbitrary distinction between these two subjects' (Haddon 1934: 100). Rivers failed to see this as a significant theoretical advance in 1911 and took anthropology in a different direction. It took two decades for Radcliffe-Brown to resurrect these ideas and use them to define a new form of anthropology called comparative sociology in an essay that gently separated him from Rivers, his mentor. It begs the question of whether Radcliffe-Brown's retrospection involved remembering Haddon and his anarchical ideas.

I have joked that Radcliffe-Brown wore Haddon's theoretical undergarments (secretly), but there is a breadcrumb trail – of the folklore variety – of facts and ideas that track Kropotkin's influence from Haddon to Radcliffe-Brown and on to his student William Lloyd Warner, director of the social research programme of the Harvard Anthropological Survey of the Irish Free State that commenced work in 1931. Warner supervised the ethnographic fieldwork conducted by Conrad Arensberg and Solon Kimball, the aim of which, according to Warner, was to apply a comparative sociology methodology in a modern, European setting (Arensberg and Kimball 1940: xiii). This is generally regarded as the beginning of modern anthropology in Ireland (see Donnan 2017: 21–22). In 2001, Anne Byrne, Ricca Edmondson and Tony Varley wrote a new introduction to a third edition of Arensberg and Kimball's report *Family and Community in Ireland* and described it as 'a detailed study of family and kin, of life and work, of mutuality in social and economic relationships among the small farmer class' (Arensberg and Kimball 2001: 2). That sentence recapitulated Haddon's combination of Kropotkin's work on mutuality with the Le Playist formula of place-work-folk in his study of small farmers and fisherfolk in the Aran Islands. Kropotkin proposed his theory of mutual aid in an article in *The Nineteenth Century* in 1890, the site of his row with Huxley. Haddon read Kropotkin before he discovered the Aran Islands in the same year and witnessed the operation of mutuality in an an-archic (self-governing) community that survived within a more advanced Anglo-Irish colony. Haddon called this a folk community, and it became the basic social unit of the ethnographic surveys of Ireland and the UK. Warner called it a traditional community, and it became the basic social unit of the ethnographic research undertaken by Arensberg and Kimball.

Finally, there is one other line of thought in Radcliffe-Brown's 1931 paper that connects him to Kropotkin and Haddon. Radcliffe-Brown (1932: 171) closed his paper by stating that an important task of anthropology was dealing with the problems that had 'arisen due [to] mingling of diverse peoples', a task Kropotkin set for geography in 1885 and Haddon incorporated into

'Incidents in the Life of a Torres Strait Islander' in 1890. Flower repeated Haddon's argument in 1894 to set the scene for an insurrection by anti-imperialist ethnologists in Ipswich in 1895.

To summarize, Haddon's ideas permeate Radcliffe-Brown's authoritative and interested assessment of the position of anthropology in 1931 and constitute, I propose, a sort of organizational memory of a time before Rivers that has slipped out of history because, in Radcliffe-Brown's words, it was ahead of its time. That is sufficient to dismiss the claim that Haddon merely facilitated the development of anthropology by others who were very different to him, and with it, the evolutionist construction of the history of anthropology that emerged in the 1990s. There were, however, important points of separation between Radcliffe-Brown and Haddon, and I focus here on two that speak to the issue of legacy. The first is that Radcliffe-Brown was engaged in a dialogue with other anthropologists within the academy, while Haddon operated in opposition to academic orthodoxy and engaged with the public through journalism, proto-cinematic slideshows, ethnographic cinema and the field club movement. Thus, while Radcliffe-Brown acted as an academic scientist, Haddon acted as a surrogate for his savage friends until, in an unprecedented collaboration with native mask-makers, choreographers and dancers, he combined the new art of cinematography with phonographic technologies to recreate their actions and voices, thereby potentially displacing the anthropologist as the privileged interpreter of other cultures. That leads into the second point of separation. Haddon did not subscribe to the idea that the comparative study of diverse cultures could lead to the discovery of general laws believed to pattern human thought and behaviour. For him, ethnological enlightenment was a matter of faith, albeit with a good dash of anarcho-utopian thought thrown in, and the function of an ethnographic experience was to generate sympathetic knowledge that disabled racism. Radcliffe-Brown understood this as an interpretative rather that inductive approach, and that brings the trail past Radcliffe-Brown to Clifford Geertz.

I read *The Interpretation of Cultures* (1973) shortly after switching from visual arts to anthropology by way of enrolling in a

PhD programme at Maynooth University, and Geertz's (1973: 5) differentiation between 'an experimental science in search of law' and 'an interpretive one in search of meaning' came to mind while writing this section. This seemed like an effective way of summarizing the difference between Haddon and Radcliffe-Brown in terms of the type of knowledge they attempted to generate. On a second reading, I was again struck by Geertz's adoption of Susanne Langer's argument that theoretical phases constituted academic trends as a pretext to argue that the failure of universal theories to account for human behaviour was a good reason to reconstruct anthropology. That sounded very like the reform programme agreed between Geddes, Haddon and Ellis in 1890, although they were dealing with biological rather than social laws. Moreover, Geertz and Haddon spoke the same language. Haddon represented anthropology in its widest aspect as an expression of his 'belief that the ethnical characteristics of a people are to be found in their arts, habits, language, and beliefs' (RIA 3,2 [1891–93]: 769) and that they needed to be studied because they gave ethnographers access to the deepest and most subtle thoughts of humanity (Haddon 1895a: 25). Geertz (2002: 10) summarized interpretive anthropology as an extension of his 'concern with the systems of meaning – beliefs, values, world views, forms of feeling, styles of thought – in terms of which particular peoples construct their existence'. Geertz (1973: 5–6) also wrote that if a person wanted to know about anthropology, they should overlook its theories and rhetoric and concentrate instead on what anthropologists did, which was ethnography. Understanding what doing ethnography involved was a route to understanding how anthropologists generated knowledge, and this is precisely what Haddon set out to do in *The Study of Man*, replacing an expert treatise by a reputable anthropologist with examples of ethnography in practice and the knowledge it generated in a range of settings. I suspect that Haddon's difficulty with treatise-writing was a factor in this decision, but that does not totally outweigh the similarity in the methodologies adopted because the same logic informed the surveys he organized.

'Doing ethnography' was a working hypothesis of the first phase of my research, that is, figuring out what Haddon was doing in Ireland between 1880 and 1901 to get a sense of what anthropology meant at that time and, more to the point, how it functioned in a period of civil and political unrest in the oldest colony. Given my focus on photography, it would have been conventional to take a well-worn theoretical path mapped by Foucault, Sekula and Tagg on one side and Said on the other. The breadcrumbs led elsewhere, however, and that brings Mead back into the story at a point located by Geertz. He challenged the idea that what a scientist did defined their science and listed the things that doing 'textbook' ethnography involved as 'establishing a rapport, selecting informants, transcribing texts, taking genealogies, mapping fields, keeping a diary, and so on' (Geertz 1973: 5–6). He did not mention photography. The camera featured only as a nescient, mechanical eye and so demonstrated how anthropology had become, in Mead's memorable phrase, a discipline of words.

I have argued that Haddon's photograph of Martin Faherty and the two women who withheld their identity was anything but nescient. It materialized a different way of making meaning, one that acknowledged resistance to empire and so represented a subversive interpretation of what doing ethnography meant in the colonial era in terms of the relationship between ethnography, social documentation and politics. August Sander explored the same problem in 'Young Farmers', a photograph of three young men on their way to a dance taken in 1914, in the region of Westerwald, it is thought. There are stylistic similarities between the two photographs and a further similarity in the ways they entered the public domain. Haddon placed his photograph in 'The Ethnography of the Aran Islands' and Sander included his in *Antlitz der Zeit* (*The Face of Our Time*), a collection considered so subversive that the Nazis suppressed it in 1936. This deserves a more detailed treatment, given Haddon's involvement with Julian Huxley in *We Europeans* (1935) and related tracts aimed at denying the scientific racism of the Nazi regime any form of anthropological legitimacy. What matters here is the consequence of both photographs. Haddon's photograph materialized a sympathy for the islanders that cost him his job on a government-funded survey of fishing grounds. Two years later, Cunningham removed him from the Ethnographic Survey of Ireland for much the same reason. As such, the photograph of Martin Faherty and the two women recalls simultaneously a subversive ethnography and an act of political oppression that justifies comparison with the acknowledged modernism of Sander.

To summarize, doing photography in the Aran Islands was, for Haddon, an act of humanizing the ethnographic subject, and that tested the political limits of organized anthropology. That places Haddon in the same trend-busting role that Geertz assumed in 1973. Furthermore, evidence of a shared belief in cultural anthropology, critical practice and a commitment to public engagement takes Haddon beyond Rivers and Radcliffe-Brown and into the company of Mead and Benedict and the glory days of popular anthropology in which *Coming of Age in Samoa* (1928) achieved what 'Incidents of the Life of a Torres Strait Islander' and 'Papuan Dances' promised.

The main problem here is that Haddon failed to complete the manifesto Ellis commissioned and left in its place a collection of deliberately popular journalism, forgotten slideshows, a collection of ten thousand photographs, three short films and associated phonograph recordings. There is nothing that matches Tylor's *Primitive Cultures* (1871), Radcliffe-Brown's *Andaman Islanders* (1922) or Malinowski's *Argonauts of the Western Pacific* (1922), and the idea of legacy is inevitably associated with the idea of a canon. That, by its nature, excludes the categorically awkward and ephemeral material that carries the memory of Haddon's revival of the humanitarian purpose of those ethnologists who, in the 1830s, stood with his grandparents in solidarity with the victims of colonialism. That was the ghost of ethnology past that haunted Huxley and the tension it generated is, to me, the defining characteristic of the culture war in anthropology in the 1890s. That war has been totally forgotten, yet the memory of humanitarian intervention – Tylor's reformist science – has persisted in the belief that each act of ethnography enacts a long tradition of radical analysis. As we pass the centenary of the foundational texts of the British tradition in anthropology, the question is whether the romance of anthropology past has any place in the economic reality of a neoliberal academy that has been forced by the murder of George Floyd to come face to face with the ghost of ethnology past.

DOES IT MATTER?

I completed writing up my doctoral research and turned my attention to the question of impact in November 2019, when the Amazon burned like never before after Jair Bolsonaro's government relaxed restrictions on colonists. Indigenous activist Celia Xakriabá made a short film in which she described the situation 'as living through a moment of legislated genocide' that surpassed even the time of colonization. Her phrasing reminded me of Haddon's use of 'legalized murder' to characterize the complicity of legislators and the executive in the extermination of the inhabitants of annexed territories. Xakriabá posted her film on the YouTube channel of Survival International as part of the Tribal Voice project, an online campaign that provides a platform for Indigenous activists to campaign against land grabs, racial violence and genocide. The project constitutes a twenty-first-century analogue of Haddon's photo-ethnographic activism, the main difference being that in 1890 limits on audiovisual technologies meant that Haddon had to act as an interlocutor – the English savage of this volume – although he adopted cinematography and phonography in 1898 as an ethnographic method that privileged the actions and voices of the people he represented. The analogous nature of these campaigns suggested that the study of racism and genocide in a historical context could become a platform for a radical intervention in the problem of racism and genocide in a contemporary context, given that Xakriabá's call for action coincided with a steady increase in racism-motivated incidents in Ireland. There was no appetite for such an approach while climate change and the #MeToo movement were seen as more pressing problems, a point made by Patrick Prendergast, Provost of TCD, in an interview with Niamh Horan (2021) that the *Irish Independent* published in July 2021; incidentally, Haddon wrote a column for the same paper. Horan's article appeared one year after George Floyd was murdered in police custody and registers how the Black Lives Matter movement brought racism and its history onto the agenda of Irish universities with an urgency that had been conspicuously absent until then.

That engagement with colonial legacies has focussed attention on the material aspects of Haddon's legacy, a collection of skulls that remains on display in a service corridor in the 'Old' Anatomy Department in TCD and an associated collection of ethnographic material from the Torres Strait and New Guinea in the National Museum of Ireland, formerly the Museum of Science and Art. Cunningham was not interested in craniology, although he built the required collection of skulls and skeletons while establishing a department of anthropology in the School of Anatomy. Meanwhile, Haddon used items of dress, ornament and dance costume from the museum to add a material dimension to his anti-racist slideshows, and that points to the purpose of the collection. His experience of population collapse in the Torres Strait generated an almost millennial belief that islanders throughout Oceania faced the same fate as the Tasmanians, and he envisaged his ethnological collections as functioning as storehouses of ancestral knowledge. Both collections are now caught up in the movement seeking the return of culturally sensitive material and human remains held in colonial-era collections in museums and universities. Community representatives lodged a claim for the repatriation of skulls that Haddon stole from burial grounds in the west of Ireland after Prendergast announced plans to 'decolonize' the campus in late 2020. He conceded that stolen skulls should be returned (see Walsh 2021a), although a working party tasked with developing the Anatomy Museum subsequently blocked repatriation on the basis that (a) the remains are archaeological rather than ethnological in origin, and (b) that provenance is uncertain, despite Haddon's written record of the theft of skulls on Inishbofin and other documentary evidence of his involvement in organized grave-robbing in the Aran Islands, Kerry and other sites. Negotiations resumed in 2022 with Provost Linda Doyle and her colonial legacies team but the board of the college endorsed a compromise with Anatomy whereby the Inishbofin remains were returned but the other half of the collection was retained pending further investigation by the colonial legacies team.

That brings us to the non-material aspect of Haddon's legacy, his anti-racist activism. As we enter a new phase of land grabs, environmental degradation, racial violence and legislated genocide at multiple flashpoints in the homelands of tribal peoples across the Middle East, South America, Africa and Asia, Xakriabiá's call for action is a good reason to revisit Haddon's ethnological project, especially his critique of anthropology as a restricted form of enquiry. His battles with Huxley, Cunningham and Macalister matter today because the issue of dissent in organized anthropology has been brought into sharp focus by the rise of practical science and the commodification of research in universities. This predates the resurgence of the Black Lives Matter movement. Keir Martin and Alex Flynn (2015) posed the problem in an opinion piece in *Anthropology Today* in 2015. They perceived a widespread and understandable fear among anthropologists in the UK that an 'engagement with political and social issues might damage the purity of anthropological theory' (ibid.: 12) and linked this to the Research Council's redefinition of impact in terms of a contribution to economic competitiveness. Martin and Flynn constructed a dichotomy between a radical tradition of innovation through engagement and a neoliberal academy that discouraged engagement, even though an engagement with pressing social issues had always been a driver of development in anthropological theory. Their article could be read as a rearguard action by traditionalists worried about the disappearance, under pressure from 'the reward structure of the contemporary neoliberal academy' (ibid.: 14; Besteman and Gusterson 2008: 62), of an anthropological nirvana imagined by Mead and Benedict. Insinuated throughout their analysis is the idea that anthropological interventions can have political outcomes and politics have become a factor in deciding which interventions are considered acceptable, suggesting that a sort of operational conditioning has become an effect of auditing procedures introduced as part of a more general reform of universities.

In 2021, Sarah Green, outgoing president of the European Association of Social Anthropologists, considered the problem of constrained knowledge-production systems in a letter published in the March edition of the *EASA Newsletter*. She described a perfect storm in which populism and a drift to authoritarianism drove a backlash against social science departments while structural changes in universities introduced auditing regimes that prioritized research income and promoted a dependence on external research funding, all of which discouraged or actively inhibited an engagement with social issues such as 'reproductive rights, LGBTQI+ issues, gender relations, asylum, and migration' (Green 2021: 4). The impact of external funding was considered in a draft report on new research models published by Alice Tilche and Rita Astuti in the January 2020 edition of the EASA newsletter. They listed new forms of knowledge-production that privileged large, externally funded projects that were 'calling into question the key principles of our discipline' by reintroducing the distinction between those who gather data and those who analyse it, the adoption of an ill-fitting science model, and commercial pressures that threaten 'the ethical integrity and epistemological underpinnings of a discipline' (Tilche and Astuti 2020: 13).

Anthropology is, it seems, going through another crisis and, taking Geertz's recommendation on board, the question is how the changes documented by Green, Tilche and Astuti are affecting what ethnographers do. In 2014, I investigated what 'doing anthropology' meant in an article for the *Irish Independent* (Walsh 2014: 20–21). At that stage I had no idea that I would, as Haddon put it, go into anthropology, but my work on the photographic archive of the Irish Ethnographic Survey focussed attention on differences between anthropology in Ireland in the 1890s and the 2010s, and this became the focus of a series of interviews with students and graduates working within and without the academy. Mark Maguire, then Head of the Department of Anthropology at Maynooth University, listed the projects that students were working on. They included 'everything from corporate speak and prison guards who train dogs to alternative medicine, civil partnerships, an poverty and indebtedness' (ibid.), and the range of research topics reflected graduate employment opportunities in education, healthcare, criminology, environmentalism, human rights and the environmental sector: anthropology in its widest sense and confirmation of Haddon's (1895a: 25) prediction that there was scope for anthropology 'even in our cities'. In addition, there was an awareness of a growing trend in the technology sector of using anthropologists as user-experience analysts. About a third of all graduates worked on academic research.

My interview notes recorded a striking similarity between the skill set I used and the problems I encountered as an organization and methods analyst, especially in my investigation in 1979 of the administration of a prison. To the consternation of my superiors in the Department of Justice, I wandered into anthropology – to rephrase an argument used by the people who criticized Haddon in 1895 – when I switched from a study of duties performed to an exploration of violence in the context of daily battles between two communities who shared a contested space, the sort of 'little wars' that Haddon witnessed in the west of Ireland. These engagements were an essential part of the ethnographic tradition, and they still happen, especially in the spaces Sarah Green identified, where marginalized groups and state agencies interact; the site of Maguire's work on migration (see Low and Maguire, 2019 for instance). The projects I reviewed in 2014, however, signalled a more general shift towards public services provision aligned with the methodologies required for the externally funded research projects identified by Tilche and Astuti. The problem here is the perception that increased instrumentalization – a combination of 'practical' anthropology and restricted systems of knowledge-production – is placing off-limits the marginal spaces traditionally explored by anthropologists and ethnologists. This shift from 'traditional' to 'practical' anthropology in an academic setting can be seen in a 2020 report on *Research and Innovation* at Maynooth University. The report conforms to the new auditing systems Green described and somewhat inadvertently confirms Tilche and Astuti's earlier findings in relation to (a) academics becoming producers of auditable outputs, including, especially, external funding, and (b) changes in the underlying structure of the discipline, including the absence of any reference to the traditional role of postgrad research in relation to innovation in anthropology. The document illustrates how the dichotomy between public engagement and academic research that Martin and Flynn observed in 2015 has morphed into a dichotomy between 'traditional' and 'practical' anthropology, and Tilche and Astuti interpreted the rise of 'practical' anthropology as a threat to disciplinary tradition.

The same conversation has been taking place in sociology. In 2021, Aldon Morris, president of the American Sociological Association, published a post on the Association's website asking members to consider an intense, decades-long debate between purists who are interested only in the dispassionate pursuit of sociological truths and emancipationists who see sociological truths as a catalyst for social change. Morris sided with the emancipationists and called on members to push the limits of knowledge-production and create 'a sociology of liberation rooted in empirical observation and theorizing from data rather than ideology' (Morris 2021). He identified 'gender discrimination and sexual harassment, racism, ableism, heteronormativity, [and] devastating class inequalities' as the pressing social issues, and I have argued that historical precursors of those issues engaged Haddon, Geddes, Ellis and their associates, including Caroline Haddon and Margaret (Haddon) Hinton. Ellis created the Contemporary Science Series as a vehicle to engage the public in a debate about these issues and asked Haddon to ground the project in a study of anthropology in defiance of a doctrine that discouraged any discussion under the name of anthropology of those issues. Their struggle bears a remarkable resemblance to that described by Flynn, Green, Martin and Morris, and this is where Haddon becomes relevant to contemporary debates about the scope and significance of anthropology.

Accordingly, I conclude this section with a final visit to Cunningham's laboratory. Galton promoted the utility of scientific anthropology by highlighting its role in the identification of criminals and, according to a report in the *Irish Times*, Haughton used this as an example of the practical application of the methods being developed in the anthropometric laboratory in Dublin. Cunningham trained Browne as a data collector and sent him to the Aran Islands to elucidate the various social problems that were fuelling anti-government sentiment and threatening the political integrity of the United Kingdom. Ten years on, Cunningham demonstrated the efficacy of his system during an investigation of the collapse in the physical condition of army recruits undertaken by the government-appointed Inter-Departmental Committee on Physical Degeneration (1903–4). This paved the way for a new era of social policy informed by social science, and that required the sort of structural links between government agencies and social scientists that characterize 'practical' anthropology today. Setha Low and Mark Maguire (2019) explored the challenge this posed for anthropologists in relation to security, which they introduced as one of the most prominent topics in contemporary anthropology. They framed their collection of essays on *Spaces of Security* with a statement about the lack of a coherent ethnographic approach to the exploration of the spaces where anthropology and security meet, and I propose that this incoherence – this lack of a sense of anthropological mission – goes to the heart of the problem with 'practical' anthropology. In summary, the current instrumentalization of anthropology in areas like security migration, climate change, public health, education, and technology-driven social programmes presents something of paradox because of the legacy of Galton and Cunningham. Contemporary anthropologists and sociologists have overwhelmingly rejected this legacy and sought comfort in its radical other whilst, according to the new radicals in the guise of traditionalists, developing disciplinary structures that marginalise voices considered too 'other' in a neo-liberal academy, a replay of the struggle Haddon and his anarcho-utopian allies in various reformist movements had with conservatives in organised anthropology and the academy. Ironically, the precarity Haddon experienced as an ethnologist at Cambridge has become a major issue for anthropologists working in an academic setting.

To finish, the persistence of Haddon's ideas, and the relevance of his experience of becoming an ethnologist entitle him to be reinstated into the story of the modernization of anthropology as a radically humanitarian voice that ought to be heard in an era when racism and its history have engaged the public like never before. The Amazon burns, genocide is legislated for and structural racism continues to claim lives while disciplinary anthropology disengages from the field and reverts to being an ideologically constrained instrument of social and economic policy. History repeats itself, and the question is whether contemporary academic anthropology, for all its practicality, can claim to be as relevant as this English savage of yore.

REFERENCES

This section prioritizes primary references (including photographic collections) and related sources in records of proceedings, reports and journalism. The object is to give some sense of the flow of ideas and influence through various networks. 'Secondary References' is a more conventional blend of contributions by individuals to journals, original works, histories and critical studies.

All material from the Haddon Papers is used with the permission of the Syndics of Cambridge University Library.

PRIMARY REFERENCES

Photography Collections

Cambridge University Museum of Archaeology and Anthropology (Haddon Photograph Collections).

Photographic collection of Andrew Francis Dixon (TCD 'Old' Anatomy, uncatalogued).

Photograph albums of Charles R. Browne (TCD Special Collections, Manuscript Library).

Photographic collection of John Millington Synge (TCD).

Photographic collection of the British Museum (Haddon Collection).

National Film and Sound Archive of Australia (Torres Strait Islanders 1898).

National Museum of Northern Ireland (Welch and Patterson).

Film/Video

Torres Strait Islanders. 1898. Dir. Alfred Cort Haddon. National Film and Sound Archive of Australia. Retrieved 23 November 2022 from https://aso.gov.au/titles/historical/torres-strait-islanders/clip1/.

Un chien andalou. 1929. Dir. Luis Buñuel. IMDB. Trailer retrieved 23 November 2022 from https://www.imdb.com/title/tt0020530/videoplayer/vi2380267801?ref_=tt_ov_vi.

Man with a Movie Camera. 1929. Dir. Dziga Vertov. BFI (British Film Institute). Trailer retrieved 23 November 2022 from https://www.youtube.com/watch?v=BtTlgxtoqhg.

The Masks of Mer. 1954. Dir. Michael Eaton. Royal Anthropological Institute.

Survival International. 2019. 'They're Killing Us with Pen and Paper'. *YouTube*. Retrieved 23 November 2022 from https://youtu.be/G_XTJIGZ_D8.

Sound Recordings

The British Library, Ethnographic Wax Cylinders (Torres Strait 1898).

Museum Collections

Haddon Collection, National Museum of Ireland (formerly Museum of Science and Art).

'Old' Anatomy Museum Collections, School of Medicine, Trinity College, University of Dublin.

Manuscripts

Haddon, Alfred Cort. 1888–89. Torres Strait and New Guinea Journal (CUL File 1029/TROVE).

———. 1890. SS *Fingal* Journal (June–Aug.), pp. 1–40 and 51–56 (CUL File 22).

———. 1890. SS *Fingal* Journal (Aran Islands), pp. 40–50 (Haddon Library File 88.H).

———. 1890. 'The Aran Islands' (Haddon Library File P.88.H).

———. 1891. SS *Harlequin* Journal (CUL File 22).

———. 1891. Draft Critique of the Imperial Institute/proposal for a bureau of ethnology (CUL File 5061).

———. 1892. Partial MS 'Ethnography of Aran Islands, County Galway' (CUL File 4062).

———. 1898–99. Torres Strait and New Guinea Journal (CUL 1030).

Correspondence (A–Z)

Haddon Papers, Cambridge University Library
Banim to Haddon, 23 January 1893, File 3058.
Banim to Haddon, 1 February 1893, File 3058.

Bettany to Haddon, 11 June 1890, File 3.
Bettany to Haddon, 6 September 1890, File 3.
Brabrook to Haddon, 18 January 1893, File 3058.
Browne to Haddon, 5 June 1894, File 4061.
Cole to Haddon, 8 July 1901, File 3.
Cunningham to Haddon, 19 February 1903, File 3058.
Daniel Lane to Haddon, 21 December [1890], File 3058.
Editor (James Knowles), *The Nineteenth Century*, to Haddon, 17 November 1891, File 5061.
Editor (Frank Harris), *Fortnightly Review*, to Haddon, 19 February 1891, File 5061.
Editor, *New Review*, to Haddon, 28 October 1891, File 5061.
Ellis to Haddon, 8 May 1890, File 3.
Ellis to Haddon, 14 May 1891, File 3.
Flinders Petrie to Haddon, 24 April 1895, File 5061.
Flower to Haddon, 17 May 1890. File 3.
Frazer to Haddon, 29 January 1891, File 3.
Frazer to Haddon, 14 November 1899, File 21/1.
Galton to Haddon, 2 December 1891, File F5061.
Garson to Haddon, 30 March 1891, File 3.
Garson to Haddon, 20 February 1893, File 3.
Geddes to Haddon, n.d., File 3.
Geddes to Haddon, 11 December [1889], File 3.
Haddon to Ernest Haddon, 12 August 1885, File 22.
Haddon to Ellis, 14 May 1890, File 3.
Haddon to Foster, 7 May 1891, File 21/2.
Haddon to Myers, 27 January 1901, File 3058.
Haughton to D22 December 1892, File 3058.
Holt to Haddon, n.d. [1891?], File 3058.
Huxley to Newton, 3 December 1880, File 21/2.
Huxley to Haddon, 1 January 1892, File 5061.
Macalister to Haddon, 18 December 1891, File 5061.
McFarlane to Haddon, 2 December 1887, File F21/2.
McFarlane to Haddon, 28 December 1887, Folder F21/2.
Milne to Haddon, 13 March 1892, File 3058.
Milne to Haddon, 14 April 1892, File 3058.
Newton to Haddon, 4 December 1880, File 21/2.
Peek to Haddon, 25 March 1892, File 3058.
O'Callaghan to Haddon, 19 May 1891, File 3058.
Ridgeway to Haddon, 16 December 1899, File 21/1.
Schmeltz to Haddon, 20 November 1890, File 3.

Schmeltz to Haddon, 21 June 1891, File 3.
Wallace to Haddon, 28 November 1887, File 3.
Welch to Haddon, May 1982, File 3058.

TCD

Haddon to Cunningham, 10 November 1889 (uncatalogued, 'Old' Anatomy, TCD).

Macalister to Cunningham, 18 December 1890 (uncatalogued, 'Old' Anatomy, TCD).

Other

Frazer to Galton, 10 October 1897 (Ackerman 2005: 101–2).

Geddes to Haddon, 10 May 1903, TROVE. Retrieved 23 November 2022 from https://nla.gov.au/nla.obj-1259871109

Haddon to Geddes, 25 December 1887, TROVE. Retrieved 14 January 2023 from https://nla.gov.au/nla.obj-1629360189

Huxley to Hooker (Huxley 1900: 204).

Huxley to Platt Ball (Huxley 1900: 284).

Records (By Date)

Anthropological Institute of Great Britain and Ireland/Council Minutes

A10 RAI Council Minutes, 10 May 1892, f: 239.

Journal of the Anthropological Institute of Great Britain and Ireland (JAI)

1879. *JAI* 8.

    Flower. 'Illustrations of the Mode of Preserving the Dead in Darnley Island and in South Australia': 389–95.

1885. *JAI* 14.

    Garson. 'The Frankfort Craniometric Agreement, with Critical Remarks Thereon': 64–83.

    Galton. 'On the Anthropometric Laboratory at the Late International Health Exhibition': 205–21.

    Galton. 'Some Results of the Anthropometric Laboratory': 275–87.

1887. *JAI* 16.

    'Miscellaneous Business of the Meeting on June 1st, 1886': 174–75.

    Galton. 'Opening Remarks by the President: Anthropological Conferences on the Native Races of The British Possessions, Being a Series of Special Meetings of the Anthropological Institute held in the Conference Hall of the Colonial and Indian Exhibition': 386–402.

Lubbock. 'The Nationalities of the United Kingdom. Extracts from Letters to the "Times"': 418–22.

1889. *JAI* 18.

Venn. 'Cambridge Anthropometry': 140–53.

Galton. 'On Head Growth in Students at the University of Cambridge': 155–56.

Galton. 'Address Delivered at the Anniversary Meeting of the Anthropological Institute of Great Britain and Ireland, January 22nd, 1889': 401–19.

Frazer and Holmes. 'Questions on the Manners, Customs, Religion, Superstitions, &c. of Uncivilised or Semi-Civilised Peoples': 431–40.

1890. *JAI* 19.

Haddon. 'The Ethnography of the Western Tribe of Torres Straits: 297–440.

'Report of the Council of the Anthropological Institute of Great Britain and Ireland for the Year 1889': 476–80.

Beddoe. 'President's Address': 481–93.

1891. *JAI* 20.

Beddoe. 'Anniversary Address': 348–59.

1892. *JAI* 21.

Galton. 'Retrospect of Work Done at My Anthropometric Laboratory at South Kensington': 32–35.

Cunningham and Haddon. 'The Anthropometric Laboratory of Ireland': 35–39.

1893. *JAI* 22.

Brabrook. 'On the Organisation of Local Anthropological Research': 262–74.

Tylor. 'Anniversary Address': 376–85.

1894. *JAI* 23.

Macalister. 'President's Address': 400–17.

1895. *JAI* 24.

Reid. 'Exhibition and Description of the Skull of a Microcephalic Hindu': 105–8.

Haddon. 'Minute of April 10: Prof. A. C. HADDON delivered an address on "Ethnographical Studies in the West of Ireland", illustrated with the optical lantern' (original formatting), *JAI* 24: 108.

1896. *JAI* 25.

Brabrook. 'Anniversary Address': 379–405.

1899. *JAI* 28 (3–4).

Rudler. 'Address Delivered at the Anniversary Meeting of the Anthropological Institute of Great Britain and Ireland, January 24th, 1899': 312–27.

1900. *JAI* 30.
> Read. 'Presidential Address, Delivered at the Anniversary Meeting of the Anthropological Institute of Great Britain and Ireland. 30th January, 1900': 6–21.

1905. *JAI* 35.
'Proceedings of the Anthropological Institute': 435–37.

1908. *JAI* 38.
Cunningham. 'Anniversary Address': 10–35.

BAAS Reports

Note: dates are given in the following format: year of publication [year of meeting].

1879 [1878]. *Report of the Forty-Eighth Meeting of the British Association for the Advancement of Science Held at Dublin in August 1878*. London: John Murray.
> Huxley. 'Department of Anthropology (Address by the Chairman)': 573–78.

1885 [1884]. *Report of the Fifty-Fourth Meeting of the British Association for the Advancement of Science, Montreal, 1894*. London: John Murray.
> Tylor. 'The President Delivered the Following Address': 899–910.

1886 [1885]. *Report of the Fifty-Fourth Meeting of the British Association for the Advancement of Science Held at Aberdeen in September 1885*. London: John Murray.
> Galton. 'Address by Francis Galton, M.A., F.R.S., President of the Anthropological Institute, President of the Section': 1206–14.
> Cunningham. 'Some Important Points of Comparison between the Chimpanzee and Man': 1226.

1890 [1889]. *Report of the Fifty-Ninth Meeting of the British Association for the Advancement of Science Held at Newcastle-upon-Tyne in September 1889*. London: John Murray.
> Galton. 'On the Advisability of Assigning Marks for Bodily Efficiency in the Examinations for Candidates for the Public Services': 471–73.
> Galton. 'On the Principle and Methods of Assigning Marks in Examinations on Bodily Efficiency': 474–77.
> Turner. 'Address by Professor Sir William Turner, M.B., LL.D., F.R.SS. L. & E., President of the Section': 756–71.
> Cunningham. 'The Proportion of Bone and Cartilage in the Lumbar Section of the Vertebral Column in the Ape and Different Races of Men': 777.
> Haddon. 'On Some Former Customs and Beliefs of the Torres Straits Islanders': 786.

Tylor et al. 'APPENDIX: Fifth Report of the Committee Appointed for the Purpose of Investigating and Publishing Reports on the Physical Characters, Languages, and Industrial and Social Condition of the North-Western Tribes of the Dominion of Canada': 797–801.

Boas. 'First General Report on the Indians of British Columbia: Introductory Note': 801–900.

1893 [1892]. *Report of the Sixty-Second Meeting of the British Association for the Advancement of Science Held at Edinburgh in September 1892.* London: John Murray.

Galton et al. 'Ethnographical Survey of the UK – First Report of the Committee': 621–53.

Macalister. 'Section H – Anthropology: President of the Section': 886–96.

Brabrook. 'On the Organisation of Local Anthropological Research': 896.

1894 [1893]. *Report of the Sixty-Third Meeting of the British Association for the Advancement of Science Held at Nottingham in September 1893.*

Galton. '1. Physical Types of the inhabitants. Photographic Portraits': 642–43.

1894. *Report of the Sixty-Fourth Meeting of the British Association for the Advancement of Science Held at Oxford in August 1894.* London: John Murray.

Brabrook. 'Second Report of the Committee of the British Association for the Advancement of Science Appointed to Organise an Ethnographic Survey of the United Kingdom': 419–29.

Flower. 'Section H – Anthropology: Presidents Address': 762–74.

Haddon. 'On the People of Western Ireland and their Mode of Life': 785.

1895. *Report of the Sixty-Fifth Meeting of the British Association for the Advancement of Science Held at Ipswich in September 1895.* London: John Murray.

'The Necessity for the Immediate Investigation of the Biology of Oceanic Islands': xciii, 93.

'Section H – Anthropology: Tuesday September 17 (Discussion on Interference with the Civilisation of Other Races)': 832.

1896. *Report of the Sixty-Sixth Meeting of the British Association for the Advancement of Science Held at Liverpool in September 1896.* London: John Murray.

Haddon. 'The Necessity for the Immediate Investigation of the Biology of Oceanic Islands': 487–89.

'Section H – Anthropology: Interim Report on the Immediate Investigation of Oceanic Islands': 929.

1898 [1897]. *Report of the Sixty-Sixth Meeting of the British Association for the Advancement of Science Held at Toronto in September 1897.* London: John Murray.

Haddon. 'The Necessity for the Immediate Investigation of the Biology of Oceanic Islands': 352.

1900 [1899]. *Report of the Seventieth Meeting of the British Association for the Advancement of Science held at Dover in September 1899.* London: John Murray.

Brabrook. 'Ethnographical Survey of the United Kingdom, Seventh and Final Report of the Committee': 493–95.

1912 [1911]. *Report of the Eightieth Meeting of the British Association for the Advancement of Science. Portsmouth: 1911 August 31–September 7.* London: John Murray.

Rivers. 'The Ethnological Analysis of Culture', 490–99 (reprinted in *Science* 34 (1911): 385–97).

1932. *British Association for the Advancement of Science: Report of the Centenary Meeting, London 1931 September 23–30.* London: Office of the British Association.

Radcliffe-Brown. 'The Present Position of Anthropological Studies': 142–71.

BAAS/Anthropological Institute

Notes and Queries on Anthropology (N&QA)

1874. *Notes and Queries on Anthropology: For the Use of Travellers and Residents in Uncivilized Lands* (1st edn). London: Edward Stanford.

1892. *Notes and Queries on Anthropology* (2nd edn), ed. J. G Garson and C. H. Read. London: Harris.

Flinders Petrie. 'No. LXXVII. – Photography': 235–36.

1899. *Notes and Queries on Anthropology* (3rd edn), ed. J. G. Garson and C. H. Read. London: Harris.

Read. 'Ethnography: Prefatory Note': 87.

Haddon. 'No. LXXVII. – Photography': 235–40.

Garson. 'Additional Notes on Photography': 244–46.

1912. *Notes and Queries on Anthropology* (4th edn), ed. Myres, J. Linton, B. W. Freire-Marreco. London: Harris.

Rivers. 'A General Account of Method': 108–27.

Sharp. 'Dancing': 217–23.

Haddon and Myres. 'Appendix: Photography': 267–70.

Other:
1909. *Anthropometric Investigation in the British Isles: Report of the Committee (being the final report on Anthropometric Method). Reprinted with additional illustrations, by permission of the Council from the Report of the British Association (Dublin) 1908.* London: The Royal Anthropological Institute.

Belfast Naturalists' Field Club (BNFC)
1893. *Annual Report and Proceedings. For the Year ending 31 March 1893, 2(3)vi (1892-93).*
    Haddon. 'The Aran Islands, a Study in Irish Ethnography': 538–39.
1894. *Annual Report and Proceedings. For the Year ending 31 March 1894, 2(4)i (1893-94).*
    Yeats, W. B. 'Irish Folk-Lore': 46–48.
    Patterson, C. 'A Few Children's Games': 48–52.
    Patterson, W. H., and Haddon. 'Report of the Ethnographical Committee': 52–54.
1895. *Annual Report and Proceedings. For the Year ending 31 March 1895, 2(4)ii (1894-95).*
    Hyde. 'Celtic Language and Literature': 204–5.
    Haddon. 'Modern Relics of Olden Time': 216–17.

Folk-Lore/Folklore: Transactions of the Folklore Society (FLS)
1890. Haddon. 'Legends from Torres Straits', *Folk-Lore* 1,1 (March 1890): 47–81.
    'Notes and News', *Folk-Lore* 1,1 (1890): 127–29.
    Haddon. 'Legends from Torres Straits. II', *Folk-Lore* 1,2 (June 1890): 172–96.
1891. Gomme. 'Annual Address to the Folk-Lore Society, November 26th, 1890', *Folk-Lore* 2,1 (1891): 1–30.
1893. Haddon. 'A Batch of Irish Folk-lore', *Folk-Lore* 4,3 (September 1893): 349–64.
1895. Haddon. 'Photography and Folklore', in 'Proceedings at Meeting of Wednesday, April 24, 1895', *Folk-Lore* 6,3 (September 1895): 221–24.

Royal Dublin Society (RDS)
1890–91. *Proceedings* (RDS 127)
    'Appendix E. Report of the Fisheries Committee': 28–29.
    'Appendix E. First Report of Survey of Fishing Grounds, West of Ireland, 1890' [presented on 13 November 1890]: 29–66.

1891–92. *Proceedings* (RDS 128)
'Appendix C. Survey of Fishing Grounds on West Coast – First Report to the Fisheries Committee. By Rev. W. S. Green, Director of the Survey' [presented 12 November 1891]: 23–72.

1891–92. *Scientific Proceedings* (RDS 7)
'Survey of Fishing Grounds, West Coast of Ireland, 1890–1891. Introductory Note by Professor A. C. Haddon M.A. (Cantab.), M.R.I.A.; Professor Of Zoology, Royal College of Science, Dublin; Naturalist to the Survey' [read 18 November 1891]: 221–24).

'Survey of Fishing Grounds, West Coast of Ireland, 1890–1891. Report on the Results of the Fishing Operations. By Ernest W. L. Holt, Assistant Naturalist to the Survey (communicated by Professor A. C. Haddon, M.A., F.Z.S.)' [read 18 November 1891]: 225–477 and plates.

1888–92. *Scientific Transactions* (RDS 4,2)
'A Revision of the British Actiniæ. Part I'. By Alfred C. Haddon, M. A. (Cantab.), M.R.I.A., Professor of Zoology, Royal College of Science, Dublin. Plates XXXI. to XXXVII [read 13 June 1888]: 297–361 and plates.

'Survey of Fishing Grounds, West Coast of Ireland, 1890. 1. – On the Eggs and Larvæ of Teleostean. By Ernest W. L. Holt, St. Andrews's Marine Laboratory' [read by Haddon 19 November 1890]: 435–474 and plates.

'Reports on the Zoological Collections Made in Torres Straits by Professor A. C. Haddon, 1888–1889. Actiniæ: I. Zoantheæ by Professor Alfred C. Haddon, M.A. (Cantab.), M.R.I.A.; Professor Of Zoology, Royal College of Science, Dublin, and Miss Alice M. Shackleton, B.A. Plates lxi, lxii, lxiii, lxiv' [read by Shackleton 19 November 1890]: 673–701 and plates.

Royal Irish Academy (RIA)

1886. *Cunningham Memoirs* 2 (RIA 1886)
Cunningham. 'The Lumbar Curve in Man and the Apes, with an Account of the Topographical Anatomy of the Chimpanzee, Orangutan, and Gibbon' [Read 8 February 1886]: 1–148 and plates.

1887–93. *Minutes of Proceedings* (RIA 1887–93).

1887-92. *Transactions* (RIA 29)
Cunningham. 'The Skeleton of the Irish Giant, Cornelius Magrath' [read 26 January 1891]: 553–61.

1889–91. *Proceedings* (RIA 3,1).
Haddon. 'Report on the Actiniæ Dredged off the South-West Coast of Ireland in May, 1888' [read 13 May 1889]: 370–74.

1891–93. *Proceedings* (RIA 3,2).
    Haddon. 'Studies in Irish Craniology: The Aran Islands, Co. Galway' [read 12 December 1892]: 759–67.
    Haddon and Browne 'The Ethnography of the Aran Islands, County Galway' [read 12 December 1892]: 768–830 and plates.
1893–96. Proceedings (RIA 3,3).
    Browne. 'The Ethnography of Inishbofin and Inishshark, County Galway', [read 30 November 1893]: 317-370 and plates.

Trinity College, University of Dublin (Uncatalogued)

Dublin Anthropometric Laboratory: Schedules of measurements and miscellaneous records.

Anthropological Laboratory: Irish Ethnographic Survey schedules of measurements 1892–97).

Anthropological Laboratory, Trinity College, Dublin: Catalogue.

Reports (By Date)

Parliamentary Select Committee (Great Britain). 1837. *Report of the Parliamentary Select Committee on Aboriginal Tribes (British Settlements)*. London: Aborigines Protection Society.

University of Melbourne. 1888. *Report of the Proceedings of the University of Melbourne for the Year 1887–88*. Victoria: University of Melbourne.

British Association. 1895. *Discussion 'On the Contact of European and Native Civilisations' Held at the Meeting of the British Association*, Ipswich, 1895 (copy filed in Haddon Papers, File 5408).

Inter-Departmental Committee on Physical Deterioration. 1904. *Report on the Interdepartmental Committee on Physical Degeneration, Vols 1–3*. London: HM Stationery Office.

Haddon, Alfred Cort. 1935. *Reports of the Cambridge Anthropological Expedition to Torres Straits, Vol. I (General Ethnography)*. Cambridge: Cambridge University Press.

Maynooth University. 2022. *Research and Innovation Report 2020*. Retrieved 8 March 2020 from https://www.maynoothuniversity.ie/research/research-and-innovation-maynooth-university/research-reports.

Newspapers and Popular Journals (By Date)

Galton, Francis. 1879. 'Psychometric Experiments', *Brain* 2: 149–57.

Kropotkin, Pëtr. 1884a. 'An Appeal to the Young I', *Justice*, 2 February: 2.

———. 1884b. 'An Appeal to the Young II', *Justice*, 30 August: 3

———. 1885. 'What Geography Ought to Be', *The Nineteenth Century* 18: 940–56.

Anon. 1886. 'The African Earthmen' [advert], *Freeman's Journal*, 20 April: 4.

Anon. 1888. 'A Morning with the Anthropometric Detectives', *Pall Mall Gazette*, 16 November: 1–2.

Davitt, Michael. 1888. 'The Starving Islanders in Arran', *Pall Mall Gazette*, 26 April: 8.

Huxley, Thomas H. 1888. 'The Struggle for Existence: And its Bearing upon Man', *The Nineteenth Century* (February): 165 [full page data not available].

Anon. 1889. 'Science Jottings: Our Monthly Look Around', *Illustrated London News*, 7 September: 310.

Anon. 1889. 'Torres Straits at the British Museum, *The Colonies and India: A Weekly Journal of General Information*, 23 October: 28–29.

Anon. 1889. 'Notes', *Nature* 40 (October 24): 626.

Reuters. 1889. 'Terrible Massacre in New Guinea: Murder of Missionaries and Boat's Crew', *Glasgow Herald*, 31 October: 7.

Anon. 1890. 'Royal Dublin Society Afternoon Lectures', *The Daily Express*, February 18: 5.

Anon. 1890. 'Contemporary Science Series', *Journal of Mental Science* 36,153 (April): 265.

Anon. 1890. 'Royal Dublin Society', *Irish Times*, 22 February: 6.

Anon. 1890. 'Royal Dublin Society', *Irish Times*, 28 June: 8.

Anon. 1890. 'Royal Dublin Society', *Freeman's Journal*, 20 November: 7.

Banim, Mary. 1890a. 'Here and There through Ireland: The Arran Islands', *Freeman's Journal*, 30 August: 9.

———. 1890b. 'Here and There through Ireland: The Arran Islands', *Freeman's Journal*, 6 September: 9.

Anon. 1891. 'Savage Art', *The Freeman's Journal*, 21 February: 5.

Anon. 1891. 'The Anthropometry Laboratory Trinity College', *Irish Times*, 26 June: 4–5.

Kropotkin, Pëtr. 1891. 'Mutual Aid among Savages', *The Nineteenth Century* 24 (April): 538–59.

Green, William, Spotswood. 1892. 'The Fishing Industry on the West Coast of Ireland', *The Graphic*, 27 February: 271–73.

Anon. 1892. 'The Belfast Naturalists' Field Club', *Northern Whig*, 24 November: 6.

Anon. 1892. 'Royal Irish Academy', *Irish Times*, 13 December: 7 .

Haddon, Alfred Cort. 1892. 'Arran Islands', in Letters to the Editor, *Irish Times*, 14 December: 6.

Anon. 1893. 'The Primitive Races of Ireland', *Northern Whig*, 17 January: 1 [Haddon's slideshow].
Anon. 1893. 'The Belfast Naturalists' Field Club', *Irish News and Belfast Morning News*, 18 January: 7 [Haddon's slideshow].
Anon. 1893. 'The Conversazione', *Dublin Daily Express*, 29 October: 6.
Anon. 1894. 'Cork Literary and Scientific Society. Dr. Douglas Hyde on Irish Folk Lore', *The Cork Constitution*, 30 November: 8.
Anon. 1895. 'Edinburgh Summer Meeting', *Glasgow Herald*, 31 August: 4.
Anon. 1895. 'Race and Civilisation', *Freeman's Journal*, 18 September: 4.
Anon. 1895. 'The British Association: Interference the Civilisation of other Races', *Glasgow Herald*, 18 September: 9.
Anon. 1895. 'The British Association, Debate on Savages – Missionary Tactics Condemned – New Population Theory – Women's Organisation', *Dundee Courier*, 18 September: 3.
Anon. 1895. 'Conquest and Conscience', *The Globe*, 18 September: 4.
Anon. 1895. 'Meeting of the British Association: Civilisation neither Railway nor Telegraphs', *Dundee Advertiser*, 18 September: 2.
Special Correspondent. 1895. 'Anthropologists and Missionaries', *Daily News*, 18 September: 4–5.
WFJ [William Frederick Johnson]. 1895. 'Belfast Naturalists' Field Club', *Belfast News-Letter*, 13 September: 7.
Anon. 1895. 'The Chief Secretary on Irelands Attitude', *Edinburgh Evening News*, 17 October: 4.
Anon. 1895. 'Mr. Gerald Balfour at Leeds', *Irish Times*, 17 October: 5.
Anon. 1896. 'Royal Irish Academy', *Irish Times*, 12 May: 6.
Anon. 1896. 'The Royal Irish Academy', *Freeman's Journal*, 12 May: 2.
Anon. 1897. 'The Saving of Vanishing Knowledge', *Nature* 55 (January): 305–6.
Anon. 1897. 'Vanishing knowledge', *The Standard*, 1 February.
Anon. 1897. 'The Fever in Inniskea', *Freeman's Journal*, 7 July: 5.
Anon. 1897. 'The Government and Belmullet', *Freeman's Journal*, 12 July: 5.
Anon. 1905. 'The Anthropological Institute', *The Field*, 18 February: 279.
Anon. 1905. 'London Day by Day', *Daily Telegraph*, 18 February: 10.
Anon. 1906. 'Round and About', *Optical Lantern and Cinematograph Journal*, 15 January: 64.

Archival/Biographical Websites (A–Z)

All websites in this section accessed 23 November 2022.
Anarchist Library: https://theanarchistlibrary.org/special/index.

Australian Dictionary of Biography: https://adb.anu.edu.au/.

Biodiversity Heritage Library (BHL): https://www.biodiversitylibrary.org.

British Museum (McFarlane Collection): https://www.britishmuseum.org/research/search_the_collection_database/term_details.aspx?bioId=37828.

British Museum (Haddon Collection): https://www.britishmuseum.org/collection/term/BIOG124027.

British Museum (Haddon Photographs): https://www.britishmuseum.org/collection/object/EA_Oc-B41-14.

British Newspaper Archives: https://www.britishnewspaperarchive.co.uk/.

Dictionary of Irish Biography: https://www.dib.ie/about.

Galton.org: https://galton.org/main.html.

Hathi Trust Digital Library: https://www.hathitrust.org/.

Irish Newspaper Archives: https://www.irishnewsarchive.com.

Irish Times Newspaper Archive: https://www.irishtimes.com/archive.

Moore Institute: https://mooreinstitute.ie/.

National Film and Sound Archive of Australia: https://www.nfsa.gov.au.

National Library of Australia/TROVE: https://nla.gov.au/nla.obj-763156135/findingaid.

Oxford Dictionary of National Biography: https://www.oxforddnb.com/.

Smithsonian Libraries: https://library.si.edu/collections.

Wellcome Collection: https://wellcomecollection.org/collections.

Secondary References (A–Z)

Ackerman, Robert (ed.). 2005. *Selected Letters of Sir J. G. Frazer*. Oxford: Oxford University Press.

Adams, James A. 1996. 'The Scottish Contribution to Marine and Fisheries Research with Particular Reference to Fisheries Research during the Period 1882–1939', *Buckland Periodical Papers* 2: 97–116.

Adams, J. R. R. 1993. 'From "Green Gravel" to "The Way That I Went": Folklife, Literature and the Patterson Family of Holywood', *Linen Hall Review* 10,3: 4–7.

Arensberg, Conrad M., and Solon T. Kimball. 1940. *Family and Community in Ireland*. Cambridge, MA: Harvard University Press.

———. 2001 [1940]. *Family and Community in Ireland*. With a new introduction by Anne Byrne, Ricca Edmondson and Tony Varley. Ennis: CLASP.

Arnold, Matthew, and R. H. Super (eds). 1973. *Complete Prose Works of Matthew Arnold: English Literature and Irish Politics, v. 9*. Ann Arbor: University of Michigan Press.

Ashley, Scott. 2001. 'The Poetics of Race in 1890s Ireland: An Ethnography of the Aran Islands', *Patterns of Prejudice* 35,2: 5–18.

Barrett, S. D. 1999. 'John Kells Ingram (1823–1907)', *Trinity Economics Papers* 99,9. Retrieved 22 October 2019 from https://www.tcd.ie/Economics/TEP/1999_papers/TEPNo9SB99.pdf.

Beckett, Ian F. W. 2004. 'Wolseley, Garnet Joseph, First Viscount Wolseley (1833–1913)'. *Oxford Dictionary of National Biography*. Retrieved 26 August 2019 from https://doi.org/10.1093/ref:odnb/36995.

Beiner, Guy. 2006. 'Memory and Oblivion', in *Remembering the Year of the French: Irish Folk History and Social Memory, 304–10*. Madison: University of Wisconsin Press.

———. 2012. 'Revisiting F. J. Bigger: A "Fin-de-Siècle" Flourish of Antiquarian-Folklore Scholarship in Ulster', *Béaloideas* 80: 142–62.

Béland, Daniel. 2009. 'Back to Bourgeois? French Social Policy and the Idea of Solidarity', *International Journal of Sociology and Social Policy* 29,9–10: 445–56.

Bell, Joshua A. 2009. '"For Scientific Purposes a Stand Camera is Essential": Salvaging Photographic Histories in Papua', in Elizabeth Edwards and Christopher Morton (eds), *Photography, Anthropology and History: Expanding the Frame*, 143–169. Farnham: Ashgate.

Bennett, G., and G. Stocking. 1997. 'Folklorists and Anthropologists', *Folklore* 108: 120–23.

Benthall, Johnathan. 1992. 'Foreword', in Elizabeth Edwards (ed.), *Anthropology and Photography*, vii–viii. New Haven, CT/London: Yale University Press/Royal Anthropological Institute.

Berger, John. 1972. *Ways of Seeing*. London: BBC.

Berry, Henry F. 1915. *A History of the Royal Dublin Society*. London: Longman.

Besteman, Catherine and Hugh Gusterson. 2008. 'A response to Matti Bunzl: Public anthropology, pragmatism, and pundits', *American Anthropologist* 110,1: 61–63.

Bourgeois, L. 1998 [1896]. *Solidarité*. Villeneuve-d'Ascq: Presses Universitaires du Septentrion.

Bowen, James. 2015. *The Coral Reef Era: From Discovery to Decline; A History of Scientific Investigation from 1600 to the Anthropocene Epoch*. Heidelberg: Dordrecht.

Bowler, Peter. 2009. 'Charles Darwin and his Dublin Critics, Samuel Haughton and William Henry Harvey', *Proceedings of the Royal Irish Academy Section C* 109,1: 409–20.

Brandt, K. 1881. 'Ueber das Zusammenleben von Thieren und Agen', *Archiv für Physliologie* 1881–82: 570–74.

Brannigan, John. 2014. *Archipelagic Modernism: Literature in the Irish and British Isles, 1890–1970*. Edinburgh: Edinburgh University Press.

Bridge, Thomas W., and Alfred Cort Haddon. 1889. 'Contributions to the Anatomy of Fishes. I. The Air-Bladder and Weberian Ossicles in the Siluridæ'. *Proceedings of the Royal Society of London* 46: 309–328.

Brinton, Daniel G. 1898. 'The Study of Man', *Science* 8,185: 82.

Bruna, Giulia. 2017. *J. M. Synge and Travel Writing of the Irish Revival*. New York: Syracuse University Press.

Carpenter, George H. 1909. 'Daniel John Cunningham', *Irish Naturalist* 18,11 (Nov., 1909): 229-231.

Carville, Justin. 2007. '"My Wallet of Photographs": Photography, Ethnography and Visual Hegemony in John Millington Synge's The Aran Islands', *Irish Journal of Anthropology* 10,1: 5–11.

———. 2011. *Exposures: Photography and Ireland*. London: Reaktion Books.

Castle, Gregory. 2001. *Modernism and the Celtic Revival*. Cambridge: Cambridge University Press.

Cattell, J. M. 1890. 'Mental Tests and Measurements', *Mind* 15: 373–80.

Chambers, William, and Robert Chambers (eds). 1889. *Chambers' Encyclopaedia 4th edn*. London: Chambers.

Chandler, Edward. 2001. *Photography in Ireland: The Nineteenth Century*. Dublin: Edmund Burke.

Clark, Anna. 2017. *Alternative Histories of the Self: A Cultural History of Sexuality and Secrets, 1762–1917*. London: Bloomsbury.

Collinson Black, R. D. 2008. 'Ingram, John Kells (1823–1907)'. *Oxford Dictionary of National Biography*. Retrieved 23 November 2022 from https://www.oxforddnb.com/view/10.1093/ref:odnb/9780198614128.001.0001/odnb-9780198614128-e-34104?docPos=12.

Cowdell, Paul, 2015. 'The Folklore Society. National and international', in *Bérose International Encyclopaedia of the Histories of Anthropology*, Paris. Retrieved 14 January 2023 from https://www.berose.fr/article611.html.

Cruft, Rev. W. G. 1915. *A History of the Haddons of Naseby*. London: Haddon & Company. Retrieved 10 June 2022 from https://thehaddonsofnaseby.com/.

Cunningham, Daniel J. 1903. 'A Scotch Radical's Experience of Ireland', *Irish Unionist Alliance* 2:163–167.

Curtis, L. Perry. 2011. *The Depiction of Eviction in Ireland 1845-1910*. Dublin: UCD Press.

Davis, Laurence, and Ruth Kinna. 2009. *Anarchism and Utopianism*. Manchester: Manchester University Press.

De Brigard, Emilie. 1995. 'The History of Ethnographic Film', in Paul Hockings (ed.), *Principles of Visual Anthropology*, 13–44. The Hague: Mouton De Gruyter.

De Mórdha, Dáithí, and Ciarán Walsh. 2012. *The Irish Headhunter: The Photograph Albums of Charles R. Browne*. Dublin: Stationery Office.

Delgado Rosa, Frederico and Han F. Vermeulen (eds). 2020. *Ethnographers before Malinowski: Pioneers of Anthropological Fieldwork, 1870–1922*. New York: Berghahn Books.

Donnan, Hasting. 2017. 'Re-Placing Ireland in Irish Anthropology', in Diarmuid Ó Giolláin (ed.), *Irish Ethnologies*, 19–35. Notre Dame, IN: University of Notre Dame Press.

Douglas, Bronwen. 2008. '"Novus Orbis Australis": Oceania in the Science of Race, 1750–1850', in Bronwen Douglas and Chris Ballard (eds), *Foreign Bodies: Oceania and the Science of Race 1750–1940*, 99–156. Canberra: ANU E Press.

Douglas, Bronwen, and Chris Ballard (eds). 2008. *Foreign Bodies: Oceania and the Science of Race 1750–1940*. Canberra: ANU E Press.

Duchenne, Guillaume-Benjamin-Amand. 1867. *Physiologie des Mouvements*. Paris.

Eagleton, Terry. 1995. *Heathcliff and the Great Hunger: Studies in Irish Culture*. London: Verso.

Edwards, Charles Lincoln. 1910. 'The Zoological Station at Naples', *Popular Science Monthly* 77: 209–25.

Edwards, Elizabeth (ed.). 1992. *Anthropology and Photography 1860–1920*. New Haven, CT/London: Yale University Press/Royal Anthropological Institute.

———. 1998. 'Performing Science: Still Photography and the Torres Strait Expedition', in Anita Herle and Sandra Rouse (eds), *Cambridge and the Torres Strait: Centenary Essays on the 1898 Anthropological Expedition* 106–135. Cambridge: Cambridge University Press.

———. 2015. 'Anthropology and Photography: A Long History of Knowledge and Affect', *Photographies* 8,3: 235–52.

Edwards, Elizabeth, and Christopher Morton (eds). 2009. *Photography, Anthropology and History: Expanding the Frame*. Farnham: Ashgate.

Ellis, Henry 'Havelock'. 1890. *The New Spirit*. London: George Bell & Sons.

Elshimi, M. S. 2017. *De-Radicalisation in the UK Prevent Strategy: Security, Identity and Religion*. London: Routledge.

Engels, Eve-Marie, and Thomas Glick (eds). 2008. *The Reception of Charles Darwin in Europe*. London: Continuum.

Eriksen, Thomas Hylland. 2021. 'Forgotten Anthropologies from the Periphery', *History of Anthropology Network*. Media release for webinar retrieved 19 November 2021 from https://histanthro.org/news/announcements/second-hoan-meeting-2021/.

Evans, E. Estyn. 1977. 'Introduction' in Bryan S. Turner, *Ireland's Eye: The Photographs of Robert John Welch*. Belfast: Blackstaff.

Fegan, E. S., and J. D. Pickles. 1978. *Bibliography of A.C. Haddon*. Cambridge: Museum of Archaeology and Anthropology.

Ferretti, Federico. 2016. 'Anarchist Geographers and Feminism in Late 19th Century France: The Contributions of Élisée and Élie Reclus', *Historical Geography* 44: 68-88.

———. 2018. 'Teaching Anarchist Geographies: Élisée Reclus in Brussels and "The Art of Not Being Governed"', *Annals of the American Association of Geographers* 108,1: 162–78.

Ferriter, Diarmaid. 2018. *On the Edge: Ireland's Off-Shore Islands; A Modern History*. London: Profile.

Forrest, Derek W. 1986. 'The Anthropometric Laboratory of Ireland', *American Psychologist* 41,12 (December 1986): 1384–5.

Flaherty, Tom. 1934. *Aranmen All*. Dublin: Hamish Hamilton.

Flueckiger, Barbara. 2016. 'Joly'. *Timeline of Historical Film Colors*. Retrieved 10 June 2020 from https://filmcolors.org/timeline-entry/1334/.

Frazer, William. 1891. 'A Contribution to Irish Anthropology', *Journal of the Royal Society of Antiquaries of Ireland* 1,5: 391–404.

Galton, Francis. 1877a. 'Considerations Adverse to the Maintenance of Section F (Economic Science and Statistics)', *Journal of the Statistical Society of London* 40: 468–73.

———. 1877b. 'Typical Laws of Heredity'. *Nature* (April 5): 492–93.

———. 1885. 'Types and Their Inheritance', *Science* 6,138: 268–74.

———. 1890. *Anthropometric Laboratory: Notes and Memoirs*. London.

Geddes, Patrick and J. Arthur Thomson. 1889a. *The Evolution of Sex*. London: Walter Scott.

———. 1889b. 'Evolution', in William Chambers and Robert Chambers (eds), *Chambers' Encyclopaedia 4th edn.*, 477–84. London: Chambers.

Geertz, Clifford. 1973. *The Interpretation of Cultures*. New York: Basic Books.

———. 1999. 'The Introduction into Anthropology of a Genuinely Historical Eye', *Journal of Victorian Culture* 4,2: 305–10.

———. 2002. 'An Inconstant Profession: The Anthropological Life in Interesting Times'. *Annual Review of Anthropology*, 31: 1–19.
Gomme, G. L. 1890. *The Village Community, with Special Reference to the Origin and Form of its Survivals in Britain*. London: W. Scott.
Gooday, Graeme. 2012. 'Vague and Artificial: The Historically Elusive Distinction between Pure and Applied Science', *Isis* 103,3: 546–54.
Green, Sarah. 2021. 'Letter from the President', *EASA Newsletter* 78: 3–7. Retrieved 1 April 2021 from https://easaonline.org/newsletter/78-0321/.
Greenway, Judy. 2009. 'Speaking Desire: Anarchism and Free Love as Utopian Performance in *Fin de Siècle* Britain', in Lawrence Davis and Ruth Kinna (eds), *Anarchism and Utopianism*, 153–170. Manchester: Manchester University Press.
Griffiths, Alison. 1996. 'Knowledge and Visuality in Turn of the Century Anthropology: The Early Ethnographic Cinema of Alfred Cort Haddon and Walter Baldwin Spencer', *Visual Anthropology* 12(2): 18–43.
———. 2002. *Wondrous Difference: Cinema, Anthropology, & Turn-of-the-Century Visual Culture*. New York: Columbia University Press.
Hadley (Haddon), Caroline. 1887. *Woodside Or, Look, Listen, and Learn*. Edinburgh: Nelson.
Harvey, Brian. 1991. 'Changing Fortunes on the Aran Islands in the 1890s', *Irish Historical Studies* 27,107: 237–49.
Haverty, Martin. 1859. *The Aran Isles: Or a Report of the Excursion of the Ethnological Section of the British Association from Dublin to the Western Islands of Aran in September, 1857*. Dublin: The University Press.
Hayward, J. 1959. 'Solidarity: The Social History of an Idea in Nineteenth Century France', *International Review of Social History* 4,2: 261–84.
Herle, Anita, and Jude Philps (eds). 2020. *Recording Kastom: Alfred Haddon's Journals from the Torres Strait and New Guinea, 1888 and 1889*. Sydney: Sydney University Press.
Herle, Anita, and Sandra Rouse (eds). 1998. *Cambridge and the Torres Strait: Centenary Essays on the 1898 Anthropological Expedition*. Cambridge: Cambridge University Press.
Hickey, Denis, J., and James. E. Doherty. 2005 [2003]. *A New Dictionary of Irish History from 1800*. Dublin: Gill & MacMillan.
Hinely, Susan. 2012. 'Charlotte Wilson, the "Woman Question", and the Meanings of Anarchist Socialism in Late Victorian Radicalism', *International Review of Social History* 57,1: 3–36.

Hockings, Paul. 1995a [1975]. 'Foreword', in Paul Hockings (ed.), *Principles of Visual Anthropology*, vii–viii. The Hague: Mouton De Gruyter.

Hockings, Paul (ed.). 1995b [1975]. *Principles of Visual Anthropology*. The Hague: Mouton De Gruyter.

Hodgkin, Thomas, and Richard Cull. 1852. *A Manual of Ethnological Enquiry*. London: BAAS.

Horan, Niamh. 2021. 'Trinity Provost's Take on Fundraising, Free Speech and a Housing Crisis Fix', *Irish Independent*, 31 July. Retrieved 23 November 2022 from https://www.independent.ie/irish-news/trinity-provosts-take-on-fundraising-free-speech-and-a-housing-crisis-fix-40639056.html

Huxley, Thomas H. 1861. 'A Lobster ; Or, The Study Of Zoology (A Lecture Delivered at the South Kensington Museum)', in Thomas H. Huxley, 1896, *Discourses Biological And Geological Essays*, 196–228. New York: D. Appleton and Company.

Huxley, Leonard. 1900. *Life and Letters of Thomas Henry Huxley, Vol. 2*. New York: D. Appleton.

Huxley, Julian, and Alfred Cort Haddon. 1935. *We Europeans*. London: Jonathan Cape.

Jones, Greta. 1998. 'Contested Territories: Alfred Cort Haddon, Progressive Evolutionism and Ireland', *History of European Ideas* 24,3: 195–211.

———. 2008. 'Nation and Religion: The Debate about Darwinism in Ireland', in Eve-Marie Engels and Thomas Glick (eds), *The Reception of Charles Darwin in Europe*, 66–78. London: Continuum.

Kearns, G. 2004. 'The Political Pivot of Geography', *Geographical Journal* 170,4: 337–46.

Martin, Keir, and Alex Flynn. 2015. 'Anthropological Theory and Engagement: A Zero-Sum Game?', *Anthropology Today* 31,1: 12–14.

Kiberd, Declan. 2000. 'Synge's Tristes Tropiques: The Aran Islands', in *Irish Classics*. Cambridge, MA: Harvard University Press, pp. 421–39.

Kropotkin, Pëtr. 1902. *Mutual Aid*. New York: McClure, Phillips and Co.

Kuhn, Thomas. 1970 [1962]. *The Structure of Scientific Revolutions*, 2nd edn. Chicago: University of Chicago Press.

Kuklick, Henrika. 1991. *The Savage Within: The Social History of British Anthropology, 1885–1945*. Cambridge: Cambridge University Press.

———. 2008a. 'The British Tradition', in Henrika Kuklick (ed.), *A New History of Anthropology*. Oxford: Blackwell, pp. 52–78.

——— (ed.). 2008b. *A New History of Anthropology*. Oxford: Blackwell.

Kuper, Adam. 2001. 'Afterword: The Usual Suspects', *Patterns of Prejudice* 35,2: 81–86.

Lancaster, W. J. 1890. *How to Be a Successful Amateur Photographer*. Birmingham: J. Lancaster & Son. Retrieved 23 November 2022 from https://archive.org/details/gri_33125013853367/page/10/mode/2up.

Langham, Ian. 1981. *The Building of British Social Anthropology: W. H. Rivers and His Cambridge Disciples in the Development of Kinship Studies; 1898–1931*. Dordrecht: D. Reidel.

Leopold, Joan. 1991. 'Victorian Anthropology by George W. Stocking, Jr', *Language in Society* 20,2: 315–17.

Long, Chris, and Pat Laughren. 1993. 'Australia's First Films 1894–96: Part Six; Surprising Survivals from Colonial Queensland', *Cinema Papers* 96: 34–37 and 65–66. Retrieved 23 November 2019 from https://issuu.com/libuow/docs/cinemapaper1993decno096.

Low, Setha & Mark Maguire (eds.). 2019. *Spaces of Security: Ethnographies of Securityscapes, Surveillance, and Control*. New York: NYU Press.

MacDougall, David. 2009. 'Anthropology and the Cinematic Imagination', in Elizabeth Edwards and Christopher Morton (eds), *Photography, Anthropology and History: Expanding the Frame*, 55–63. Farnham: Ashgate.

MacFarlane, Alan. 2009. 'A Cambridge Department: Some Ethnographic Notes'. Retrieved 23 November 2022 from https://nanopdf.com/download/a-cambridge-department-some-preliminary-notes-towards-an_pdf.

MacKenzie, Norman. 1975. 'Percival Chubb and the Founding of the Fabian Society', *Victorian Studies* 23,1: 29–55.

Maddock, Kenneth. 1994. 'Through Kropotkin to the Foundation of Radcliffe-Brown's Anthropology.' *Red and Black: An Anarchist Journal* 24 (1994): 14–15.

———. 2002. 'Radcliffe-Brown, A.R.', in Alan Barnard and Jonathan Spencer (eds), *Encyclopaedia of Social and Cultural Anthropology*, 700–703. London and New York: Routledge.

Malinowski, Bronisław, 1954. *Magic, Science and Religion and Other Essays*, 2nd edn. Garden City, NY: Doubleday.

Masefield, John. 1916. *John M. Synge: A Few Personal Recollections with Biographical Notes*. Letchworth: Garden City Press.

McCormack, William J. 2000. *Fool of the Family: A Life of J. M. Synge*. London: Weidenfield and Nicolson.

McLaughlin-Jenkins, Erin. 2001. 'Common Knowledge: Science and the Late Victorian Working-Class Press', *History of Science* 39,4: 445–65.

Mead, Margaret. 1995 [1975]. 'Visual Anthropology in a Discipline of Words', in Paul Hockings (ed.), *Principles of Visual Anthropology*, 3–10. The Hague: Mouton De Gruyter.

Meijer, Miriam Claude. 1999. *Race and Aesthetics in the Anthropology of Petrus Camper (1722–1789)*. Amsterdam: Editions Rodopi.

Meller, Helen. 2008. 'Geddes, Sir Patrick (1854–1932)'. *Oxford Dictionary of National Biography*. Retrieved 26 August 2019 from https://doi.org/10.1093/ref:odnb/33361.

Messenger, John C. 1966. 'Man of Aran Revisited: An Anthropological Critique', *University Review* 9: 15–47.

Michelson, Annette (ed.), and Kevin O'Brien (trans.). 1984. *Kino-Eye: The Writings of Dziga Vertov*. Berkeley: University of California Press.

Moriarty, Christopher. 1996. 'The Reverend W. S. Green: A Pioneer in Fisheries Research and Development', *Buckland Periodical Papers* 2: 155–68.

Morrell, Jack, and Arnold Thackray. 1981. *Gentlemen of Science: Early Years of the British Association for the Advancement of Science*. New York: Clarendon.

Morris, Aldon. 2021. 'Emancipatory Sociology: Rising to the Du Boisian Challenge'. Retrieved 23 November 2022 from https://www.asanet.org/annual-meeting-2021/theme-and-program-committee.

Morris, Brian. 2018. *Kropotkin: The Politics of Community*. Oakland, CA: PM Press.

Murray, John. 1878. *Handbook for Travellers in Ireland, Fourth Edition*. London: John Murray.

O'Connor, Clifford. 2005. *A People's History of Science: Miners, Midwives and Low Mechanics*. New York: Bold Type.

Ó Giolláin, Diarmuid (ed.). 2017. *Irish Ethnologies*. Notre Dame, IN: University of Notre Dame Press.

Okuefuna, David. 2008. *The Wonderful World of Albert Kahn: Colour Photographs from a Lost Age*. London: BBC Books.

O'Sullivan, Tanya. 2015. 'The Perception of Place and the "Origins of Handedness" Debate: Towards a Cognitive Cartography of Science in Late-Victorian Dublin', *Endeavour* 39,4: 139–48.

Pearson, Karl. 1924. *The Life, Letters and Labours of Francis Galton, Vol. 2: Researches of Middle Life*. Cambridge: Cambridge University Press.

Pease, Edward R. 1925. *The History of the Fabian Society*. New York: P. Dutton.

Poliakov, Leon. 1974. *The Aryan Myth: A History of Racist and Nationalist Ideas in Europe*. London: Chatto & Windus.

Porter, Andrew. 2004. 'Chalmers, James (1841–1901), Missionary and Explorer'. *Oxford Dictionary of National Biography*. Retrieved 11 February 2020 from https://www.oxforddnb.com/view/10.1093/ref:odnb/9780198614128.001.0001/odnb-9780198614128-e-32344.

Praeger, R. Lloyd. 1949. *Some Irish Naturalists: A Biographical Note-Book*. Dundalk: W. Tempest.

Prendergast, Patricia A. 1969. 'Chalmers, James (1841–1901)'. *Australian Dictionary of Biography*. Retrieved 11 February 2020 from http://adb.anu.edu.au/biography/chalmers-james-3187/text4781.

Proudhon, Pierre J. 1863. *The Principle of Federation*. The Anarchist's Library website. Retrieved 23 November 2019 from https://theanarchistlibrary.org/library/pierre-joseph-proudhon-the-principle-of-federation.

Pruner Bey, Franz Ignaz. 1861. 'Mémoire sur les Négres', *Société d'Anthropologie de Paris* 1.

Pyenson, Lewis, and Susan Sheets Pyenson. 1999. *Servants of Nature: A History of Scientific Institutions, Enterprises and Sensibilities*. London: HarperCollins.

Quiggin, Alison Hingston. 1942. *Haddon the Head-Hunter: A Short Sketch of the Life of A. C. Haddon*. Cambridge: Cambridge University Press.

Quiggin, Alison Hingston, and Ethel S. Fegan. 1940. 'Alfred Cort Haddon 1855–1940', *Man* 40: 97–100.

Radcliffe-Brown, A. R. 1923. 'The Methods of Ethnology and Social Anthropology', *South African Journal of Science* 20: 124–47.

Reclus, Élie. 1891 [1885]. *Primitive Folk: Studies in Comparative Ethnology*. Originally published as *Les Primitifs: Etudes d'ethnologie comparée*. London: Walter Scott.

Renwick, Chris. 2009. 'The Practice of Spencerian Science: Patrick Geddes's Biosocial Program, 1876–1889', *Isis* 100,1: 36–57.

———. 2012. *British Sociology's Lost Biological Roots: A History of Futures Past*. Basingstoke: Palgrave Macmillan.

Robinson, Tim. 1997. *Stones of Aran: Labyrinth*. Harmondsworth: Penguin.

———. 2006. *Connemara: Listening to the Wind*. Dublin: Penguin Ireland.

Rockett, Kevin, and Emer Rockett. 2011. *Magic Lantern, Panorama and Moving Picture Shows in Ireland, 1786–1909*. Dublin. Four Courts Press.

Rose, Gillian. 2012. *Visual Methodologies: An Introduction to Researching with Visual Materials*. Los Angeles: Sage.

Sachse, J. F. 1896. 'The Joly Process of Colour Photography', *Proceedings of the American Philosophical Society* 35,151: 119–22.

Seebohm, Frederic. 1883. *The English Village Community, Examined in its Relation to the Manorial and Tribal Systems, and to the Common or Open Field System: An Essay in Economic History*. London: Longmans, Green & Co.

Sekula, Allan. 1986. 'The Body and the Archive', *October* 39: 3–64.

Seligman, Charles. G. 1940. 'Dr. A. C. Haddon, F.R.S', *Nature* 145: 848–50.

Shankland, David (ed.). 2014. *Westermarck: Occasional Paper No. 44 of the Royal Anthropological Institute*. Published in association with the Anglo-Finnish Society. Canon Pyon: Sean Kingston.

Shepard, Elizabeth. 1987. 'The Magic Lantern Slide in Entertainment and Education, 1860–1920', *History of Photography* 11,2: 91–108.

Sloane, Nan. 2018. *The Women in the Room: Labour's Forgotten History*. London: Bloomsbury.

Spencer, Herbert. 1873. *The Study of Sociology*. London: H. S. King.

Steele, Tom. 2007a. *Knowledge is Power! The Rise and Fall of European Popular Educational Movements, 1848–1939*. Bern: Peter Lang.

———. 2007b. 'French Radical Freemasonry, Scientific Positivism and the Rise of the Universites Populaires.' Retrieved 23 September 2018 from http://www.leeds.ac.uk/educol/documents/000000157.htm.

Stephens, Edward. 1974. *My Uncle John: Edward Stephen's Life of J. M. Synge*, ed. Andrew Carpenter. London: Oxford University Press.

Stephens, Lilo. 1971. *My Wallet of Photographs: The Photographs of J.M. Synge Arranged and Introduced by Lilo Stephens*. Dublin: Dolmen.

Stocking, George W. 1971. 'What's in a Name? The Origins of the Royal Anthropological Institute (1837–71)', *Man* 6,3: 369–90.

———. 1987. *Victorian Anthropology*. New York: Free Press.

———. 1995. *After Tylor: British Social Anthropology 1888–1951*. Madison: University of Wisconsin Press.

Stocking, George W., and Alfred Cort Haddon. 1993. 'The Red-Paint of British Aggression, the Gospel of Ten-per-Cent, and the Cost of Maintaining our Ascendancy: A. C. Haddon on the Need for an Imperial Bureau of Ethnology, 1891', *History of Anthropology Newsletter* 20,1: 3–14. Retrieved 3 June 2017 from https://repository.upenn.edu/han/vol20/iss1/3.

Synge, John Millington. 1958. *John Millington Synge: Plays, Poems and Prose*. London: Dent.

———. 1979 [1907]. *The Aran Islands: With Original Photographs by the Author*. Oxford: Oxford University Press.

Tagg, John. 1988. *The Burden of Representation*. London: Macmillan.

———. 2009. *The Disciplinary Frame: Photographic Truths and the Capture of Meaning*. Minneapolis: University of Minnesota Press.

Tanner, J. M. 1981. *A History of the Study of Human Growth*. Cambridge: Cambridge University Press.

Taylor, Isaac. 1889. *The Origin of the Aryans: An Account of the Prehistoric Ethnology and Civilisation of Europe*. London: Walter Scott.

Tilche, Alice, and Rita Astuti. 2020. 'Draft of Good Practice Guidelines in Collaborative Research: "Data" Ownership, Authorship and Power', *EASA Newsletter* 75: 12–19. Retrieved 30 January 2020 from https://easaonline.org/newsletter/75-0120/guidelines.

Topinard, Paul. 1885. *Éléments d'Anthropologie Générale*. Paris: A. Delahaye et É. Lecrosnier.

Urry, James. 1972. '"Notes and Queries on Anthropology" and the Development of Field Methods in British Anthropology, 1870–1920', *Proceedings of the Royal Anthropological Institute of Great Britain and Ireland, 1972*: 45–57.

———. 1989. 'Reviewed Work: Victorian Anthropology. by George W. Stocking', *Man* 24,2: 364–65.

———. 1993. *Before Social Anthropology: Essays on the History of British Anthropology*. Chur: Harwood Academic.

Vermeulen, Han F. 2015a. 'History of Anthropology Panels at the 14th Biennial EASA Conference, Milan, Italy, July 20–23, 2016 and the Refounding of HOAN', *History of Anthropology Review*. Retrieved 3 April 2020 from http://histanthro.org/news/observations/history-of-anthropology-panels-easa-milan/.

———. 2015b. *Before Boas: The Genesis of Ethnography and Ethnology in the German Enlightenment*. Lincoln: University of Nebraska Press.

Vertov, Dziga. 1923. 'Kinoks: A Revolution', in Annette Michelson (ed.) and Kevin O'Brien (trans.), 1984, *Kino-Eye: The Writings of Dziga Vertov*, 11–21. London, Los Angeles and Berkeley: University of California Press.

Vibart, H. M., and James Falkner. 2004. 'Edward, Prince of Saxe-Weimar (1823–1902)'. *Oxford Dictionary of National Biography*. Retrieved 25 June 2015 from https://doi.org/10.1093/ref:odnb/32976.

Walsh, Ciarán. 2013. 'Charles R. Browne: The Irish Head-Hunter', *Irish Journal of Anthropology* 16,1: 16–22.

———. 2014. 'An Anthropologist Walks into a Bar and Asks, Why is this Joke Funny?' *Irish Independent*, 4 January: 20–21.

———. 2021a. 'The Case of the Missing Skulls from Inishbofin', *RTÉ Brainstorm*, 14 April. Retrieved 23 November 2022 from https://

www.rte.ie/brainstorm/2021/0411/1209153-skulls-inishbofin-stolen-return-head-hunter/.

———. 2021b. 'Don't Kick That Skull or the Dead Will Come after You!' *RTÉ Brainstorm*, 26 August. Retrieved 23 November 2022 from https://www.rte.ie/brainstorm/2021/0825/1242817-ireland-folklore-skulls-human-remains-dead-bodies-graveyard-cemetery/.

———. 2021c. 'Anarchy in the UK: Haddon and the Anarchist Agenda in the Anglo-Irish Folklore Movement', in Matthew Cheeseman and Carina Hart (eds), *Folklore and Nation in Britain and Ireland*, 78–99. London: Routledge.

———. 2022. 'Artist, Philosopher, Ethnologist and Activist: The Life and Work of Alfred Cort Haddon (1855–1940)'. *Bérose International Encyclopaedia of the Histories of Anthropology*, August.

Weir, Neil. 2006. 'Hinton, James (1822–1875)', *Oxford Dictionary of National Biography*. Retrieved 20 June 2020 from https://www.oxforddnb.com/view/10.1093/ref:odnb/9780198614128.001.0001/odnb-9780198614128-e-13354.

White, Paul. 2003. *Thomas Huxley: Making the 'Man of Science'*. Cambridge: Cambridge University Press.

Winters, Christopher (ed.). 1991. *International Dictionary of Anthropologists*. New York: Garland.

Whyte, Nicholas. 1999. *Science, Colonialism, and Ireland*. Cork: Cork University Press.

Wilson, Edmund B. 1901. 'Aims and Methods of Study in Natural History', *Science* 13,314: 14–23.

WORKS BY HADDON

Haddon, Alfred Cort. 1880. 'Greek Fret'. *Nature* 23: 9–10.

———. 1887. *Introduction to the Study of Embryology in 1887*. London: C. Griffin.

———. 1889. 'Zoological Notes from Torres Straits', *Nature* 39: 285–86.

———. 1890a. 'Incidents in the Life of a Torres Straits Islander', *Lippincott's Monthly Magazine: A Popular Journal of General Literature, Science, and Politics* 45 (January–June): 567–72.

———. 1890b. 'Manners and Customs of the Torres Straits Islanders', *Nature* 42: 637–42.

———. 1890c. 'Papuan Dances', *Lippincott's Monthly Magazine: A Popular Journal of General Literature, Science, and Politics* 46: 386–91.

———. 1891. 'The Tugeri Head-Hunters of New-Guinea', *Internationales Archiv für Ethnographie* 4: 177–81, Plate xv.

———. 1893a. 'The Aran Islands, County Galway: A Study in Irish Ethnography', *Irish Naturalist* 2,12: 303–8.

———. 1893b. 'Secular and Ceremonial Dances of the Torres Straits Islanders', *Internationales Archiv für Ethnographie* 6: 131–62, Plates xi–xiv.

———. 1893c. 'Rambles in the Natural History Museum 1', *Irish Daily Independent*, 26 December: 5.

———. 1893d. 'Rambles in the Natural History Museum 2', *Irish Daily Independent*, 27 December: 5.

———. 1893–94. 'Rambles in The Natural History Museum: 1 Introduction; 2 Classification; 3 Polyps; 4 Queer Partnerships; 5 Stone Lilies; 6 Various Shells; 7 Fishes; 8 Ancient Reptiles and their Degenerate Descendants; 9 Sea Cows and Whales; 10 The Wandering of Animals', *Irish Daily Independent* (December 1993–February 1894).

———. 1894a. 'Science and the Woman Question 1–3'; 'Boys and Girls'; 'Children's Toys and Games 1–7', *Irish Daily Independent* (October–November).

———. 1894b. 'Science and the Woman Question', *Irish Daily Independent*, 22 October: 5.

———. 1894c. 'Children's Toys and Games II: The Bull-Roarer', *Irish Daily Independent*, 20 November: 6.

———. 1894d. 'Children's Toys and Games III: "Draw a Pail of Water"', *Irish Daily Independent*, 27 November: 6.

———. 1894e. 'The Identification of Criminals', *Irish Daily Independent*, 27 December: 6.

———. 1895a. 'The Study of Anthropology', *University Extension Journal* (no data available, copy in CUL File 4008).

———. 1895b. *Evolution in Art; as Illustrated by the Life-Histories of Designs*. London: Walter Scott.

———. 1898. *The Study of Man*. New York/London: G. P. Putnam's Sons/Bliss, Sands & Co.

———. 1899. 'The Cambridge Expedition to Torres Straits and Sarawak', *Nature* 60 (August): 413-416.

———. 1901a. *Head-Hunters: Black, White, and Brown*. London: Methuen.

———. 1901b. 'Rev. James Chalmers ("Tamate")', *Nature* 64 (9 May): 33.

———. 1906. 'A Plea for the Investigation of Biological and Anthropological Distributions in Melanesia', *Geographical Journal* 28,2: 155–59.

———. 1934. *History of Anthropology*, 2nd edn. London: Watts.

———. 1935. *Reports of the Cambridge Anthropological Expedition to Torres Straits I (General Ethnography)*. Cambridge: Cambridge University Press.

Haddon, Alfred Cort, and Alison H. Quiggin. 1910. *History of Anthropology*. London: Watts.

Haddon, Caroline (as Anonymous). 1884. 'The Future of Marriage', *Modern Thought: A Religiious, Political and Social Magazine* [no volume data found].

Haddon, Kathleen. 1929. 'In the Gulf of New Guinea', *Life* 24: 268–70.

INDEX

• • •

Note: There are over 850 terms containing 'anthropolog' so the historiography of Haddon's entry into Anglo-Irish anthropology is indexed in terms of a debate on scope and definition between reformers intent on reconstruction and their practical opposites in anatomy.

Aborigines Protection Society, 14, 18, 53, 63, 66, 75, 79–80, 84, 233
academic anthropology, 2, 15–16, 23, 50, 84–85, 128, 130, 143, 231, 250
  crisis in, 9, 201, 232, 246–50
  disciplinary folklore, 4, 21–21, 28, 91–92
  forgotten' histories, 13–16, 49, 84, 159, 178, 214, 227, 233
  neoliberal academy, 9, 233, 243–245
After Tylor (Stocking), 13–15
  precarity in, 49–51, 84, 192–93, 250
agency, 7, 22, 157, 171, 214
American Sociological Association, 248
anarchy and anarchists, 18, 48
  anarcho-utopian networks, 63–64, 101, 151, 194, 227, 230–31, 239
  an-archy as, 48, 62, 97, 101, 229, 238
  Ellis and, 61–62, 66–67
  Geddes and, 43, 47–49, 53
  Haddon family and, 18–19, 21
  Kropotkin and, 8.10, 19.52.57, 47–48, 52
  Proudhon on, 48, 62
anthropography, 6, 134–37, 147, 151, 196
Anthropological Institute of Great Britain and Ireland, 16, 42, 69, 95–96, 141
  Aran Islands and, 177, 184, 186
  cinematography in, 205–7
  culture wars and, 4, 66–72, 82–83, 112, 207
  Ethnographic Survey of the UK, 141, 143–44
  ethnography in, 71–72
Anthropological Laboratory, TCD, 127–28, 146
  academic anthropology and, 127–28
  photographic albums, 12, 128, 131, 184–85
Anthropological Society of London, 53–54, 66, 69, 140
anthropology. *See also*
  Anthropological Institute of Great Britain and Ireland; Section H
  Haddon, A. C., entry into, 27–30, 33, 40, 42–47, 49–52, 59, 64
  historiography of, 1–4, 12, 17–18, 20–21, 44, 49, 67, 84, 123, 150, 178, 207–8, 222, 231

reconstruction of, 2, 13, 22, 58, 59, 62–64, 80, 97, 101, 108, 130, 137–38, 184, 192–194, 202, 220, 227, 230, 240

reform, reformists, and, 2, 7–8, 20–21, 45, 47–49, 50, 54–55, 58, 64, 79, 84, 101, 174, 189, 201, 240–46, 249

science as, 22, 48, 110–14, 146, 149, 231

scope of (definitions and doctrines), 3–9, 30, 40–45, 54–56, 65, 68–72, 77, 82–85, 110–14, 138, 145, 150, 195, 201, 235, 246–248

Anthropometric Laboratory of Ireland, 22, 89–92, 108, 109, 115

consortium, 111, 130

anthropometry, 109–10, 124
  Cunningham and, 112
  Flower and, 114–15
  Galton and, 112–25, 145
  laboratories for, 22, 91, 113–15, 126, 128
  photography compared to, 197–98
  skull-measuring and, 111

Aran Islands, Ireland, 88, 98, 106, 127–28, 229
  anarchism and, 101, 227
  Balfour and, 93–95, 102, 105, 107, 124, 149
  ethnicity *vs.* race on, 129–30, 145–240
  ethnography of, 12, 127–138, 144, 148, 156, 166, 177, 185–187, 195, 198, 218, 241
  evictions, 99, 147–148, 186–187
  famine on, 104–5, 131, 186–87
  Green, William Spotswood, 93–96, 102–106
  political unrest, 93, 105
  skull-measuring on, 130, 132, 134, 146, 231
  slideshow of, 103, 105, 180–85, 216–17, 232
  social conditions, 92, 135–136, 144, 151, 249
  Synge and, 223, 225–27
  visual anthropology on, 2–3, 129, 153, 166–68

Arensberg and Kimball, 238

avant-garde, 224, 228, 232, 235

BAAS. *See* British Association for the Advancement of Science

Baker, Aidan, 12, 92, 179

Baldwin, Walter Spencer, 210

Balfour, Alice 'Blanche,' 149, 192

Balfour, Arthur James, 93–95, 102–5, 149

Balfour, Gerald, 149, 187

Banim, Mary, 99–100, 102, 105, 106, 147, 187

Beddoe, John, 96, 130

Bennett, Gillian, 90

Bérose International Encyclopaedia of the Histories of Anthropology, 20

Bigger, Francis Joseph, 214–16, 220–22

biosociality, 13, 31, 56–57, 63, 173

Black Lives Matter movement, 244–45

Boas, Franz, 42–44

Brabrook, Edward, 71
  Anthropological Institute and, 82–83, 141, 145
  Ethnographic Survey of the UK and, 141–44, 150

British Association for the Advancement of Science (BAAS), 66, 231–32. *See also* anthropology; ethnology; Section H
  embargo on Oceania research, 11, 80–81

British Museum, 30, 55, 71, 75, 140, 195
  Torres Strait expedition (1888), 2, 10, 28–29, 33–34, 34, 38–39, 38–41, 44, 139–40, 162–63, 176

Browne, Charles R., 145
  academic anthropology and, 128, 249
  Aran Islands and, 12–13, 22, 66, 108, 123, 126–133, 136, 147–148
  ethnographic methods and, 97, 124, 142–44, 148–50
  photographic albums of, 12, 128–131, 155, 165–166, 183–85, 198, 231

Cambridge University, 49, 66, 92, 121
  anthropology *vs.* ethnography in, 1–2, 4, 9, 21, 28, 50–51, 65, 68, 83–85, 128, 192, 237
Camper, Petrus, 116–18
Castle, Gregory, 223
cephalic index, 111
Chalmers, James 'Tamate,' 38–39, 79
Chartism movement, 54–55
cinematography, 159, 200–203, 208–12, 239
  Anthropological Institute, 206–7
  de Brigard, 30, 165, 213, 227
  cinema, art of, 189, 195, 206–7, 219, 224, 227–28
  ethnographic, 227–28
  Griffiths on, 15, 210, 213–14
  Mead on, 17, 159, 200, 209–10
  modernism and, 207–8, 224–25
  phonography and, 200–201, 203, 210, 243
class, 53, 54–55, 67, 73, 170–171, 238, 248
class war, in sciences, 19–20, 48–49, 64
collections. *See* colonial legacies
colonialism, 2, 14–15, 21, 23, 37–39, 48, 58, 68, 76, 97, 99, 125, 134, 150, 158, 178, 202, 215, 222–222, 227
  anticolonial, 3–4, 11–12, 14, 22, 208, 224, 230–231, 233
  consequences of, 40, 64, 73–74, 77, 178, 202

decolonialization, 76, 208, 222, 224, 228, 244
'oldest colony,' 2, 187, 194, 208, 224, 241
post colonial, 214, 222, 232
problem of representation and, 178, 201, 213–14, 241
solidarity and, 57–58, 133–134, 213, 230–232, 242
colonial legacies, 20–21, 23, 39–40, 162, 233–234, 244–245
communities, folk, 88, 92, 101, 107–8, 238
comparative anatomy, Cunningham and, 109–10, 116–17
comparative sociology. *See* sociology
Contemporary Science Series, 7, 14, 58–61, 169, 192, 248
craniology. *See* skull-measuring
cultural nationalism, 30, 130, 183–84, 215
  ethnology and, 222–23
culture wars, 4, 8, 19–20, 67, 112–14, 131, 242–43
Cunningham, Daniel J., 91, 115, 118–19, 121, 131
  anthropometry and, 112
  Browne and, 127–28
  comparative anatomy and, 109–10, 116–17
  Haddon, A. C., and, 144, 148–49
  Home Rule and, 148
  practical anthropology and, 249
  on race, 116–17, 148
  study of Ireland by, 32–33, 123, 125

dance, 12, 165, 190
  art and, 168–69, 174, 191–92
  of Malu Zogo-Le, 17, 204–5, 232
  Papuan, 202, 215, 221
  'Papuan Dances,' 188–89, 191, 193, 202, 210, 212, 224–25, 228, 242
  Patterson, Clara, 11, 17, 208, 215, 218–21
  religion and, 188–90

'Secular and Ceremonial Dances,'
  191–92, 194–95, 201, 206, 211
 singing games and, 11, 215,
  218–22, 228, 236
De Mórdha, Dáithí, 12, 97, 129, 130
Delgado Rosa, Frederico, 20.
discrimination, 220
 racial variation and, 116–17
Dixon, Andrew Francis, 98, 103,
  166–68

Edwards, Elizabeth, 199–201, 210, 214
Ellis, Henry "Havelock," 2, 10–11
 anarcho-utopian networks and, 59,
  61–62, 66–67, 90, 194
 on an-archy, 62
 Contemporary Science Series and,
  7, 13–14, 49, 60–63, 66, 107, 139,
  169–70, 174, 191–92, 248
 on evolution, 61, 191–92
 Fellowship of New Life and, 61
 on gender, 62, 189, 220
 Haddon, Caroline (aunt), and, 18,
  24, 61, 171, 248
 Huxley on, 54, 58
 reconstruction of anthropology
  and, 59–64, 132, 137, 138,
  240–42
 on sex, 59
 social reform (reconstruction) and,
  54, 61–62, 202, 248
 Synge and, 225
 as utopian, 59, 61–62, 64
ethnocentrism, 21, 158, 224
Ethnographic Survey (Ireland), 12,
  151–52, 193, 228, 246
Ethnographic Survey (UK), 110,
  130–31, 140, 150–51
 Anthropological Institute and, 128,
  141, 144, 217
 BAAS and, 197, 216–17
 BNFC and, 197, 215–16
 failure of, 193
 Folk-Lore Society and, 141–42

ethnography. *See specific topics*
ethnography, of Aran Islands, Ireland,
  12, 127–138, 144, 148, 156, 166,
  177, 185–187, 195, 198, 218, 241
Ethnological Society of London, 53,
  64, 66, 69, 80
ethnology, ethnologists and, 4, 6, 16,
  31, 44, 84–85, 157, 174
 Aborigines Protection Society and,
  53, 63, 75, 79, 233
 Enlightenment and, 19, 116, 118
ethnology, Haddon, A. C., and, 97,
  150, 170
 in Anthropological Institute, 71–72
 anthropology *vs*., 4, 6, 39–42, 64,
  65–73, 82, 85, 113–14, 118, 245
 Aran Islands and, 22, 92–93,
  98–103, 106–08, 128, 130–35,
  145, 151, 186, 234
 BAAS and, 43, 66, 69, 79–82, 85,
  113–14
 Boas, 41–43
 Bureau of Ethnology, 14, 57, 138,
  140, 143–44, 149, 171, 174, 193
 colonial legacies, 244
 cultural anthropology as, 3, 8, 9,
  85, 130, 207, 235–37
 cultural nationalism and, 3, 30,
  221–23
 dance and, 41, 202
 'dangerous features,' 4, 10, 11, 19,
  53, 57, 62, 63–64, 69, 75, 79–82,
  84–85, 108, 158–59, 208, 223,
  239, 242–43, 247
 lectureship in, 1, 9, 11, 21, 28,
  50–51, 65–67, 83–84, 159, 250
 modernism and, 3, 30, 86, 208, 250
 philosophy and, 178, 212–13, 239
 Synge and, 208, 226
 Torres Strait and New Guinea, 2,
  10, 29, 33, 35–39, 42, 44, 46 160
 visual, 12, 158, 160–62, 164–65,
  168–69, 175, 186, 199, 201, 207,
  232

eugenics, 8, 123, 124–25
  Anthropometric Laboratory of Ireland and, 119–20
  Galton and, 29–30, 109–10, 114–15, 124
  Ingram, Geddes, and, 123
European Association of Social Anthropology (EASA)
  Green, Sarah, 246–68
  Tilche and Astuti, 246–48
evolution
  art and dance in, 14, 63, 74, 169, 190–92, 201
  biosociality and, 13–14, 31, 48, 56–57, 63, 143–44, 173
  debates, 63, 67, 69, 86, 122, 195, 201, 235
  eugenics and, 110, 112, 119, 125
  race, class, gender, and, 67, 171–72
  race, empire and, 4, 15, 49, 116, 213, 215
  sex of, 14
  social, 6, 7, 48, 136–38, 170
  social reform and, 14, 47–48, 56–57, 60–61, 64, 67, 74–75, 85, 150, 192, 196
  'survival of the fittest' and, 48, 54, 228
evolutionist historiography, 15
  Haddon, A. C., and, 3, 15, 48–49, 63, 67, 79, 110, 130, 213–14, 220, 239

Fabian Society, 1, 18, 52, 61, 171, 230
Faherty, Michael, unnamed woman and, 154, 157, 198, 241
Fellowship of the New Life, 61
Flower, William Henry, 29, 41, 44, 50, 155
  anthropology (history of), 69–71
  anthropometry and, 114–15, 120
  on genocide, 73–75, 239
  Haddon, A. C., and, 9–10, 29, 34, 38, 41–44, 47, 49–58, 80, 91, 96, 134, 141–43

  photography and, 155, 197, 206
  practical science and, 114–15, 124, 128
Floyd, George, 20–21, 23, 233, 244
folk
  community, 92, 101, 238
  'folk' vs. 'savage,' 7
  'place-work-folk,' 8, 137, 189, 193, 238
folklore, folklorists and, 7, 82, 90–91, 177, 189, 206
  Hyde, Douglas, 187–88, 228
  Torres Strait and New Guinea, 17, 43, 140, 168, 221
folklore, Haddon, A. C., and, 5, 7, 63, 90–92, 97, 106, 187, 189, 193
  anthropology vs., 90
  Aran Islands, 135, 157, 178
  Belfast Naturalists' Field Club, 185, 208, 214–23
  ethnology and, 8, 17, 113
  nationalism and, 208, 215, 221
  photography and, 157, 177–78, 197
Folk-Lore Society, 43, 128, 141–42, 157, 218–19
  Ethnographic Society and, 128, 150, 217, 141144
  Gomme and, 62, 89–90, 106, 206
  Haddon, A. C., and, 8, 16, 43, 89–90, 128, 150, 231–32
Foster, Michael, 32, 35, 56, 79, 95, 139–40, 168–69
Frazer, James G., 10, 50, 138, 235
  Lectureship in Ethnology and, 9, 65–68, 71, 82–85, 233
  Torres Strait and, 2, 42, 50, 81–82
Freemasonry, 2, 10, 19, 52–53, 88, 190–91, 194, 202, 212

Galton, Francis, 30, 40, 71, 74, 112–13, 121, 234, 249
  Anthropometric Laboratory, Dublin, 11, 22, 29, 86, 109–11, 121–25, 145–46

INDEX

on colonialism, 74
Cunningham and, 110, 115, 119–21, 131, 139, 151, 249
eugenics and, 8, 29–30, 109–10, 114–15, 120, 124
Geddes *vs.*, 111, 123
Haddon, A. C., and, 50, 81, 108, 128, 130, 140–42, 150–51
International Health Exhibition, 120, 145
photography and, 44, 72, 112–14, 124, 164, 170, 197, 234–35
quantitative, hard science methodology of, 44, 72, 112–14, 124, 164, 170, 197, 234–35

Garson, John George, 116, 139–44, 150–51, 195–98, 235

Geddes, Patrick, 8, 18, 123
anarcho-utopian networks and, 43, 47–49, 53, 187
biosociality of, 31, 56–57, 63
correspondence with, 27–28, 43, 46–48
influence of, 9–10, 18, 64, 139, 189–90, 193, 239
Reclus, Élisée and, 19, 47, 76
sociology of Le Play, 8, 61, 190, 194
solidarism and, 51–52
Thomson and *The Evolution of Sex*, 14

Geertz, Clifford, 233
doing ethnography, 240
Haddon, A. C., and, 239–40

gender, 171, 173, 189, 246
agency, 171, 224, 236
anarchism and, 18–19
discrimination and, 10, 220, 248
feminism, 62, 90
sexual politics, 171

genocide, 14, 171
colonialism and, 21, 74–75, 243
imperialism and, 5–7
Tribal Voice project, 232–33, 243, 250

geography, 19, 33, 47, 57, 145, 235
of Aran Islands, 135–37
in *History of Anthropology*, 193–94

Gomme, Laurence, 62, 206
Folk-Lore Society and, 89–90

grave-robbing
in Inishbofin, 91–92, 97, 134
repatriation and, 244–45

Green, William Spotswood, 93–96, 102–6

Griffiths, Alison, 15, 210, 213–14

Haddon, Alfred Cort. *See also* Torres Strait and New Guinea
Anthropology, a manifesto by, 5–9, 10, 14, 16, 49, 61–67, 82–83, 90, 107–8, 133, 136–37, 145, 169, 174, 187, 189, 212, 221, 222, 231, 235, 237, 245, 248
anticolonial activism, 3–4, 11–12, 14–15, 22, 58, 158, 208, 230, 233, 241, 244
anti-racist activism, 14, 21, 57, 64, 158, 171, 188, 193, 233, 236, 239, 241, 250
anti-slavery activism, 1, 14, 21 79, 158, 170, 202, 231
colonial legacies and, 21, 23, 233–34, 244–45
critique of imperialism, 6, 11, 13, 50, 57–58, 64, 74–75, 85, 97, 138–39, 171, 187
education in art, 160–61
education in ethnology, 29, 34
education in photography, 166–67
education in zoology, 30–32
employment in anthropology, 50–51, 83, 151–52, 192–93
family influence of, 1, 10, 14, 18, 34, 79, 159–61, 170–72, 175
humanitarian tradition and, 1, 14, 18, 21, 67, 73–75, 79, 85, 158–59, 171, 194, 202, 234, 242, 250

journalism column of, 5, 10, 64, 76, 80, 158, 170–74, 194, 213, 215, 220, 239, 242, 244
marine biology career of, 2, 10, 21, 27, 44, 49, 55, 89, 90, 93, 95, 97, 101–2, 106–7, 110, 131, 194
as modernist, 3, 22, 203, 207–8, 222–27, 231
philosophy and, 4, 10, 20, 67, 72, 116–18, 173–74, 178, 188, 192–94, 201–2, 208, 213–14, 227, 229, 230, 235
photography, a manifesto by, 11, 22, 178, 194–97, 200–201
Haddon, Arthur (brother), 161, 168
Haddon, Caroline, (socialist aunt), 10, 18–19, 21, 52, 173, 224
Ellis and, 18, 24, 171, 248
Haddon, Caroline (mother, author), 1, 161
Haddon, Ernest (son), 159–61, 206
Hadley as, 161
Haddon, John (father, illustrator), 161
Haddon, John (grandfather), 21, 34, 161
antislavery activism of, 14, 79, 158, 170, 202
Haddon, Kathleen (daughter), 199
hard science doctrine, 3, 110, 233–35
Harvard Anthropological Survey of the Irish Free State, 129, 238
Haughton, Samuel, 26, 31, 121–24, 146, 150, 249
head-hunters, 46–47, 92, 191, 210–11, 224–25, 230
Hinton, Margaret Haddon (aunt, Fabian), 18, 21, 52, 171, 248
HOAN (History of Anthropology Network), 20
Hockings, Paul, 164
Hodgkin, Thomas, 79–81
Home Rule
anthropology and, 22, 33, 93–94, 99, 102, 106, 110, 114, 122–24, 131–32, 145–50

general elections, 76, 149, 186–87, 215
Haddon, A. C., as sympathizer, 110, 123, 151, 183, 187, 228
Killing Home Rule, 148–49, 187
killing with kindness of, 148–51, 187
humanitarian, 21, 85, 119, 171, 178, 202
Huxley, Thomas Henry, 9, 187
biology and anthropology, 30, 44, 47, 53–54, 63, 77, 110, 148, 194, 201
capitalism defense of, 19–20, 54–55, 63–64, 73, 85, 243
fisheries research and, 30, 49, 94–95, 104
Geddes and, 19, 47, 55–57, 64, 173
Haddon, A. C., and, 1, 10–11, 30, 49, 55, 57, 58, 64, 107, 140, 223, 235, 245
Imperial Institute and, 53, 58, 75, 76–78, 85, 131, 140–41, 149, 193
Kropotkin *vs.*, 47–48, 52, 57, 173, 238
political influence, 55–57
reform of science, 54, 55, 60, 85–86, 171–73
Torres Strait and, 2, 32–35, 44
Hyde, Douglas, 15, 187, 214–17, 222–23, 227–28

imperialism, 5–6
critique of, 13, 57–58, 64, 74, 138–39, 171
Imperial Institute, 120
indigenous activism, 232–33, 243, 245, 250
Ingram, John Kells, 122–23, 146, 148
Inishbofin, grave-robbing in, 91–92, 97, 134
initiation ceremony
Freemasonry and, 190–91
of Malu Zogo-Le, 191, 211–12
Insurrection in Ipswich session. *See* Section H

International Health Exhibition, 120, 145
Irish Ethnographic Survey, 12, 128–29, 151–52, 193, 246

Jones, Greta, 15, 30, 49, 59, 63, 110, 130, 171, 208, 215, 220

Kearns, Gerry, 19, 23, 47, 52
Kiberd, Declan, 130
Kropotkin, Pëtr, 7–8, 10, 18–19, 51–52, 59, 61–64, 90
  Aran Islands and, 22, 48, 62, 101, 227–29, 238
  Huxley *vs.*, 47–48, 54–55, 57
  influence of, 10, 18, 57, 107, 173 193, 202, 238–39
Kuklick, Henrika, 15, 30, 110, 130
  on eugenics, 119
  The Savage Within, 4, 48–49

laboratories
  for anthropometry, 29, 89, 91–92, 101, 108, 113–14, 130, 145, 191, 219, 249
  mobile, 22, 33, 44, 123–24, 126
  at TCD, 11, 22, 115, 119–28, 127, 146
lantern slides. *See* photography
Leopold, Joan, 15–16
Le Play. *See* Geddes
Lippincott's Monthly Magazine, 57, 103, 188, 210, 227, 229
literary modernism, 3, 12, 30, 130, 215, 225
  scientific racism and, 223
  of Synge, 15, 208, 222–23
"little wars," 97, 247
London Missionary Society (LMS), 34, 38
  anthropology and, 76–77, 80
  influence of, 38–39, 79
  Missionaries of, 2, 29, 34, 38

Macalister, Alexander, 116, 124, 140, 212

Macfarlane, Alan, 84
magic lantern slideshows. *See* photography
Maguire, Mark, 23
  Setha Low migration and, 247, 249
Malinowski, Bronislaw, 37–38, 165
Malu Zogo-Le, 11, 208–10, 213
  ceremonies of, 17, 191, 208, 210–12, 214, 225
  dance of, 17, 22, 204–5, 227–8, 232
McFarlane, Samuel, 10, 29, 34, 37–39, 160–61
Mead, Margaret, 3, 201–2, 232, 242, 245
  on discipline of words, 22, 164–65
  on ethnographic film, 17, 159, 164, 200, 241
#MeToo movement, 244
Michael O'Donnell, John, 156
missionary infrastructure, expeditions and, 37–38
mobile laboratories, 123–24, 126
modernism, 3, 201, 223–24, 228–29, 242. *See also* literary modernism
modernist, 3, 22, 203, 207–8, 222–25, 227, 231
Morrell, Jack, and Arnold Thackray, 19, 75, 79–81
Morris, Aldon, 248
Morton, Anna, 52–53
mutuality, 48, 55, 238

naturalist field club movement, in Ireland
  Aran Islands, 99, 187–88
  Belfast, 11, 53, 99, 103, 142–3, 152–53, 166, 177, 184–86, 214–28
  Dublin, 31, 215, 225
  Synge, 225
Notes and Queries on Anthropology (photography), 164, 185, 195–99, 209–10

O'Callaghan, David, 182–83, 187
Oceanographic research, 10, 28, 33, 44
Ó Giolláin, Diarmuid, 15–16, 30, 130, 215, 223

'Papuan Dances.' *See* dance
Paris Commune, 47–48, 52, 66
Patterson, Clara, 11, 17, 208, 215, 218–21
performed ethnography, 22, 201, 224, 228
Petrie, Flinders, 68, 73, 77, 85, 197
phonography, cinematography and, 200–201, 203, 210, 243
photo-ethnography, 200–201, 203, 205, 208, 210, 239, 242–43, 243
  methodology in, 194–95
photography, 2–3, 41, 162–63, 199
  in 'The Ethnography of the Aran Islands,' 135–36, 154–57, 185, 241–45
  fieldwork and, 167–68
  instantaneous, 164, 183–84
  magic lantern and, 10, 22, 158, 175, 176–78, 202, 206–7
  in *Notes and Queries on Anthropology*, 11, 22, 178, 194–95, 196–97, 200–1
  slideshows, 3, 17, 80, 157, 164, 174, 176–78, 184, 186–88, 201, 239, 242
  technology of, 165–68, 176, 178–79, 209
'Photography and Folklore,' 177, 197, 206
'physicals' *vs.* 'culturals,' 66, 68–70, 73, 82–83, 85, 101, 110, 130–31, 138, 148, 207
post-evolutionism, 14, 48, 61, 67, 112, 113, 196, 231, 235
Praeger, Robert Lloyd, 30, 56, 214–15, 222, 224–25, 228
Prichard, Cowles, 79–80, 110, 116, 118–19

Primitive Folk, 62
Principles of Visual Anthropology, 104, 164
professionalization, of anthropology, 114–15
progress, of simple societies, 220
protection, of simple societies, 1, 73–74
psychology, 47, 59, 81, 135, 145, 170, 212
  psychological, 63, 232, 234–36

Quiggin, Alison Hingston, 3, 9, 10, 32, 34, 36, 56, 78, 84, 92, 95, 111–12, 130, 157, 159–61, 171, 193, 222, 237

race, 4, 15, 49, 61, 67, 114, 124, 188, 213
  Anthropometric Laboratory of Ireland and, 33, 91, 110, 120, 128–9, 139
  on Aran Islands, 129–30, 135
  classification of, 70, 96, 114–15
  Cunningham on, 116–17, 148
  Haddon, A. C., on, 57, 76, 95, 150, 170–73, 172–73, 190
  Home Rule and, 146–48
racism, 14, 23, 236, 243–34, 248, 250
  anti-racism activism, 11, 64, 148, 188, 193, 239
  colonialism and, 158, 171, 233–34
  scientific, 22, 30, 86, 115, 223, 224, 231, 241–42
Radcliffe-Brown, A. R., 18, 59, 231–32, 235–38
  'Anarchy' Brown, 18
  Haddon, A. C., influence on, 239–40
  Haddon, A. C., on, 235–39
  Kropotkin and, 238
Radical and radicals, 2, 19, 52, 54, 233–4, 277
  definitions of, 2–3, 20, 48, 231, 250
  Radical *vs* reactionary, 23, 85, 231
  Traditions, 85, 243, 245–49

RDS. *See* Royal Dublin Society
reactions, from periodicals, 76–78, 120–23, 178–79, 185, 205–6, 215–16
Reclus, Élie, 10, 19, 62, 107, 227
Reclus, Élisée, 19, 47, 51–53, 62, 76, 187
religion, 53, 62, 237
  anthropology and, 118–19
  dance and, 188–89
  ethnology and, 83
  Haddon, A. C., and, 7, 42, 76, 190
Renwick, Chris, 8, 31, 52, 54–57, 123, 137, 201
repatriation campaign, 244–45
representation, 185, 200, 202, 213, 232
  'burden' of, 160
  colonialism and, 201–2
  ethnographic, 161, 178, 205–6, 221, 224, 231
revolution, 54, 61, 187
  in anthropology, 46, 48
  cinematography, 224–25
  Huxley, in science, 49, 54, 56, 60, 85
  Kuhn, scientific, 4, 16
  photography, 165
revolutionaries, 8, 48, 61, 229
ritual, 2, 159, 165, 190, 200, 202, 212–13, 220, 224, 236
Rivers, William H., 231
Royal Dublin Society (RDS)
  Aran Islands and, 97, 98–102
  fisheries research, 16, 26, 29, 31–32, 56, 90, 93–95, 102–34, 191
  gender, 31, 220
  Home Rule and, 102–6
  'Native Life in New Guinea,' 176, 179, 188, 224
  photography, 166
  'Savage Art,' 191
Royal Irish Academy, 16, 26, 218–19
  anthropology, 116–17
  anthropometric laboratory and, 29, 91, 121–24
  Ethnographic survey and, 34, 127–28, 132–33, 138, 142, 148–50, 184–85, 191
  fisheries research, 31, 43, 55–56
  Unionism and, 123, 148, 149
Rudler, Frederick W., 68–69

savage, 4, 7, 68, 72, 178–79, 188–92, 205, 212–14, 220, 232
  Synge and, 225
  a very English, 4, 202, 228, 230, 239, 243, 250
Section H, 64, 67. *See also* British Association for the Advancement of Science
  Cunningham and, 112–13 116, 121, 127–28
  Ethnographic Survey of the UK and, 141–43, 216–17
  fieldwork and, 118, 128, 141–43
  Galton and, 112–13, 121
  Haddon, A. C., (slideshows), 157, 177, 184, 186
  history of, 69–73
  Ipswich, 11, 67, 73–78, 80–86, 99, 174, 187 144, 195, 231
  Rivers and, 231
  Torres Strait, 18, 28, 34, 40–42, 44, 88–89
'Secular and Ceremonial Dances.' *See* dance
sex and sexuality, 14, 18–19, 59, 62, 67, 117, 171, 212, 224–25, 236, 248
Shackleton, Alice, 10, 31, 220
Shankland, David, 20, 23
singing games. *See* dance
sketches, 2, 17, 33, 92, 96 101, 162–63, 167–68
  as ethnography, 45, 98, 157, 160–64, 174, 177, 200
  illustration, 99, 103, 155, 191

INDEX

skull-measuring, 11, 18, 43, 46, 72, 86, 90, 93, 111, 137, 150, 170, 177, 222, 226
  on Aran Islands, 12–13 22, 130–32, 146, 231
  craniology, 47, 66, 91, 96, 112, 114, 131–40, 140, 143, 149, 151, 185, 244
slideshows. *See* photography
social anthropology, 3, 7–8, 20, 48, 67, 82–84, 110, 114, 124, 130, 175, 212–14, 231, 235–36, 238, 245–46
socialism, 1, 8, 19, 51, 52, 54–55, 61–64, 73, 171, 227–28, 231
  Huxley *vs.*, 148
  state, 95
Sociological Society, 8, 237
sociology, 6, 19, 20 248, 51
  anthropology and, 8, 9, 13, 43, 46–48, 59–60, 64, 68, 77–78, 85, 110, 186, 195, 235–37, 249
  Aran islands and, 135–38, 147, 150
  comparative, 13, 43, 46–48, 66, 236–38
  crisis in, 123, 236, 248
  Cunningham and, 111, 115–16, 119, 143, 145, 249
  Ellis on, 60–64
  Eugenics and, 114, 123, 131
  evolution and, 48, 130–31, 235–36
  Geddes and, 8, 27, 43, 46–48, 64
  Haddon, A. C., on, 6–9, 13, 20, 64, 136–38, 186, 190, 221–22, 237
  Home Rule and, 123, 147–51
  Kropotkin and, 7–8, 189–90
  Radcliffe-Brown and, 59, 232, 235, 238
  social survey, le Play, 8, 11, 56, 151
  Spencer on, 63
solidarism, 51, 63, 66, 230–31
Stocking, George W., 4, 30, 54, 66, 69–70, 208
  After Tylor, 13–15, 48–49, 59, 63, 110, 130, 174, 195

Survey of Fishing Grounds, West Coast. *See* Royal Dublin Society
survival, of the fittest, 48, 54, 228
sympathies, for islanders, 133–34, 148–49
Synge, John Millington
  anarchism and, 227
  Haddon, A. C., and, 23, 208, 222, 225–27
  Jones on, 15
  Photography and, 235
  Skulls in TCD, 226

tabu, bourgeois society and, 211, 224–25
Tasmania, 74, 76, 80–81, 116, 117, 244
taxonomy, descriptive, 8, 29, 31, 160
TCD. *See* Trinity College, Dublin
technology, 170, 247, 249
  cinematic, 165, 207, 209–11
  photographic, 165–68, 176, 178–79, 199, 209
'tedious' texts, 22, 155, 159, 168, 173, 197
Topinard, Paul, 71, 117, 146
  doctrine of, 71–72, 74, 82–83, 85, 110, 144–45, 150–51, 193, 201
Torres Strait (1898), 50, 221, 235
  BAAS embargo, 80–82
  ethnographic experiments, 195, 199–201, 204–11
  Haddon and, 11, 14, 17, 191, 208–14, 225
Torres Strait and New Guinea (1888-89), 2, 4, 10, 17, 21, 27–43, 47, 80–81, 90, 98, 140, 244
  Boas and, 158
  Caroline Haddon and, 171
  Colonial Legacies of, 244–45
  Ellis and, 61, 171
  ethnographic experiments in, 159, 159–63, 165, 167, 169, 174, 176, 179, 195, 199–201
  Geertz and, 242

Haddon, A. C., on, 57, 82, 97, 168, 171, 188, 190–94
Huxley and, 32, 34
Kropotkin and, 64, 238–39
Mead and, 242
Synge and, 225
Tribal Voice Project, 233, 243
Trinity College, Dublin (TCD), 244
   Anthropological Laboratory of, 127–28, 146
   Anthropometric Laboratory of Ireland of, 22, 91, 115, 126, 128
   Colonial Legacies of, 244–45
   Unionism and, 110, 123, 124, 131, 145, 147–48, 151, 187, 249
Tylor, Edward Burnett, 43, 50, 174, 234
   Anthropological Institute, 64, 66–67, 141
   'anthropological rotation,' 71–72, 84
   Boas and, 41–44, 70, 140, 142, 158
   'physical' *vs* 'culturals,' 66, 68, 82–85, 101, 111, 131, 138, 144
   Quaker heritage and, 11, 110
   Section H and, 70, 112

United Kingdom (UK), 8, 245. *See also* Ethnographic Survey (UK)
   Anarchy in, 19, 52, 76, 187
   Ireland, 93, 108
   threat of Home Rule and, 76, 131, 146, 151, 249
university extension movement, 19, 53, 166, 220. *See also* Ellis

Journal of, 82, 187
Reclus, Freemasonry, and, 52–53

Vertov, Dziga., 225, 228
visual anthropology, 174, 214. *See also* cinematography; photo-ethnography; photography
   Haddon, A. C., and, 3, 22, 162–64, 242
   illustration, 158, 168–69, 175, 191–92
   Principles of Visual Anthropology, 159, 164–65, 200–202
   'tedious' writing comparison, 2–3, 155–59, 168–69, 173–74, 196, 199, 232
   Visual Anthropology, Journal of, 213
Visuality, 210, 213

Warner, William Lloyd, 233–34, 238
Welch, Robert John, 103, 166–67, 179, 184, 207, 209, 218, 220, 277

Xakriabá, Celia, 243

Yeats, William Butler, 220, 226, 229

zoology, 43–44, 55, 69, 80, 89, 96, 160, 172, 194, 199, 213–14, 219, 220
   'former zoologist,' 14–15, 30, 109–10, 157, 165, 213–14, 222, 227, 230–32
   Haddon, A. C., switch from, 1–3, 9, 10, 27–35, 44, 107

www.ingramcontent.com/pod-product-compliance
Lightning Source LLC
Chambersburg PA
CBHW070911030426
42336CB00014BA/2365